MAKING
HAYE

MAKING HAYE

THE AUTHORISED DAVID HAYE STORY

ELLIOT WORSELL

Quercus

First published in Great Britain in 2011 by
Quercus
55 Baker Street
7th Floor, South Block
W1U 8EW

Picture Credits

p1 © Jerome Haye
p53, p109, p163 © Cressida Jade
p255 © Richard Pelham, *Sun*
p331 © Andrew Couldridge, Action Images

A CIP catalogue record for this book is available
from the British Library

HB ISBN 978 1 78087 020 5
TPB ISBN 978 1 78087 021 2

10 9 8 7 6 5 4 3 2 1

Text designed and typeset by
Ellipsis Digital Limited, Glasgow

Printed and bound in Great Britain by
Clays Ltd St Ives plc

For my grandads

CONTENTS

PART 4

PART 5

PART 6

PART 7

PROLOGUE

Fighter and writer stand alone and nervous in a Hamburg lift, quietly counting down the hours until battle, all the while pretending not to worry.

PROLOGUE
BY DAVID HAYE

I first met Elliot Worsell eight years ago at Bethnal Green's York Hall. He was just a teenager at the time. Don't worry, though, this isn't one of *those* stories. The author of this book had just finished secondary school and was a few months into life at college when we first came into contact at Britain's home of prizefighting. Like me, he was a boxing fan. Unlike me, Elliot was also a writer. He was seventeen.

As for me, I was watching rather than fighting that December night in Bethnal Green, and had recently been crowned English cruiserweight champion, a title that meant a lot to me at the time, but was something I always viewed as a stepping stone to bigger and better things. I wanted cruiserweight and heavyweight titles of the world variety and, even at that early stage of my career, I was already telling *everybody* about it. I was twenty-three.

I knew of Elliot and his online boxing writing and, in fact, I first became familiar with his name when he decided to use an incredibly imaginative and somewhat disrespectful phrase to describe my unorthodox boxing style in September 2003. It didn't bother or upset me, as I knew it was par for the course following a poor performance. Everybody else was taking shots after the fight in question, so at least Elliot was creative with it. It was just unfortunate that the first fight of mine Elliot covered from ringside also happened to be one of my shakiest performances as a professional, and it's fair to say he made me know all about it. I was knocked down for the first time in my career against Lolenga Mock and, while many were quick to write me off and find the next bandwagon to jump aboard, Elliot, despite an initial teenage tantrum, decided ultimately to stand by me and continue the journey. So, thankfully, by the time we did properly meet face-to-face in late 2003, I was already a fan of his writing and, I think – no, *hope* – Elliot would say the same about my boxing.

The first thing that struck me about Elliot upon meeting him was how young he looked. He wasn't your typical ringside reporter, and I'm sure I wasn't the first person to notice that fact. In between discussing the up-and-down fortunes of Roy Jones Jr and my own ambitious career plans, I asked Elliot how old he was, and he replied, 'Seventeen', much to my surprise. Still, I never asked for ID or for him to point me in the direction of his parents, nor did I feel the need to have this youngster prove anything to me. Many people wouldn't have taken him seriously, given his age, but I could see the potential genius in what he was writing, even at that early stage. Elliot briefly interviewed me that day at York Hall and, although I find it difficult to recall much of the detail, his presence struck a chord with me; I liked the fact that this young kid was following boxing and, more importantly, my own career, with such passion and enthusiasm.

We stayed in touch beyond that first interview, me fighting and Elliot writing and, given the similar circles we were now mixing in, future appointments unfolded naturally. Each time we met I was happy to give him a bit of my time and he was eager to give me a bit of his ear. As time passed, and I began to realise the extent of the knowledge and interest Elliot possessed, we – trainer Adam Booth and I – allowed him even greater access.

PROLOGUE

Subsequently, Elliot's boxing knowledge, and knowledge of my own career and tendencies, has grown over the years, and he is now an integral part of my team. Aside from his ongoing and successful writing career, he has helped formulate and strategise my assault on world heavyweight and cruiserweight titles, and has been there in the shadows at every pivotal stage of my professional boxing life. He has spent time with me at home with my family, experienced the ups and downs of training camps, and has even been present in those tense moments when most fighters choose to be left alone.

We always discussed Elliot one day going ahead and writing a book about his time spent with me and, with that very much in mind, I felt it was important to introduce him to the real 'Hayemaker' and allow him unprecedented access to situations kept hidden from the public at large. Key moments that stick out for me are the final few hours he spent with me in a Paris hotel before I boxed Jean-Marc Mormeck for the world cruiserweight titles, and then the final hours we shared in a Nuremberg hotel two years later, when I stood up to the seven-foot Russian giant Nikolay Valuev with the WBA world heavyweight belt on the line. Elliot has become a long-standing part of the pre-fight entourage and, therefore, is better positioned than anybody to recall and analyse my path to world titles, as both a cruiserweight and a heavyweight. There really is nobody else capable of writing this story.

These are his, and only his, observations, and many of them were even hidden from me for a number of years. As a result, when I finally read the manuscript I was rediscovering moments, conversations and situations that I'd long forgotten, as well as gaining an insight into how Elliot has viewed my antics along the way. I got a kick out of revisiting the highs and lows and viewing them through the critical eye of somebody else, somebody I respect. It's one thing recalling my story the way I saw it, but it's another thing entirely to see it chronicled by someone who has followed me all the way and grown close to me.

I first read *Making Haye* on an eight-hour flight back from Miami. All potential toilet breaks were ignored. I had just completed the first stint of training for my world heavyweight title unification fight in July, and the book brought the importance of the fight fully into focus. It gave me the chance to contemplate what I had achieved, ponder what had gone right and wrong in the process, and then realise just what a fantastic position I was about to find myself in.

Everything in this book is accurate and beautifully written, and the content remains pure and unvarnished. It is personal, yet also critical. Despite our close relationship, Elliot doesn't try to sugar-coat situations and, as you will soon discover, is brutally honest with both his observations and opinions. Some of the book's content made me nostalgic and happy, certain passages made me cringe, and other parts made me sad. All in all, though, I am just immensely happy that this major part of my life has been documented by a man whom I've learnt to trust.

PART ONE

A ten-year-old David Haye steps through the doors of the boxing gym for the first time and immediately challenges all-comers.

CHAPTER ONE
KNOCKOUT KINGS

He had one voice for the world and another voice for me. To the untrained eye and ear, the two were hard to tell apart, but, over time, loyalty and understanding allowed me to notice and embrace the subtle difference. He also had two dreams. One was the kind he'd casually describe to the world, while the other was of a darker variety and remained locked up for much of his adult life. We'd hear the first dream countless times, of course. Ten years of age and belly full of fight, young David Deron Haye returns from Lambeth's Fitzroy Lodge Amateur Boxing Club and declares to his mother Jane and father Deron that one day he will deliver the heavyweight championship of the world to the mantelpiece of their family home in Gatehouse Square, Bermondsey. Although it shamelessly flirted with sporting cliché, Haye often outlined the aforementioned scenario with unshakeable confidence and clarity.

The boxer's second dream, however, dabbled in far more surreal and disturbing territory, and many years later would arrive at my doorstep as a byproduct of long-term trust and loyalty.

'In this dream I look like David Haye, but don't feel like David Haye,' he'd tell me. 'I think I'm in my twenties, but cannot be sure. I'm wearing a pair of white shorts and red gloves and am standing in the centre of a boxing ring throwing punches at thin air. The canvas is thick and sticky like treacle. I don't know why I'm punching, but can't seem to stop.

'I look across the ring at my opponent, but it's hard to make out his face or recognise the name on his trunks. His face is a blur. Completely anonymous. It's freaky. He just stands there and lets me punch. He doesn't even come after me or block. I feel terrible. My punches are long, slow and all wrong. Everything I do is sloppy and lethargic. I try closing the gap on my opponent, but my punches always fall short, no matter how close I try to get. The punches get worse and worse, and remind me of the kind of shots I'd throw as a little kid starting out at the Lodge. The weird thing is, I look great physically and my abs have never been more defined. I'm in the best shape of my life, but I can't throw punches properly.

'I then start sweating and become distracted. I nearly trip over the arms of some ringside photographers poking under the bottom rope, and then realise the ring-card girls are waving and flirting with me at ringside. They're not even pretty, though, and it starts to jar me. They're ugly as hell. I find myself wondering why they were picked for the job and it pisses me off. Everything just feels wrong and out of place. I haven't even been hit yet, but I feel like I've lost. Everybody laughs at me. I can't do what I was born to do.'

It was then that Haye would wake from his slumber, wipe the sweat from his brow and dart in haste towards the bathroom mirror. He'd run his trembling hand across his face, checking for any sudden bumps and bruises, before firing left jabs and right crosses at an invisible tormentor. He sought confirmation and reassurance, a sign that reality still cast him as an aspiring boxer with the world at his feet. This recurring dream would nudge Haye at various intervals in the lead-up to fights, and each time the boxer would be forced to wake, sit bolt upright, remember and realign. He never liked to tell people about it, so would instead adopt his other voice and visualise a bare mantelpiece in Gatehouse Square and two proud parents expecting a delivery.

My own boxing dream also centred on the idea of satisfying loved ones on a wet afternoon in a nondescript living room, situated far closer to Aldershot, Hampshire, than Bermondsey, south London, mind you. The vision entailed stepping inside a time machine and enjoying, if only for one day, the so-called golden era of prizefighting that youth had robbed me of ever experiencing. I dreamed of watching Muhammad Ali with my grandfather, and Sugar Ray Leonard with my father. We'd congregate in a similarly modest room to the one Haye planned to decorate with a world heavyweight title, and would relish the chance to deride Ali's hopes of defeating Sonny Liston in 1964, before bouncing around deliriously as Marvin Hagler and Thomas Hearns launched leather-coated grenades at one another in 1985. Instead, by 2003, boxing's obsessive need to self-harm had perturbed perfectionists, those who had experienced the good times, and bemused newcomers – the kind who, like me, were chasing the promise of our own Ali or Leonard. The idealised boxing dream had become a prolonged nightmare, and very few were sticking around long enough to wake up and shadow-box in front of a mirror for reassurance.

My father Graham still enjoyed watching prizefighting on television, but often didn't know or care to know who was fighting or for what prize. Boxing in the twenty-first century had already managed to confuse and isolate even its staunchest followers, and my father had now been lost and bemused for many years. A one-time fan of both Ali and Sugar Ray, he wasn't about to relearn the intricacies of a sport that had once meant so much both to him and to an entire lost generation. The fact that he couldn't tell you the names of current world champions was boxing's problem, not his. Twenty years ago he, and everybody else, would have found such an examination far easier to ace. This was, after all, now a sport corrupted by greed, and boasting upwards of eight world champions in any one of its seventeen weight classes. And yet, given that I was only fourteen years of age at the time, proclamations of the so-called golden age never stirred me too much. I simply didn't know any better.

'You should have seen Sugar Ray in his prime,' my dad would boast. 'He was like a smaller version of Ali, but was even more exciting to watch. He had everything.'

'Well, have you heard of Roy Jones, Dad?' I'd ask in response, keen to slug him back.

My father frowned, muttered and rubbed his chin. He nodded his head in a way that suggested, 'I should know this – I should know everything my snot-nosed son knows.'

'His name rings a bell,' said my father, clearly fibbing, but revealing just enough to remain on a level playing field.

'Well, he's amazing,' I purred. 'I think he's the best fighter *I've* ever seen.'

'What's so good about him then?'

'He's just so athletic and talented. He can win fights with one hand behind his back. He's the quickest fighter of all time, I reckon. Did you know he can land six left hooks in one second?'

My father didn't dare argue. A walking encyclopaedia on anybody nicknamed 'Sugar', he realised the lights were dimmed when it came to Jones. He'd never heard of him, never seen him, and, until thirty seconds ago, didn't care for him, either, irrespective of the American's standing as an acclaimed former middleweight, super-middleweight, light-heavyweight and soon-to-be heavyweight world champion. Boxing had done this to my father. Boxing had turned him prematurely senile.

Despite his extraordinary hook and look, Pensacola's Roy Jones Jr was never included on any editions of *Knockout Kings*, the

Playstation 2 video game my brothers and I routinely laboured over in preference to homework. Needless to say, this oversight bugged me annually. I'd warn my brothers Adam and Alex, 'If you thought I was elusive with those other fighters, wait until you see how much I piss you off with Roy', but, alas, the spectacle never materialised. Regardless, Jones was my favourite boxer – my Leonard, my Ali – and was the recipient of the kind of love and admiration I'd yet to offer woman or pet. If we'd been afforded the space in our dual bunk-bed room, posters of Jones' six-pack would have undoubtedly and unashamedly adorned the walls.

Roy's routine exclusion from *Knockout Kings* failed to prevent me from applying the gifted American to the ever-expanding roster of customised fighters, of course. The game's basic yet vital editing facility allowed idle layabouts to add their own boxers – even themselves – into the game's pool of playable characters, and such an opportunity was never lost on my brothers and me. A self-confessed boxing anorak from an early age, I'd waste little time drawing up a list of ditched fighters – Roy, Mike Tyson, Kostya Tszyu and Thomas Hearns, to name a few – and then, like *Blade Runner*'s Dr Eldon Tyrell, would go about providing each with a beating heart and soul. The greatest compliment I could bestow on any professional boxer was to include them on my *Knockout Kings* roster and lavish their face and body with the sense of authenticity only a true perfectionist could muster. I wanted a jheri-curled Hearns to catapult the right hand like he did in '85, and needed Tszyu to appear with his trademark ponytail intact, and for it to dance gleefully along with each powerful combination he threw. I was a stickler for the finer points and could never understand why nobody else in the family shared my obsession for pixilated pugilists.

'You're missing the boxing,' warned Nita, also known as Mum, upon successfully prising my hands from a control pad and serving up a plate of food at the kitchen table one Friday afternoon in June.

'What boxing?' I enquired, mind still on the contours of Tszyu's hair.

'Amateur boxing, I think.'

'Oh.'

Mum was right. We were watching the 2001 World Amateur Championships from the Odyssey Arena in Belfast, and Roy Jones Jr was nowhere in sight, hence my blasé approach. The BBC had showcased the event in its entirety, and we were now in the final throes of the seven-day tournament. Four Ukrainians, two Uzbeks, two Turks, two Romanians, two Russians, one Kazakh, one Bulgarian, one Frenchman and one Englishman made the finals that year, but, on the whole, it was plain sailing for the cruising Cubans, who dominated the majority of weight classes from light-flyweight (48kg) to super-heavyweight (over 91kg). Almost four hundred boxers from a record sixty-seven countries competed at the Odyssey Arena, including six reigning world champions, four current European champions and no fewer than twenty-three medallists from the 2000 Sydney Olympics.

'That David Haye's fighting in the final tomorrow, isn't he?' asked Mum, as she provided the finishing touches to meals for the rest of the family.

'Yes, he is,' I replied, moments before the BBC, as if eavesdropping, conspired to run a sequence of highlights from Haye's tournament so far. He was *the* Englishman.

The Bermondsey-born fighter boxed for the East End's Broad Street Amateur Boxing Club at the time and, along with bronze medallist Carl Froch, had illuminated the games for BBC viewers. In fact, the twenty-year-old Haye's appearance in the heavyweight final marked the first time an English fighter had ever reached the climactic stage of amateur boxing's most demanding international competition. This all meant very little to me at this stage, of course. I just wanted to see Roy Jones, and perhaps introduce my father to his miraculous left hook while I was at it.

Nonetheless, Haye's semi-final victory over Uselkov was enthralling in a way most other amateur fights weren't. A victor by twenty-seven points to fifteen, Haye appeared at times as though he wasn't sure whether he should be attacking or defending, but demonstrated both actions with a conviction that belied his scatty technique. He didn't seem able to control the God-given gifts he'd been blessed with, including fast and powerful hands and over-sized limbs, yet made each rudimentary swing count. This immense athletic specimen seemed as though he'd been moulded from elastic and was able to bend, twist and contort in ways that other fighters, especially rigid European ones, were unable to. He had a relaxed and liquid nature to his supple boxing style, something fight fans often described as the 'American way'. Dare I say it, the Englishman appeared almost Jones-like at times.

Haye also helped me overcome my phobia of amateur boxers going the distance. Packing dynamite in both fists, but especially the right, he was never content until his opponent was prematurely sniffing canvas. He fought with an intensity and impatience lost on or diluted by other, perhaps better-schooled amateur fighters, especially the Cuban masters. Haye was an out-and-out destroyer, a pugilist developed and destined for the brutal demands of the professional game. Amateur opponents lucky enough to last the distance with him, including Uselkov, only did so because their cranium was supported by an outer padding of headguard. Remove the wall of protection and Haye would have been knocking *everybody* out cold. The combination of speed and power was vicious and, though wild and agricultural at this stage, represented early building blocks most fighters would sacrifice a right arm for.

I sat and watched the television that afternoon as an exhausted

Haye, holding an icepack to his right bicep, attempted to rationalise his stunning rise to silver medal position through an interview with Mike Costello of the BBC. As well as looking like a killer between the ropes, it was Haye's humble and self-deprecating style outside the ring that captivated both my mother and me. In all honesty, her highness was never a massive fan of violence at the best of times, so was always swayed more by a well-constructed sentence than a well-picked punch combination. Though barely free from his teenage years, Haye already excelled at both, much to our mutual pleasure.

The sound of Haye's words entering my eardrums roused as much instant gratification as the first time I listened to Jimi Hendrix's *Electric Ladyland* as an after-the-event teenager. He was everything I wanted in a fighter and so much more. Cool and clever, of both sight and sound. A pin-up with a penchant for a punch-up. Catch him at the right angle, through squinted eyes, and you might even think you were watching Hendrix in gloves.

By the time the BBC interview finished, I realised I'd been sitting in front of an empty plate for approximately ten minutes and scampered upstairs to kickstart more productive pursuits.

'I've got someone new to make,' I said to my brother as the door slammed shut behind me.

'Who?' asked Alex, far less intrigued than I would have liked him to be. I grabbed the control pad from his hands and took the pilot's seat for this one. My masterpiece.

'I'm creating David Haye,' I said.

'Who?'

'The English guy boxing in the final tomorrow. He's going to be brilliant.'

'The heavyweight?'

'Yeah, but I think I might put him in as a light-heavyweight. He's too small and skinny to ever be a proper heavyweight.'

'Okay,' said my brother, as he climbed to his feet and wandered off towards the door. This major breakthrough was clearly far less of a eureka moment for him than it was for me.

'Who is he fighting tomorrow?' he said.

'Odlanier Solis,' I replied. 'The Cuban.'

'Oh. Well, he's lost that then, hasn't he?'

The question was rhetorical, of course. Even an uneducated peasant like my brother knew the score with the Cubans when it came to amateur boxing. I was on the verge of announcing Haye as my greatest fighting creation to date, and yet could do nothing about his inevitable defeat the following day.

Odlanier Fonte Solis was six months older than David Haye and had already twice beaten Cuban legend Felix Savon. The 21-year-old phenom was considered Cuba's next great amateur heavyweight and the continuation of a tradition established by Savon and Teofilo Stevenson before him. Solis wasn't only expected to beat Haye comfortably, but was also nailed on to win future World Championships and Olympic Games. Such achievements were considered landmark moments in the careers of British boxers, yet Solis and his superiors looked upon tournament wins as merely part of the duty. The absurd concept of failure in élite-level competition was deemed an unforgivable sin back home in Havana. Like many great Cubans before him, winning was something taken for granted, not praised. With the bar set higher than for most of his peers, Solis, thankfully, had the skills to continually rise above.

The heavyweight favourite's semi-final victory over Sultan Ibragimov was an exhibition of the art of clean and concise amateur theft. Originally starting the contest in Ibragimov's pocket, Solis was quick on the draw, and happy to rely on his snappier hands and reflexes to rob points from his bemused opponent. Solis beat a sustained rhythm on the head of Ibragimov, knocking the southpaw this way and that before soaring into a significant points lead.

Once the head-start was established and Ibragimov's fire extinguished, Solis dropped down the gears and began to immerse himself in the exquisite art of cruise control. This was something at which the Cubans were considered masters, and entailed the winning boxer, more often than not the Cuban, removing their foot from the gas pedal and gracefully gliding through the remainder of the contest, ensuring they received as little punishment as possible. Switching to his back foot, Solis soared around the ring like a malevolent figure-skater, darting back and forth to land solitary jabs or lead right hands whenever he became tired of moving. Stuck in the mud and irreversibly behind on points, Ibragimov was now obsolete in the contest.

Whenever a Cuban hit cruise control, the opponent was better off waving the white towel and heading home. If a Cuban didn't want to get hit, there was no way to argue the point. With defence the priority, Solis pick-pocketed Ibragimov in the fourth and final round to claim a 23–13 verdict at the bout's conclusion.

In a battle of the bands, England's Haye would take to the stage in a thrash metal quartet, while Cuban Solis would calmly ride the rhythm of an eleven-minute instrumental jazz groove. Haye was explosive and unpredictable, a feral mix of athleticism and testosterone. The domesticated Solis, meanwhile, was four teaspoons of measured perfection. He moved better than any other heavyweight in the world and was able to swim in and out of range with sophistication and savvy. Both boxed with their hands tantalisingly by their side, yet the Cuban performed steps for a reason, as Haye trampled on toes and reacted rashly to changes in the direction of the wind.

That's not to say the Englishman was a silent bystander in Saturday's dispute, of course. After all, the best way to beat well-schooled, production-line perfection appeared to be via inconsistent and almost insane imperfection. Haye possessed that, at least, in abundance. Solis had revised the textbook back-to-front, while Haye lazily skim-read, dipping in and out of chapters, only focusing on bits that snagged his interest.

Yet, despite a fourteen-year-old's blindly positive perspective, very few others forecast the Brit taking home gold that weekend. Even the fighter himself, burnt out from a rigorous schedule in Belfast, had doubts going into the biggest fight of his amateur boxing life.

Haye told the BBC on the morning of the fight: 'Mentally I feel very strong and together, but physically it's a different story. I feel really knackered. I've had three fights on the spin without a day's rest, and my body's aching.

'If you want to become the best in the world, this is all just part of it. You've got to put your body through it and sacrifice.'

'Come on, the fight's starting,' hollered our matriarch, as she attempted to fill the living room with as many interested Worsells as possible on Saturday, 9 June. I was already front and centre, of course, eyes locked on the tiny black box in the corner of the room. Normally nonplussed by the sometimes messy nature of a four-round amateur bout, the 2001 World Amateur Championships heavyweight final, and a certain mixed-race Englishman, had, by now, managed to capture our collective attention.

Although the rest of my family shared different levels of interest in the fight, it was heartening to see everybody congregate in the same room and support a British boxer. This kind of communal get-together didn't happen often in the hectic household, especially with boxing as the focal point and a twenty-year-old stranger as ringleader.

Regardless, the fight started and all eyes were on Haye, a man overflowing with nervous energy and bad intentions. He waved his fists around like a sugar fiend in a sweet shop, unsure what to buy from the pick 'n' mix rack. Stinging jabs began to pierce the guard of Solis as Haye's unparalleled hand speed presented the Cuban with a dimension he'd yet to encounter in the tournament. Unwilling to let Haye tee off with jabs, Solis simply upped the pace and charged the gangly Englishman behind a high-held guard.

Then, just as Solis opened up in a neutral corner, Haye found the bingo shot in the form of a scything uppercut that caught the favourite on the unprotected point of the chin. Seemingly unconscious for a split second, Solis reeled back on unsteady legs and scrambled for both his bearings and his pristine reputation.

'He's got him!' I screeched at the television. 'Solis is hurt!' The rest of the family joined in and implored Haye to finish the wounded bull across the ring. However, while in a professional ring Haye would be well within his rights to garnish his uppercut with a fusillade of finishing blows, such primitive instincts are forbidden in the amateur game. Rather than a clean knockdown signalling a count, in amateur boxing the standing eight-count is administered whenever a fighter appears hurt or shaken. Forgetting all about code and clarity for a split second, Haye performed a manic charge in pursuit of the finish.

Thankfully, for the sake of Solis' health, the referee hastily intervened and restored order. Even the poker-faced Solis would have a tough time denying he was hurt by Haye's lethal right hand, though.

In the ensuing mêlée, Haye went back to the neutral corner on the referee's instructions and a shell-shocked Solis received his first and only standing count of the championship, with just twenty-five seconds gone in the final.

'I haven't seen a Cuban hit like that in living memory,' swooned BBC commentator Jim Neilly.

'I've never seen *anybody* hurt like that in the whole competition,' added co-commentator and former WBC world bantamweight champion Wayne McCullough.

Upon the restart, Haye soared to a 7–2 lead and continued to wail away on a subdued Solis. He first got busy with manic right crosses and left hooks, before wisely settling down behind his trusty jab. Stunned, but now stoic, Solis kept his hands high and soaked up whatever Haye spat his way. He remained calm and composed throughout, and occasionally inserted counterpunches amid Haye's fury.

Nevertheless, the Englishman settled for a 9–4 lead after the first round concluded, an advantage he would have no doubt gratefully accepted if offered to him before the bout. Nobody beforehand expected Haye to accelerate past the fast-starting Cuban, let alone press shuffle on his mind with a chilling uppercut.

David started the second round with more of the same vigour, as he zapped lefts and rights into Solis' mid-section from long range. Leaping in and out like a free-spirited puppet on an overlong string, Haye utilised superior foot speed to negotiate positions Solis simply could not match. The Cuban wasn't agile enough to close the distance, and Haye's freakishly long arms were primed to touch flesh and vest from afar.

Problems occurred for Haye when his own pace slowed and he began looking for pit stops, however. If the Brit failed to unload from distance, Solis would sense the reluctance, step forward and ransack his punching zone. Once there, the Cuban swiftly revealed just why he was such a highly regarded talent. Demonstrating punching instincts unmatched by anyone in the amateur game, Solis knew when to throw each shot and did so with an uncanny sense of timing and purpose.

Haye, meanwhile, was being weighed down by introspection and anxiety at this point. Still narrowly ahead in the contest, the Briton's pre-fight injuries became more of an issue with each point Solis clawed back. Suddenly, adrenalin had leaked from our hero's body, and his first-round uppercut seemed a lifetime ago. The adversary in front of him had eradicated the incident from his memory, and now Haye, too, was questioning whether the first-round flashpoint had ever even occurred. His mind was a fog of uncertainty and self-pity, his legs unsteady and punches unsure. With a minute to go in the second round, Solis had sneaked his way back into the fight at 11–11. By the time the bell sounded for the end of round two, Haye was 19–15 down. Solis had scored fifteen points in two minutes, and was now in pole position to grab the medal everybody expected him to win.

Haye's sloppiness continued into the third round, too, as he nailed thin air with awkward lefts and rights, only to be promptly punished for his sins by Solis counters. With thirty seconds gone in the round, Haye dallied by the ropes and copped a couple of punches for his troubles. Believing the underdog to be flagging, the referee jumped in and counted the fighter in red. Embarrassed more than hurt, Haye bent at the waist and stretched out, an act of defiance perhaps performed in the hope of returning some pep to his gasping limbs.

Hands now by his thighs, Haye slung frantic punches in the general vicinity of Solis, but was no longer a threat or feature in the bout. The power had vacated Haye's fists and his attacks were more pesky than purposeful. Experienced beyond his years, Solis quickly sensed this and attempted to close the show.

Checking his invisible watch and calling 'time', the referee then provided Haye's lifeless body with a chance to reanimate backstage. He waved off the contest and rubber-stamped a merciful end to Haye's gruelling championship. The runner-up merely smiled and shrugged at the bout's conclusion, well aware that only his body's inability to perform had forced him to settle for second place. As talented and as adaptable as Solis proved throughout, Haye's frustration was a result of tiredness rather than inferiority. The score at the time of the stoppage was 31–17, a convincing victory in the amateur ranks, yet meaningless should the two have been pros.

'Most people would have been knocked out cold by *that* uppercut,' Haye told the BBC in the aftermath. 'I've knocked out over twenty people with that same shot, and Solis did well to come back. I hit him with the shot and thought the fight was all over. He staggered back and was still a bit "gone", but he managed to recover. I actually did further damage to my bicep when throwing that shot, so I think the punch actually hurt me as much as it hurt him.

'No excuses, though, as the better man won on the day. I'm sure that if the referee had let us continue after the uppercut, my right hand would have been fine to finish him off. That's just the way it goes sometimes.'

All the post-fight talk was of Haye excelling at the next Olympic Games, scheduled for summer 2004 in Athens. The BBC pundits gushed at the thought of a 23-year-old Haye taking the world by storm on the grandest amateur stage of them all. They believed Haye's shock triumph in Belfast offered a precursor to what this bubbling ball of hostility could deliver in three years. However, unlike Solis, the fresh-faced British torchbearer had other options and, cock-blocked at the moment his life-changing uppercut landed, didn't require further evidence to realise fame, fortune and freedom would ultimately be found in a professional ring.

Cuban hero Solis would have been a far safer bet for the 2004 games, of course. Immediately after defeating Haye, the victor was rushed back to Havana, gold medal and first major championship ticked off his extensive to-do list. Just as many had predicted beforehand, Solis had now arrived as Cuba's next great amateur boxing superstar. Still only twenty-one, he had the time and tenacity to reign for years, winning multiple world and Olympic titles in the process. He was young, impressionable and spirited – exactly the way Fidel Castro liked them.

Upon returning to Havana, Solis could have expected to receive a bicycle or second-hand car for his achievements, depending on how the figures added up and how his heavyweight gold measured against those of fellow Cuban gold medallists Mario Kindelan (lightweight), Guillermo Rigondeaux (bantamweight), Yan Bartelemi (light-flyweight), Diogenes Luna (light-welter-weight), Lorenzo Aragon (welterweight), and Damian Austin (light-middleweight).

Bold Brits Haye and Froch were hailed for their ability to hang tough in the final days of the tournament and eventually grab medals – making history in the process – whereas Solis' gold was equalled by six others and unfairly judged against past successes. It was little surprise, therefore, that the Englishman standing in second place on the podium wore a broader grin than the surly Cuban posing at the highest point, a gold medal swinging from his neck. If Haye had got his way and chinned the determined champion in the opening round, Solis would have returned home a silver medallist without any mode of transport. Haye's silver medal, on the other hand, was treated as gold and, rather than viewed as a disappointment, would potentially act as his key to riches and glory in the professional game. In a poignant turn of events, Solis' superior gold medal would ultimately restrict his freedom and opportunity to test himself on the pro stage, yet the defeated Haye was now offered the chance to experience everything hidden from his great Cuban rival. If amateur boxing success merely offered the golden ticket to the chocolate factory, Haye may have triumphed, even in defeat.

CHAPTER TWO
GROWING PAINS

'Boxing promoters are all cunts by nature,' David Haye would later tell me. 'When it comes time to sign with one of these cunts, it's all about choosing which one is the lesser cunt.'

By the end of 2002, a 22-year-old Haye had a choice to make. Dust had collected on his world championship silver medal and the Olympic Games had never seemed further away. Immune to the advice of England head coach Ian Irwin, an injured Haye fled the Commonwealth Games in Manchester earlier that summer, on account of a bicep tear picked up in his first-round bout, and then promptly switched his focus from the Olympics to the professional ranks. Consequently, sharks began to circle, each unaware of the deep-rooted cynicism already coursing through the veins of England's latest amateur star. Even at the tender age of twenty-two, Haye respected none of his many professional suitors, but would eventually pinpoint Eugene Maloney, brother of Frank, as the most tolerable of gathering evils.

Part of the appeal of signing professional terms with Maloney seemed to be the sense of creative control it placed in the hands of both Haye and Adam Booth, his trusted amateur trainer, mentor and pro manager. Keen to plot their own destiny from day one, Haye and Booth were presented with the reins to their own sleigh, while Maloney merely provided the sketchbook upon which both could doodle. Haye was keen to agree to a deal which stretched no further than twelve months, and was adamant he'd be free to once again roam when the contract expired. Although most promoters look for at least a three-year commitment on any deal involving a potential pro star, Haye wouldn't budge and demanded a clearly signposted exit door if things weren't flying the way he pictured them. It quickly became evident that horror stories of the past made this pro newcomer more wary of the threat of promoters than of the punch power of early opponents.

While some fighters chose to shower promoters with expletives, the term 'loser' was more commonly applied to the likes of Tony Booth, a journeyman boxer from Hull, well accustomed to falling short against younger foes. Quite simply, Booth was someone who lost fights with more style and grace than anybody else in boxing. It was what he did best. Defeats were his stock in trade and the USP that kept his schedule busy and pockets full. On 8 December 2002, the night pro debutant David Haye requested his services, Booth proudly puffed out his chest to forty-one professional victories and seventy-two defeats, with eight draws providing some semblance of balance.

A sucker for a late-notice brawl, Booth was the kind of fighter who routinely received the call to box fresh-faced prospects with only hours to spare. Although a cruiserweight by trade, Tony had also campaigned at heavyweight, light-heavyweight and any other division that coughed a modest fee his way.

Fighting Booth was presumably a lot like punching your dad. His hair was grey and thinning, his body snug and comfortable, and his demeanour warm and peaceful. Amusingly, he'd often clown and showboat inside the ring, as though the basics came easy to him and he was merely *deciding* to lose.

On one Friday afternoon in December a phone rang and Booth immediately and instinctively picked up.

'When? How much? Who? Oh, okay. Yeah, I'll be there,' went something like his response.

Sealing the deal with a nod and invisible handshake, Booth accepted the late-notice challenge of becoming David Haye's first professional opponent. In little over forty-eight hours he would come face-to-face and blow-to-blow with one of Britain's most prodigious and hard-hitting amateur stars. In the meantime, Booth put the phone down, shrugged his shoulders, and prepared himself for a day's work with Hull City Council.

Haye's beating of Booth took place forty-five minutes before the advertised time on the entrance tickets, as the BBC, having signed him to a ten-bout deal, were keen to showcase their hot new cruiserweight protégé that afternoon on *Grandstand*. When the broadcast kicked off at midday, Booth was pictured already in the ring, while Haye jigged, smiled and strutted towards his first pro meeting. He entered the hall wearing a black Puma sweatshirt, arms slashed and neck hole baggy and loose, the general appearance reminiscent of a slightly more fashion-conscious Mike Tyson. Like the 'Iron One', Haye thrived on the idea of boxing's black basics and the purity of the violence he was about to exact.

'He doesn't seem like he's got a single nerve in his body,' beamed BBC commentator and former WBC world super-middleweight champion Richie Woodhall. 'I'm impressed just watching him walk to the ring.'

Woodhall spoke for us all. Merely seconds into the scheduled six-round contest, Richie and the rest were slack-jawed at the speed and athleticism on display, as a bamboozled Booth did all he could to escape and survive numerous Haye onslaughts. He was hit by any number of elaborate shots, including slashing right hands and big roundhouse punches, and none of it seemed fair. To the uninitiated, Haye might have been beating up a shyster plumber for a job-not-so-well-done, such was the disparity in athleticism and ambition.

Blinded by speed, Booth dropped to one knee in the first round and then, at the conclusion of the second session, withdrew from the contest due to a rib injury. It came as no surprise to anyone who'd grimaced at the hurting he had to endure.

'For a kid of twenty-two he was unbelievable,' said Booth in the aftermath. 'He's very fast and heavy-handed. He keeps his hands low, but he's got such long arms and it's difficult to get to him. It's an awkward style that reminds me a lot of Tommy Hearns. He hits like him, too.

'It's the first time I've seen David fight, but I think he'll go all the way and become a world champion. The problem they'll have now is persuading fighters to get in the ring with him.'

The wise old man was right. Blighted by his own impatience, and everybody else's fear of fighting him, Haye's first professional tests ranged from the plucky to the deplorable, peaking with ballsy Frenchman Saber Zairi and hitting excruciating lows of American heavy bags Roger Bowden and Vance Winn. Haye shimmied into the fourth round against Zairi, but folded Bowden, Winn and Greg Scott-Briggs in the very first bars of the opening round. Another Brit, Phil Day, gallantly lasted into the second round with the Londoner in Reading.

A student of the sport, Haye accepted the fact that beating up the unlikely lads was an essential part of the game and shared similarities with a teenager's rise through adolescence. It wasn't pleasant, it didn't seem warranted and, at times, he'd feel antagonised, break out in spots, skip classes and hate where both life and the establishment were taking him. In order to make it to graduation, though, Haye had no choice but to struggle on through the ennui, the deepening voice and inevitable growing pains.

CHAPTER THREE
JELLY BABIES

As far as dress rehearsals go, an early encounter with middleweight Howard Eastman was about as daunting as they came. Landing a free spirit like Eastman as a first interview subject was akin to being Peter McNeeley the night Mike Tyson decided he wanted to fight again upon release from jail. The task was overwhelming, thankless, ill-advised, perilous and incredibly intimidating. Lo and behold, Battersea's Eastman would be the first man in the chair for this aspiring sixteen-year-old fight writer and, unlike Pete the 'Hurricane', I wouldn't be handed a penny for my pain.

Working under the guise of an internet scribe, and paid merely in compliments and credentials, I made my way to the Norwich Sports Village in July 2003, an English literature student with one eye on a career in journalism. Eastman happened to be defending his European middleweight crown against French veteran Hacine Cherifi that evening, and I had somehow been approved to cover the event from ringside by Andy Woollatt and Ben Carey, the UK-based editors of fight site eastsideboxing.com. Of course, my father had no problem getting behind the wheel and driving me the five hours it took to reach Norfolk, and showed even less hesitation when asked to stand behind a camera lens, find his spot by the ring canvas and click away. Writer and photographer, we were, above all else, fans masquerading as pros, and neither of us cared a jot. Father and son were ringside and had earned it. Though evidently not *everyone* agreed.

'They're even letting schoolkids turn up and cover these things nowadays,' scoffed one journalist, as he conveniently arrived in time for the main event and arrogantly glanced over to where I had been sat covering a forgettable undercard for five hours straight. He'd brought his wife with him that night too, presumably to hold his biro in the manner she once gripped his penis three decades previously. Rest assured, while I still lived with my parents and blagged my way into eighteen-certificate movies, I was convinced I already knew more about boxing than most of the tabloid Tyrannosauruses who sauntered in late with a blank notebook, stare and soul.

Eastman successfully stopped Cherifi in eight rounds that night, having dished out a steady stream of clubbing blows, and then, as the dust settled on pro victory thirty-eight, there was a weak and reluctant knock on his dressing-room door. Nervous and unsure how Eastman would play me, I made my way inside the changing room and sat at the fighter's feet, watching intently as he removed hand wraps and applied an ice pack to a brewing bicep injury. Save for a mesmerising bleached blond beard, Eastman's face was unmarked, a sign of both his underrated defence and leathery skin.

Renowned for his unpredictability and oddball nature, both inside and outside the ring, the truculent Eastman coped with journalists about as well as he cornered slick counterpunchers. The rambunctious champion rarely smiled, wasn't a fan of quotable quips and revelled in the bizarre and awkward. Research told me Howard had lived on the streets of London from age sixteen to eighteen and owned thirty pet parrots, one of which was called 'Tyson'. No amount of research could prepare me for what lay ahead, however.

'How determined were you to replicate the success of Felix Trinidad and Keith Holmes in stopping Cherifi tonight?' I asked, matter-of-factly, as Eastman finally locked eyes and horns with me.

'Only God could sum up my performance tonight,' said the champion, burying his head in a soaking-wet towel. 'Put in front of me was a highly rated opponent and I overcame him.'

I nodded, smiled, then looked down to consult my notebook for advice. Sensing I was lost without it, Eastman snatched the pad from my hands and proceeded to close it and place it on his lap. He then gestured with his hand for me to continue.

'Do you think that was the sort of performance that will entice Bernard Hopkins into a fight with you?' I said, rocked, unsteady and now working on sheer fighting instinct.

'Who knows?' replied Eastman. 'I hope so. What do you think?'

'I think it will,' I said, hands trembling, unsure what was to come next. 'You won the fight by stoppage, but didn't blow Cherifi away or do anything that would have scared Hopkins off.'

I stopped in my tracks, mouth still open, Eastman's squinting eyes fixed firmly on mine. The words sounded different in my head. Had I really just unintentionally offended a professional fighter sitting only a matter of inches away from my straight and pretty nose? Perhaps sensing my sudden and deep regret, Eastman mercifully smiled and nodded.

'I think you could be right,' he said. 'I gave Hopkins a performance tonight that will have him thinking he can beat me – *but he won't*. I did what I had to do and fought well below my powers, but a victory is a victory. Tonight you only saw fifty per cent of the real Howard Eastman, and against Hopkins or [William] Joppy you will see the other fifty per cent.'

Eastman wiped his face with the towel once more, then placed his bony mitt on my shoulder. I jumped.

'How old are you, brother?' asked the boxer, like a West End doorman.

'Sixteen,' I replied. 'Seventeen next month.'

'Really?' he said. 'That's real good. So you're a big boxing fan?'

'Yes. You're one of my favourite fighters, and this is the first interview I've done with a boxer.'

'I'm sorry I couldn't have been more exciting for you tonight then,' said Eastman.

Before I could grovel, the champion winked and tapped me on the shoulder once more. I watched as his own shoulders loosened up and his angular head moved closer to mine, as though now relishing the interrogation I was about to present him with. He handed me back my notebook.

'Tell the world the door has been opened, my friend,' preached Eastman, towering over me, presumably to ensure my spelling was correct. 'It has been *knocked down*. I no longer have to keep banging on doors. William Joppy and Bernard Hopkins *have* to fight me. I *demand* that those fights take place. I fought the wrong fight against Joppy first time, but still won. I'll fight differently next time and win by an even bigger margin. As for Hopkins, he is a coward. Let him fight me. They say British fighters are bums, they say they can't fight, well let them come fight me. I'll show them all.'

As Eastman exposed the whites of his teeth and extended his hand, I felt proud to be British and relieved to be still alive.

Having conquered the supposedly impenetrable Eastman in July, I spent the next two months running up my parents' phone bill and rattling off numerous fight previews, reports and interviews. A schoolboy dipping into the make-up bag of a genuine sportswriter, I snared unlikely chats with IBF world heavyweight champion Chris Byrd, WBA world bantamweight champion Paulie Ayala and light-welterweight warrior 'Irish' Micky Ward in the first few weeks of this unpaid and potentially fruitless quest for approval in the land of the lost.

'You're from England, right?' asked Ward, midway through a thirty-minute, transatlantic phone interview. 'I've been getting a lot of interviews from England recently.'

'It's probably because of the Gatti fight,' I replied, referring to the Lowell slugger's legendary May 2002 blockbuster with the late Arturo Gatti.

'Yeah, that's probably it,' said Ward. 'I think you might be the youngest reporter from England yet, though. Are you at school or something over there?'

'I'm at college. I've got exams in a couple of weeks.'

'Oh, really? That's great. I wish I'd concentrated harder at school. I might not have had to fight for a living.'

By the time I'd got around to verbally massaging his ego, Ward was thirty-seven years of age and in the process of hauling himself through the rigours of training for a third battle with Gatti. Win or lose, the likelihood was that Ward would retire and stay on the shelf of survivors for good, acting on the advice of doctors, family and friends. His eyesight was already on the wane and his speech slurred more with each conversation I had with him. With that in mind, I felt honoured to speak to the man before his inevitable exit and decline, aware of the debt I owed him for that sterling first clash with Gatti.

'It's still the best fight I've ever seen,' I told him.

'That's very nice of you to say that,' said Ward. 'I'll tell you what, give me your home address and I'll send you a signed picture from the fight. It will cheer you up while you're studying.'

Two weeks later a signed picture of Ward and Gatti trading blows in Connecticut arrived through my parents' letterbox. Scribbled haphazardly in gold marker pen, the message read: 'To Elliot. Keep up the studying. "Irish" Micky Ward.' Wishing he had the same option, I knew Ward meant it.

David Haye's seventh professional fight would take place on Friday, 26 September 2003. My new-found online power and profile allowed me access to the fight, and Haye's own discovery of twenty-first-century self-promotion helped stretch his fan base beyond readers of newspapers and viewers of the BBC. His next fight was also set to take place in Reading and, with the Rivermead Leisure Centre a mere twenty-minute drive from home, my father and I were once again asked to attend and pretend.

Meanwhile, Haye had now followed my lead and was also whoring himself out on boxing websites, posting recklessly on forums under various monikers, including 'Dhaye' and 'David_Haye'. The fighter would frequently log on and discuss the pressing matters of his own career with all those residing on said forums, no question unanswered and all criticism welcome. It appeared as though this interaction with fans on boxing forums boosted both Haye's ego and his profile and, often posting out of sheer boredom and curiosity, the fighter quickly established a reputation as someone who was keen to listen, eager to promote the sport and unafraid of tackling sensitive topics. He was humble, self-deprecating and unassuming. He didn't think himself above any of the fans worshipping his cyber slippers and never once cussed anyone out for throwing up their keyboard as shield and offending him.

Taking advantage of Haye's candour, I soon discovered his email address and contacted the boxer in the hope of securing an interview ahead of or after his seventh pro contest. Within a day, Haye replied to my request and assured me of an interview once he'd 'sparked out' his unfortunate next victim. Following Eastman, Ward, Ayala and Byrd, David Haye would be my fifth subject.

Haye's seventh, meanwhile, would be Lolenga Mock, a Congolese swarmer nicknamed 'Lumumba Boy' and famed for entering boxing rings in leopard-print trunks, complete with detachable tail. If such an image sounds at all humorous or gimmicky, I can assure you the free-swinging wild man could flat-out *fight*. Traditionally a light-heavyweight, Mock was sturdy enough to live and survive in the presence of larger foes, and possessed a jaw that had enabled him to go twelve years without being stopped. By 26 September 2003, the night he travelled to England to face Haye, Mock's professional record stood at a handsome 21–6–1.

It quickly became apparent that Mock was the first genuine test of Haye's career and represented his first interesting assignment as a pro. Yet, while most considered the bout a sizeable risk, the consensus was that the Londoner, by far the bigger man, possessed the size and smarts to keep the squat African in check over the six-round distance. Also, while Mock had twenty-one wins to his name, only seven were registered by stoppage, a stat that revealed a clear lack of punch power on the part of the African. With some doubting the strength of Haye's chin, the choice of the light-fisted Mock as an opponent seemed to veer wisely on the side of caution.

Huddled at ringside in Reading, my father and I watched Haye box in the flesh for the first time and, as it turned out, so nearly the last, as a marauding Mock instantly swung with all he knew, tail blowing in the wind and respect left at the door. Haye impressively used his foe's aggressiveness against him in the first round, as he dropped Mock with a well-placed right hand, before running into trouble in a memorable second stanza.

'Get your bloody hands up, David!' barked my father from ringside, shattering our already flimsy veneer of professionalism. The snarls and stares of nearby photographers forced my father back behind his lens, but his calls were a warning of things to come for Haye. Never a fighter to tuck up behind a traditionally high-held guard, Haye's hands had drooped to an all-time low, perhaps the result of a ridiculously one-sided opening session.

Then *it* happened. Rolling forward with an ungainly stagger, Mock closed his eyes and bowled over an ambitious right hand, thrown like a novice swimmer practising the front crawl. Within a split second the punch bounced off Haye's forehead and sent the Londoner's legs into spasm and his mind into another realm. The crowd collectively gasped as Mock bounced away and Haye sprawled to the floor, no longer able to trust either his legs or his brain. He was a mess of uncoordinated limbs and contradictory thoughts, playing hide and seek within the confines of his own confused mind.

Disaster had struck, and Haye's notorious Achilles' heel once again came back to haunt him. I looked on, mouth agape and eyes bulging, and wondered how my favourite young prospect would dig himself out of this predicament. I focused solely on his legs at this stage and vividly remember how his right leg looked as though it was about to suddenly snap and pop out from beneath him. Haye had no control over his movements and appeared to be operating on broken, malfunctioning limbs. The fighter struggled to one knee, then dozily grinned at both his corner and the referee. Rather than a smirk of confidence, though, Haye's demeanour instead resembled that of an alcoholic at closing time. He was smiling out of delusion and skewed senses, rather than any genuine happiness or confidence. As Mock revved up his engine in a neutral corner, it was clear to everyone that Haye was about to be beaten up and stopped for the first time in his young professional career.

Loading up on each shot with all his might, Mock now performed in a trance of victory. Upon the restart, he threw punches without rhyme or reason, knowing full well Haye had neither the legs nor the smarts to argue for much longer. Unable to stand properly, let alone muster his own retort, he sought refuge once more on the ring canvas, this time by grabbing at Mock's waist and body-slamming him to the floor. It was a freestyle form of time-wasting, as Haye landed directly on top of his stunned opponent and remained content to stay there for a few seconds before the referee tried to drag both men to their feet. The tumble wasn't scored a knockdown in either fighter's favour, yet it allowed Haye priceless time to reconcile with time zone and location. The tumultuous second round ended and, as trainer Adam Booth looked to resuscitate Haye's body and mind in the corner, everybody in Reading was thankful for the cue to breathe.

Ominously, Haye retained his baggy stance in the third round and appeared intent on keeping Mock at bay with quickly slung left jabs and the occasional right hand. He didn't commit to much and wasn't in a position to take chances. Haye instead showed a surprising calm to manoeuvre Mock around the ring for three minutes, limiting the African's opportunities in doing so.

Haye continued into the fourth round with similar restraint, relying purely on his left jab and the sporadic luxury of a right cross. By reducing his punch output, Haye was subsequently suppressing his desire to once again become embroiled in a street fight.

Enough of this nonsense, thought Mock, with an impatient sigh and swing. Sensing he was once more being quietened in the contest, the African began to brawl again with abandon. He shut his eyes, stumbled inside punching range and unleashed right hands, many of them missing, but the odd one or two glancing off Haye's naked shoulder or dome. Still unsure of how to deal with his opponent's frenzied attacks, the Brit instinctively backed up with arms down by his sides and caught one of Mock's right hands on the temple. Our man retreated, in panic rather than pain, and was bullied around the ring by a frantic Mock, keen to take his second chance at finishing the contest. Mock harried and hustled, windmilling punches with a sense of both desperation and impatience, as Haye stepped away and regained composure.

Then, as if slow-motion had allowed David to seize his opportunity, an energised Mock blindly staggered forward into an almighty right uppercut. Mock promptly faltered to the ground with a loud thud as Haye untangled himself from his opponent and skipped to a neutral corner. The African rose, took a deep breath and did his best to lock pupils with referee Mark Green. Bizarrely, an unconvinced Green merely frowned, shook his head and waved the contest off, declaring Haye a sudden and surprising stoppage victor.

Most ringsiders were incredulous, unsure why Mock had been deemed unfit to continue, and upset that an emerging classic had been halted before the pivotal third act. Haye also shrugged and shook his head at the bout's conclusion, in a manner that suggested he agreed with the complaints. Ever the lethal finisher, Haye would have loved nothing more than the chance to end the fight more conclusively. Nevertheless, the victor had managed to power through the fog of his first professional knockdown and remove his head from the vice at the point at which his eyes began to bulge. If critics found plentiful ammunition in his patchy defence and suspect resistance, Haye's display of bravado and punch power endeared the Londoner to all.

'Great finish, David,' I enthused afterwards, as I bravely approached the shattered boxer, moments before the night's main event was about to begin. Perhaps unsurprisingly, Haye's occupied ears, distracted by other surrounding voices, failed to register my generous compliment. I nudged him on the arm in the hope of grabbing his attention. It worked.

'Watch the arm,' yelped David, as he finally spun around. 'Go easy on the arm.'

'Oh, sorry,' I said. 'Are you okay to do an interview? It's me, Elliot.'

'Now's not a good time,' replied Haye, still engaged by those at ringside. 'Shoot me an email when you get home and we'll sort something out. I'll be able to think straight then.'

I accepted the rearranged appointment and shook David's hand, once more bringing a pained wince to his face. 'Careful, my hand is still sore,' barked the fighter, as he briskly pulled away.

'He just doesn't have it,' I whinged to my father two hours later in a McDonald's car park. 'There were rumours that he didn't have the greatest chin before this fight, and now *this* has happened. I can't see how he can get around the problem.'

'He did well to come back, though,' said my father. 'Everybody thought it was over when he got knocked down. I could see it in his eyes that he was hurt.'

'Yeah, but he shouldn't have been struggling with a guy like that,' I spat back, still annoyed that Haye had brushed me off post-fight. 'What's going to happen when a genuine cruiserweight or heavyweight whacks him on the chin?'

Though I was too inexperienced to have been aware of this at the time, one of the disadvantages of watching a fight from ringside is the sheer immediacy of it all. There is no capacity to view or digest an instant replay, and each judgement is a byproduct of gut instinct and emotion. My recollection of this particular fight was that Haye had been nailed clean on the chin and had flopped like a pack of cards in the hand of an inebriated dealer. Each time Haye was buzzed thereafter, the same fate threatened to engulf him. Dejected and bloated on fast food, I was already preparing the post-mortem in the form of my fight report, a damning assessment centred on Haye's inability to withstand a heavy shot to the chops.

However, upon returning home and rewatching the fight video, I soon reached an entirely different conclusion. Originally thinking Mock's right hand had trimmed the Londoner's suspect beard, I later discovered, on reflection, that the shot had instead grazed his forehead, thus upsetting his equilibrium and sending him off-kilter. I'd seen similar shots destroy the senses of sturdy heavyweights and knew the potential for damage. Although perhaps not as definitive as a shot to the chin, anything glancing off the top of one's head can be equally destructive.

'Dad, come and take a look at this,' I shouted into the living room, tape on pause and revitalised by this new discovery in the case. Haye made no excuses for the knockdown afterwards, yet I'd already scrambled one together for him. Contrary to popular opinion, Haye's chin wasn't even cracked once during the fight.

Leaving the c-word alone for a moment, I decided to backtrack and base my report around Haye's defensive inadequacies and the shortcomings of his hands-down approach. Of course, many of my favourite fighters boxed with low-held hands, so the style never particularly bothered me, but Haye's laziness with it clearly led to his near downfall in Reading. Whereas in previous contests his stance was at least loosely comparable to some of my boxing heroes, against Mock he wallowed in an ill-advised style all of his own. I searched long and hard for the words to describe it, aware that no other fighter could provide comparison. It was then that, suddenly, like a Mock right club, it struck me from out wide. 'At times,' I wrote, 'Haye resembled an arthritic attempting to walk a jelly baby to school.' I'd done it. My first *mildly* original line. The fifteen-hundred-word report wrote itself from that point on, though I later stalled to ponder how Haye would react to it. After all, the report and accompanying putdown were set to hit the World Wide Web with my byline attached. A blossoming internet junkie, Haye would no doubt stumble across the piece and the name of its architect on his idle travels.

Three days later and twenty-four hours after my report – 'walking jelly babies' included – hit the online boxing bubble, I received an email from David Haye. Yes, *the* David Haye. The email was ostensibly in response to my request for an interview, yet the subject line had curiously changed to 'LOL'. Aware of what the phrase meant in internet-speak, I jumped on my computer and opened the email as quickly as my shoddy dial-up connection could manage, keen to discover what had made the fighter apparently Laugh Out Loud.

'Sorry I couldn't do the interview on Friday,' went Haye's email. 'I hope I wasn't too rude to you after my fight. I was still a little bit "gone" and didn't know what was happening or who I was talking to. I read your report and loved it – especially the line about jelly babies. Think of some questions and we'll do this interview ASAP. Don't sugarcoat them – I can take it.'

I gradually opened my eyes, uncrossed my fingers and breathed, still alive and seemingly in line for an interview. Better yet, I'd received confirmation that Haye was both accessible and secure enough to appreciate a punch-line amid so much incoming negativity. This ride could be fun, I thought to myself. So, with that, I quickly forgot any nagging doubts and reclaimed my seat on the emptying bandwagon, now every bit a fan of the person as I was of the fighter. If there were soon to be inevitable question marks surrounding Haye's ability to ship punishment inside the ring, there was little doubt he could take what was dished out away from the office. Just go easy on handshakes.

CHAPTER FOUR
NINE LIVES

We reconvened at York Hall, Bethnal Green in December 2003, the fighter dressed for a night on the tiles and the writer sitting ringside with a notebook and pen in hand. David Haye was four weeks on from a stunning minute-and-a-half demolition of Lincoln's Tony Dowling to win the English cruiserweight title, a deadly deed committed at the very same venue. He'd left his title at home that December night, but appeared eminently more accessible than he'd done when beating Mock and, indeed, Dowling. There were no gloves or distractions in sight, and the newly crowned English champion seemed content to linger and mingle at the back of the hall while a night of boxing was showcased in the ring.

Meanwhile, Haye's trainer and manager, Adam Booth, was guiding another of his boxers, Stephen Smith, through final preparations ahead of a bout with relentless Northampton scrapper Alan Bosworth. The pair were set to meet over ten rounds for the English light-welterweight title, and both boxers saw the belt as the culmination of tough careers, as opposed to a stepping stone to loftier titles. There was, of course, no doubt as to the status the same belt carried for cruiserweight titleholder Haye. Proud to have won his first pro strap in November, Haye was already on the hunt for bigger and better accolades.

With only a burgeoning love of Roy Jones Jr in common, I sensed the time was right and patiently waited for my moment, keen to distance myself from the look of a teenage deviant on the warpath for a scribble or a smile. Eventually, I strode confidently over to the new English champion and extended my hand, just as the pros would.

'Hi David,' I said with a grin. 'It's me, Elliot.'

'What's up, mate?' replied Haye, as he shook my hand and backed away from the gathering crowd.

'Did you see the Roy Jones fight the other week?' I asked, referring to Roy's lacklustre decision win over Antonio Tarver to once again reclaim the WBC world light-heavyweight crown.

'Yeah, I did. I couldn't believe how bad he looked. I think dropping all that weight has hurt him. He didn't look anything like the Roy Jones of old. I was really worried that he might lose. He just didn't have *anything* there.'

While both Haye and I marvelled at Jones' 2003 destruction of John Ruiz at heavyweight, we shared extreme concerns for our hero's move back down the divisions. Fast approaching thirty-five years of age, Jones wasn't in a position to skip up and down the weights, gain and drop muscle mass and remain fresh, sprightly and as good as old. In dropping 20lbs to face Tarver, a forlorn Jones appeared drawn in the face, creaky in movement and empty in the tank.

'He should have just stayed at heavyweight,' said Haye. 'There was actually no need to drop down and face Tarver. Roy had already won something like seven belts as a light-heavyweight. What's the point in going back down to your old division and just reclaiming one of them? A win over Tarver does nothing for Roy's legacy and yet he risked his life by dropping back down and fighting him. It all came down to pride in the end.'

It seemed that the trauma of watching twelve rounds shared by

Jones and Tarver had upset Haye's fighting Utopia. Suddenly the world around him no longer made sense. Unassailable superstars appeared beatable.

'And what about you?' I asked. 'What's next?'

'I'll probably defend my English title in January,' added Haye. 'I'm not bothered who I fight, I'll take on anyone in Britain who thinks they can beat me. It's only getting harder to find opponents, though.'

I finished scribbling Haye's quotes into my notebook, and inadvertently created a lull in our conversation, lengthy enough to allow Haye to sweep in with a counter-shot of his own.

'How old did you say you were?' he asked.

'I've just turned seventeen,' went the reply.

'It's pretty strange to see someone so young follow boxing the way you do. So you go to all the fights, do you?'

'Yeah, well, the ones I can get into.'

'Are you going to Danny's [Williams] rematch with [Michael] Sprott in January?'

'No, I don't think so. I'll probably have difficulty getting a credential.'

'Don't worry about that. Adam [Booth] is Danny's manager and we'll get you in. Give me a call in a week to remind me, but we'll definitely get you a seat, if you want to go.'

A six-round heavyweight bout was in mid-flow as I entered the Wembley Conference Centre that January night and, conscious of disturbing anyone's view of the violence, I settled for a place in the cheap seats to begin with. It didn't bother me, of course. This was, after all, the distance from which I was accustomed to viewing fights. Up ahead I spotted David Haye sitting amongst the superior beings at ringside, head sporadically rotating left and right, as though wary of hit-men who might be out to collect a cheque for his head.

As the fourth round came to an end, Haye spun around in his seat and glanced back at the mass of peasants behind him. Homing in on my bottle-green jacket, he waved, pointed and beckoned me forward. Turned out it was me he was looking for. Those in close proximity stared in disbelief as the boxer invited me to cheat and join him at ringside. Somewhat embarrassed, I shrugged, mouthed an apology, stepped over a rotund man's legs and made my way towards a better view.

Once there, Haye was all smiles and flash watches as he showed me to my seat and gained satisfaction from the fact he'd performed his good deed for the day. I sat down in row B and, for starters, watched Dagenham's featherweight prospect Kevin Mitchell physically abuse a far smaller and inferior victim inside one round.

Meanwhile, Haye's trainer Adam Booth, clearly in the middle of something important, made his way towards us, like me, doing his best to avoid any outstretched limbs that blocked his path.

'This is Elliot,' said Haye, as he introduced me to his distracted mentor.

'Oh, really?' replied Booth with a handshake. 'I've heard *lots* about you.'

'Good things, I hope,' went my response.

'No,' said Booth, with a surprisingly stern and straight face. 'Not all good things.'

I waited for the accompanying grin, cheeky wink or the 'just kidding' punch on the arm, but none of these arrived. Booth was tetchy, serious and paranoid in his dedication to the night's impending battle. Before I could probe his frosty character further, Booth was waved off somewhere else and skipped to his next role as manager of the evening's main event champion. He may have muttered a 'goodbye' or flicked a passing gesture, but I never heard or saw either. This was boxing, and Booth had a job to do. Haye's wingman was determined and ambitious in a way that only a young trainer and manager could be. New to the sport and widely lambasted for playing such a significant role in the development of a future fighting star, Booth was having to prove himself and exhibit qualities in a tired institution blind to youthful invention and talent.

A former university lecturer, amateur boxer and footballer, clean-cut Booth first came into contact with a sixteen-year-old Haye in 1996. Working as a young trainer at the time, Booth one day took friend and fighter Chris Okoh down to the Fitzroy Lodge Amateur Boxing Club in pursuit of sparring partners. Okoh was a twenty-seven-year-old Commonwealth cruiserweight champion, and a man of imposing physical stature. Comparatively childlike, the cocksure Haye nevertheless accepted the invitation to spar. Rounds quickly passed and Booth soon forgot who was champion and who was the teenage upstart. Haye dazzled against Okoh and blurred the line between veteran and prospect. The twenty-eight-year-old Booth was suitably impressed and keen to invest in the Haye rise, eventually befriending, nurturing, mentoring and teaching the youngster through his temperamental teenage years.

Booth was now thirty-five – educated, articulate, forward-thinking – and boasted the looks of a man better suited to the lead role in a Robert Downey Jr biopic than the lonely corner of a ring in a boxing gym. His face didn't fit, and I soon realised that Booth was uncomfortable in his role as promising trainer and manager. He was skittish and wary of trusting or believing anyone. Booth was proving himself in a dying sport and was spared any favours or approving backslaps from the condescending old guard.

By the time the main event's participants were wheeled out, both Haye and Booth positioned themselves front and centre of row A and slipped on their game faces. Booth had been in British heavyweight champion Danny Williams' corner for his most recent battle with Michael Sprott in Reading, but had to sit out this third match, acting only as the Brixton fighter's manager. Williams was back with old trainer Jim McDonnell, a former European featherweight champion and a man with vastly more ring experience and trade kudos than Booth.

We all watched as Williams sleepwalked through twelve rounds with Sprott, unable to shift out of first gear and launch anything resembling a meaningful attack. A curious display, which included plenty in the way of showboating and tongue-poking, but little in the way of punching, landed Williams a decision loss at the climax. His British and Commonwealth titles went home with Reading's Sprott, the busier man and someone Williams had twice defeated already.

My attention throughout was divided between wincing at the dire spectacle inside the ring and admiring the sight of Haye and Booth advising, guiding, motivating and rallying their flagging friend in oversized trunks. Both displayed the kind of technical nous and clarity of voice that were often absent when one would eavesdrop on advice bellowed from ringside. Every nugget the pair launched Williams' way appeared to make sense, yet the eighteen-stone heavy-weight could do nothing to act upon it. Haye roared his voice hoarse in desperation, while Booth, the more concise and composed of the two, broke down events with an impressive accuracy and understanding.

The most revealing aspect of this whole farrago, however, was the clear frustration and regret that lingered in the voices of both Haye and Booth. While Haye was annoyed at his pal for not being able to soar through the gears like he could, the young cruiser-weight was also desperate to heed his own advice in the ring some-time soon. He wanted to be involved in similar fights, meaningful twelve-rounders for worthwhile titles, and was adamant he wouldn't flatter to deceive the way his friend had.

Booth, on the other hand, had seen his own professional boxing career evaporate after breaking a leg playing football. Boxing as a light-welterweight for Lynn Amateur Boxing Club, Booth won forty of forty-eight bouts and was on the brink of signing pro terms with leading British promoter Micky Duff at the time of the break. Gifted in the ring and on the football field, Booth now had to settle for preaching moves from either the corner or row A, as a flock of dying vultures scoffed and derided his every move. Aloof though he undoubtedly was, I couldn't help but sympathise.

I was back in the press row come February, waving through black suits at Haye, as the fighter took his seat in the VIP area of Sheffield's Ponds Forge Arena. We had accidentally met once more, this time in the name of seeing lovable cruiserweight crash dummy Carl Thompson, now thirty-nine years of age, regrettably get pounded into dust and subsequent retirement by the younger, fresher and faster South African Sebastian Rothmann.

Tel-Aviv-born Rothmann was the IBO cruiserweight champion and had already shattered the hopes of British boxers Mark Hobson, Crawford Ashley, Garry Delaney, Rob Norton and Kelly Oliver in previous WBU title defences. Yet to hit thirty and fully reach his potential, Rothmann had lost only once in twenty pro bouts and was considered a danger to Thompson's health. He was cocky, flash and had a knack of mercilessly beating opponents up round after round before delivering the *coup de grâce* when the finish line was agonisingly in sight. In short, Rothmann was the worst kind of foe for any sagging veteran.

Enter Bolton's Thompson, who returned from assumed retire-ment in 2003 to register three low-key victories over journeymen Phil Day, Hastings Rasani and Paul Bonson. Hardly the kind of form-line to strike fear into the gut of a dominant champion, of course, yet Thompson received his shot at the belt through repu-tation, rather than any standout recent wins. Although rapidly approaching forty years of age, Thompson always guaranteed a dust-up, irrespective of whether he ended fights with his arm raised or in a sad heap on the canvas. As if impervious to pain and fatigue, Thompson was the real-life bogey man, a lump of flesh shot and stabbed countless times, yet still somehow able to continue stumbling forward in a daze of stubbornness. Of course, most considered Carl to be shot at thirty-nine, his speed and balance having deserted him on the evidence of three lacklustre comeback bouts. The former champion now tottered rather than prowled around the ring, his coordination hampered by years of brutal altercations and blows to the brain. He was shaken and stirred by punches that once brought only a shrug from his broad shoulders. Yet, with the closure of Carl the assumed order of the day, none of us could look away. The only man in the building who appeared to show zero affinity for Thompson was IBO champion Rothmann, a leering and languid box-fighter with a desire to make mincemeat of Carl's frail physique.

Through the first three rounds of their bout, it seemed Rothmann was on course to do just that, too, as he prodded for openings and powered sledgehammer shots into the wrinkled features of the beloved antique in front of him. One right hook in the fourth round buckled Thompson's knees and forced him to slump towards the ropes, touching down momentarily in the process. Rothmann smirked, spun away and raised his arms in delight at registering the first knockdown of the bout. Hands down, chin jutted forward and tongue occasionally protruding in ridicule, Rothmann peppered Carl at the restart, then shook his head like a father taunting a toddler with a rattle.

Despite the champion's overt display of arrogance, though, Thompson was still somehow alive and punching. As many can attest, that's often enough for Carl. With the end seemingly in sight, a dazed Thompson suddenly exploded with a Hail Mary right hand to the exposed chin of Rothmann, which, followed by a jarring uppercut, dramatically dropped the champion into the ropes at the bell to end round five. Referee Richie Davies administered a count and, in a stunning turn of events, Thompson's never-say-die spirit and concussive power had dramatically swung the bout back around in his favour.

Having barely survived the tumultuous fifth round, Rothmann smartened up through the middle sessions, stuck his jab and right hand in Thompson's face and distorted the Briton's grill whenever he forced the issue too much. Stung by Thompson's power, Rothmann's tongue remained in a closed mouth and childish taunts made way for a new-found maturity and concentration.

The onslaught had once again become worryingly one-sided by the ninth round, as Rothmann snatched his second wind, bounced around in jubilation and then dumped multiple jabs onto the welcome mat of his ageing adversary. Sensing his man was on the way out, Rothmann tagged Thompson with a cuffing right hand and watched as the challenger groggily swayed back against the ropes on unsteady pins.

The champion proceeded to shuffle forward and throw a stream of rights in the direction of Thompson, before stepping back for a better look, perhaps to entice the challenger to foolishly relax and open himself up.

The action then seemed to freeze, as the fading home favourite aimlessly lurched forward from the ropes. In one seamless movement, Thompson sucked it up, capitalised on the momentary lull, touched Rothmann with a measuring-stick jab and then pulverised the visitor with one of the hardest and loudest right crosses my young eyes and ears had ever witnessed. Grin eradicated, Rothmann took the punch flush on the jaw and dissolved head-first onto the canvas in a humiliated heap.

Although he somehow bravely made it to his feet, Rothmann was in no position to continue and could only wobble back into the ropes as referee Davies waved the contest over. Carl Thompson was back from the dead. Again.

Intoxicated by the hit he'd provided us all with, I blindly followed the ringside press hounds towards Thompson as he departed the ring and stumbled into his dressing room. Sceptics turned believers, the ringside faction had formed a humbled shield around Thompson as he made his exit. While most reporters were told to hold back and wait for their signal, my youthful looks allowed better access and a free ride inside the new champion's changing room.

'Let's go and see Rothmann,' declared Thompson, before he'd de-gloved, changed, showered and consulted the increasingly anxious doctor on hand. 'Where is his changing room?'

Utilising my better knowledge of the venue's layout, I shot my arm in the air and signalled for Thompson and his team to follow me towards the South African's place of recovery. Once there, Thompson and Rothmann immediately met in an embrace of blood, sweat and mutual respect.

'I'm sorry I showboated like that,' said the shirtless former champion as he slumped down on the wooden bench supporting his frail pins. 'I didn't mean any disrespect by it. I do that in all my fights. Nothing personal.'

'It's fine,' said Thompson. 'Believe it or not, you actually helped me by doing that. I could see you smiling and poking your tongue out, and I thought, right, this guy's going to get it now. All those taunts just drove me on, mate.'

They both laughed and tapped fists in appreciation of what they'd just shared.

'Maybe I need to stop doing all that stuff then,' said Rothmann. 'I usually just do it to motivate myself, y'know?'

'Exactly,' said Thompson. 'I knew why you were doing it. I knew you were only doing it because you felt tired or because you were hurt. That's why it just made me come on stronger. I loved watching you do that.'

The pair separated on doctor's orders, though one got the impression they could have continued chatting long into the night.

On my way out of the new champion's court I bumped into Haye as he relaxed in the corridor ahead of his own appointment with the king. He had provided on-air comments for the BBC and was as mesmerised by Thompson as the rest of us.

'I've never seen anything like that before,' said Haye. 'I thought he was finished about ten times during the fight and yet he kept coming back. You've seriously got to spark that guy clean out to stop him. He's incredible. I honestly don't know how he does it.'

'You don't want too many of those fights in your career, though,' I replied.

'No way,' said Haye. 'You don't want *any* of those if you can help it. That's not my kind of thing at all.'

One month later, Haye blitzed a terrified Hastings Rasani in 137 seconds of the very first round in Wembley. He remained unbeaten in the process.

PART TWO

David Haye prepares to face Carl Thompson and preserves his precious hands in ice buckets while on training camp in Bournemouth.

CHAPTER FIVE

BIG BALLS

I was told a boxing gym could be found in London's West End, within the four walls of a peculiar place known as The Third Space. Eyes inquisitive and frown forming, I waited for the punchline. Eager to investigate and ensure I wasn't being set up, I later discovered this building doubled as a fitness centre and played host to the rich and famous, as well as a certain young prizefighter. I still wasn't convinced. The Third Space? If a boxing gym with that name had ever opened in Philadelphia, Smokin' Joe Frazier would have been a synchronised swimmer. The name alone brought to mind *Twin Peaks* – dancing dwarves, claret curtains, chewing gum and Kyle MacLachlan's tape recorder. Situated along Shaftesbury Avenue, the place sounded otherworldly, in both name and reputation.

This would be like no other boxing gym I'd ever encountered. The Third Space, so the myth went, was an entirely different interpretation of old boxing folklore. Rather than train amongst the grunts and sweat of fellow fighters, young cruiserweight hope David Haye was happier preparing alone for fights in the basement of central London's swankiest fitness club. Fight posters were nowhere to be seen and, rather than preach the ills of distraction, The Third Space seemed to promote and employ them, as female instructors were kitted out in tight spandex outfits, accentuating their impressive forms and head-turning capabilities.

Nothing was cheap, dirty or macho about The Third Space. Lights were dimmed, colours were sensual and nobody shouted or screamed. You had to search hard to hear the thwack of leather on flesh or the guttural scream of a fighter crippled by a well-placed liver shot. Entering the building, you could be forgiven for thinking you'd aimlessly wandered into a library, spa, portal into the future, or a unique combination of all three.

Rather than park down on seats, visitors were ushered towards huge rubber yoga balls, perfectly shaped to guarantee a comfortable rest. Meanwhile, city men and women entered through turnstiles, flashing their cards, wallets and blinding white teeth.

'I'm here to see David Haye,' I told the female receptionist at the front desk. 'He told me to meet him for an interview.'

I was advised to take a seat on the inflatable silver scrotums and did as I was told. I plumped my backside down and waited, all the while flicking through a copy of the *Financial Times*, as though I genuinely cared about what was inside. Whereas copies of *Boxing News* or *The Ring* could be found in most boxing gyms up and down the country, *The Third Space* catered for a different kind of readership. Unable to even comprehend how one might read and enjoy the *Financial Times*, my mind instead recalled why I'd found myself in this strange place to begin with.

'Come and spend the day with David and me,' Adam Booth had said over the phone two days before. 'You can do a feature on him for *Boxing News*. I think the time is right now.'

'Why is that?' I asked.

'Keep it quiet, but it looks like the Carl Thompson fight is on. We're looking at a date in September, but it seems very close to being agreed. It's going to be for the IBO title, now that David has secured a ranking.'

BIG BALLS

By the time I was sitting alone on a space-hopper in The Third Space, the fight had been signed and sealed and a 10 September date was in the works. Though only ten bouts into his fledgling professional career, Haye had secured the bout he'd been working towards, far earlier than many expected.

To get the ball rolling, in May he'd impressively defeated former IBF world cruiserweight champion 'King' Arthur Williams inside three rounds to nab an IBO ranking. It was the finest performance of Haye's career to date and the first indication that he was ready to butt heads with the division's rhinos. Sure, Williams was spitting copious amounts of debris at thirty-nine years of age, but the American veteran still presented tangible risk and had mixed in a far higher class. Through nearly three rounds of action, Haye was as perfect as a young prizefighter could be, and barely took any leather in return. He made it look easy.

Thompson, like Williams, was thirty-nine and considered on the slide. He was a weathered force, renowned for shipping unsightly doses of punishment before rallying back. Youth and speed appeared to be his kryptonite and Haye possessed both in abundance. An air of inevitability surrounded the September match-up, and the assumption was that the two fighters had effectively signed up for an agreed passing of the torch. Haye and Thompson were both now under the same Fight Academy promotional banner and, while Thompson's fights remained eminently watchable, Haye was considered the future star and long-term company breadwinner. An IBO ranking and handshake sealed the deal, and both fighters knew their respective roles in the impending battle. Everybody seemed happy. Well, *nearly* everybody.

'Believe it or not, my mum doesn't actually want me to fight Carl,' said Haye, as he finally sat down alongside me on his own super-sized gobstopper at The Third Space. 'My parents have been big fans of Carl for years now, and they didn't want me to ever fight him. We used to watch his fights back in the day, including the ones he had with Chris Eubank, and our family would always support him. My mum really liked him as a person, too. I think he's an even nicer guy now that he's allowed me a shot at his belt.'

Haye was never afraid to express his admiration for Thompson, despite the fact that some may have interpreted it as a weakness or character flaw. He had no problem declaring how much he respected Thompson's fighting skills or how much he liked the person behind the gloves. Haye was human, after all. Yet, behind this veneer of mutual respect, I discovered a far more sinister and cold reason for wooing Thompson to a fistic sleepover.

'It doesn't matter how much I like somebody, I'm still going to try and violently knock them out,' said Haye. 'I'd support Carl against anybody else, but in this fight he's getting destroyed. Right now he's stopping me get something I want. He's stopping me make money and fulfilling my dream of becoming a world champion. I'm going to destroy him and I'm going to do it quickly. I don't want to punish him for a long time – I just want to clean him out quick.'

We walked from The Third Space reception, over the glass floors offering a dizzying view of the swimming pool below, down the stairs and then through a corridor, which presented the first indication of potential combat. The red walkway that connected the boxing portion of the gym to the rest of the complex was decorated with images of Muhammad Ali and Mike Tyson, two fighters who had made an everlasting impression on the psyche of a teenage Haye. Then, once memories of Ali and Tyson passed, the boxing gym and adjoining punch bags came into view. The ring was empty, the bags motionless, and standing apart from a gathering of vein-busting weightlifters was the solitary figure of coach Booth, the man armed with the task of masterminding Haye's planned destruction of Thompson.

There was an invisible line separating Haye and Booth from those who paid to pump iron and stare longingly into mirrors for hours on end. Nobody bugged them on days like this. The fighting pair were a welcome part of The Third Space set-up, and would often mingle and interact with staff; yet, when it came time to go to work, the two preferred to be as distanced from the crowd as possible. Nobody else could possibly help these two rule-breaking trailblazers. Only Gary Logan, the former Southern Area light-middleweight champion and personal trainer at the complex, could cast an analytical eye or valued morsel of advice without fear of backlash.

Despite the serious connotations of business, however, both fighter and mentor appeared to find it difficult to conduct a session without a certain amount of jocularity. They didn't do silence, and Haye, especially, was strangely at his most focused and effective when distracted.

'I was born with a black eye,' he said, while extravagantly skipping in front of a large mirror. 'There are early pictures of me as a child, and even in those I look like a boxer who had done ten rounds before being born. Everyone used to mention how monged-up my face looked and how I had that rugged look of a fighter through my early years. My party piece was whacking people with my fists. I was always walking around the house punching things, and it became a bit of a family joke. You had a little one-and-a-half-year-old kid and everyone wanted to feel how hard he could hit. I couldn't even walk at this point, but everyone knew I could dig. Punching tables and kneecaps was how I spent my early years growing up.'

After working up a sweat, Haye showed me the contours of his hands and held them under the only available light for closer inspection.

'I've busted that one a few times already,' he said, as he pointed to his middle knuckle, a sharp, raised lump which jutted out from his hand with an ugly sense of independence. The fighter's hands were riddled with calluses and rough edges, and his dry skin felt like sandpaper to touch. The tools of a killer, Haye's hands were every bit as threatening to look at as they presumably were to taste and, while a relatively smooth and unblemished face contradicted his harsh profession, the boxer's unmasked weapons presented plentiful evidence of many years of cracking leather and kneecaps.

'My mum and dad were big boxing fans and would always leave tapes around with boxing or kung-fu action on them,' said Haye, as Booth meticulously wrapped and protected the boxer's fists as though they were precious minerals discovered at the bottom of an ocean. 'While other kids my age were watching *Sesame Street*, I was watching Jackie Chan movies.'

If Big Bird forever remained a mystery, a ten-year-old Haye found solace in the company of Nigel Benn, Naseem Hamed, Roy Jones Jr and James Toney, all of whom were name-checked that afternoon. Haye rarely showboated like Hamed, but often switched between replicating Jones and Toney. It was time for Toney that afternoon, as Haye remained fixed with his feet and slung stinging shots at Booth's red pads. In between each blurring combination, Haye would share a joke with his trainer or perhaps mock his own technical deficiencies and inability to land the desired dig. The rust was apparent in Haye's punches, sluggish movement and pedestrian pace, yet neither man was particularly flustered or frustrated at this stage. Even with twenty-ounce gloves on, Haye was hitting quicker and sharper than most could with a bare fist.

'Don't worry,' Booth whispered to me, as his fighter rested in between rounds. 'He's looked a lot worse than this before. Believe it or not, this isn't actually *that* bad.'

Booth's revelation was followed by a chuckle between the pair, as I took a moment to fully digest what he'd said. If this was Haye on a *bad* day, I could only imagine what kind of force would be generated in the coming months. Suddenly I felt incredibly sympathetic towards Thompson's expected plight. On natural talent alone, Haye was already playing hopscotch on Thompson's limitations. Training merely presented the challenger with the chance to extend the gap and accelerate further past the champion.

Booth's hard-nosed approach to his pupil seemed to stem from his exposure to the many great ring wizards of the 1980s. His favourite fighter was Sugar Ray Leonard and his go-to fights were those involving Leonard and any one of Marvin Hagler, Thomas Hearns or Roberto Duran. The celebrated antics of the 'Fabulous Four' hooked a teenage Booth to the charms of the ring and he'd never looked back. The experience also offered him an elevated view of boxing, a perfect and perhaps unfair vision of what the sport could and *should* be. As awesome as Haye could appear in spurts, at twenty-three, he was still some way short of becoming Booth's Leonard.

'Leonard could do *everything* in the ring,' said Booth, as we watched Haye rhythmically pound away at a nearby heavy bag. 'There has never been a fighter more versatile or natural. He was born to fight. You can go through his career and find a fight for every different style. He could box, move, counterpunch, push forward, fight aggressively, fight inside and slug it out. There was never one position or situation that made him uncomfortable.'

The best way to animate Booth was to mention the 'Fabulous Four'. He had an opinion and story on each fighter and fight, and his eyes lit up whenever pressed to retell it. Though Leonard remained a clear favourite, he was also full of admiration for the three rivals who combined to make the American champion so great. Traces of all four kings would be imprinted on the brain of Haye over the coming years, but we agreed Hearns offered the best direct comparison to the man standing in front of us that afternoon. Like 'The Hitman', Haye was blessed with a gangly and unorthodox build, which allowed him to sling punches up from beyond the eye-line of his unsuspecting opponent. Perhaps more crucially, Haye, like Hearns, was a master in the meat-and-potatoes of the sport, the jab followed by the right hand, or what's commonly known as the old-fashioned one-two. Both set their victims up with a piercing left lead before leaping in with a jack-hammer right hand. They shared a disjointed, staccato and explosive quality, the kind of style that always promised tension, whether in victory or defeat. Haye didn't resemble Hearns that day, but maybe the time would come.

As Booth remembered the night he watched Leonard and Hearns box live at a packed cinema in Carshalton, I couldn't help but feel envious of the iconic images against which he was able to judge Haye. Like my father, Booth boasted a cleaner and more idealised view of the boxing world than I did. He'd seen the sport when it was all it claimed to be. He'd been part of the glory years, the times that bespectacled grandparents discuss when bouncing grandkids on their knee. I'd since watched it, of course, but Booth had *lived* it.

From time to time ex-pro Logan would also peer over the fence and offer his own recollections of the fights that had left such an everlasting impression on the pair as young boys and lifelong friends. I could have listened to the trainers reminisce for days. When Booth talked about 'the science' his eyes and words handcuffed your attention.

'I think in order to become a truly great fighter you either need to be frighteningly clever or ignorant,' said the trainer. 'You have to be one or the other, and can't be stuck in between. Someone like Leonard was incredibly clever and could think his way through fights better than anybody, whereas someone like Duran was incredibly ignorant, and knew nothing else but fighting. He was a fighter to the core and would break his opponents down through sheer stubbornness. Duran didn't mind getting whacked repeatedly in the head to come out on top, but Leonard was clever enough to realise there were other ways to victory. The average fighters get stuck in that middle ground between being intelligent and ignorant.'

I needed more examples.

'Someone like Audley Harrison thinks he's intelligent like Leonard, but he's not,' said Booth. 'He doesn't have all bases covered like Leonard did. So what is Audley? He's not ignorant. He's not stupidly brave. That's why Audley looks confused and petrified whenever a glove lands on him. That leaves him in that dangerous middle ground. You can still be a good fighter in that middle ground, but I question whether he'll ever become great.'

I didn't even need to ask Booth the next question, as he'd already processed the request himself.

'I don't know about David, either,' said Booth. 'Some days I think he's frighteningly intelligent and other days I think he's frighteningly ignorant. I think it's something that will reveal itself in time. As of right now, we're still waiting to see where he falls. I don't think it's a case of choosing. He is what he is.'

Following an afternoon's leather abuse, Haye showered, changed and waltzed along Shaftesbury Avenue to a small café, relatively empty given the time of day. He slung his rucksack down on a chair, pulled out his mobile phone and began scrolling through the many messages he'd missed while grafting. A frown of concentration formed across his brow as Haye focused hard on the information in front of his nose. He muttered messages under his breath, a method of fully digesting the words and meanings. He didn't mind that the entire café could overhear, either. Haye was in the zone, and required maximum concentration to complete this task. Thankfully, a cherubic waitress from somewhere in Scandinavia, armed only with a notebook and a smile, broke Haye's trance.

'Are you ready to order?' she said. Haye looked up from his phone, snatched the menu from its holder and, within seconds, had made his decision. He plumped for the chicken caesar salad and then threw the menu across to me. It landed on my lap and, never one for big or particularly quick decisions, I merely went for the simple times-two option.

'Where are you from?' asked Haye, as he returned the menu to the waitress. 'Actually, let me guess. Say something . . .'

Embarrassed, the waitress hid behind her shoulder and twirled her hair in a pinky, unsure what to say and why she should say it.

'Read out your phone number, home address or something,' said Haye, as his fingers hovered over his own phone in anticipation. 'I think you come from Sweden.'

The waitress shook her head and signalled for Haye to guess again. 'Okay then,' he continued, taking a closer look. 'How about Poland?'

Wrong.

'Switzerland?'

Nope.

'Madagascar?'

What?

'Afghanistan?'

Sensing this fool was getting nowhere, the waitress shut her notebook and put Haye out of his misery. 'I am from Moldova,' she said, 'and your order will be ready in ten minutes.'

'I was going to say that next,' protested Haye, as the waitress pivoted and left the table.

The beaten boxer then slid his phone away from his grasp, as though aware he needed to create distance for sanity's sake. 'She was only a low seven anyway,' he said. 'She looked better from the back than the front. I did like her accent, though.'

Haye's unique form of birdwatching was something that continued during our time at the café – rating women as they passed by the window – and would keep the fighter entertained through much of life, in fact, as he revelled in an innate ability to judge females to the nearest decimal point.

'I'm glad this Thompson fight is happening now,' said Haye, switching lanes while sipping on a fruit juice. 'I was really starting to give up on British boxing before this fight was signed.'

'What do you mean?' I asked.

'Well, I always got the impression from watching boxing back in the day that everyone was out to prove they were the best. That's not the way it is any more, though, and it's a shame. In Britain we have a few decent fighters who are all claiming to be the best. If that's the case, why aren't they fighting each other to prove it?

'There are always a million reasons not to fight someone, but the main reason that most fights should happen is to basically prove who is the best fighter. That should outweigh all the excuses a fighter tries to make. I still maintain that any fight can be made if the two fighters seriously want to make the bout.'

Haye's date with Thompson was made easier to arrange due to the fact that both were now aligned with the same promotional company, thus removing any politicking excuse. Natural fighters, Haye and Thompson were never likely to refuse the opportunity for a rendezvous, while promoters Fight Academy were aware that they were about to stage a massive domestic blockbuster and, potentially, the passing of the torch from veteran champion to rising prospect.

'I'd like to change the way British boxing is,' added Haye, as he peered out the window, either in a show of deep thought or in order to make his next assessment on the female form. 'In an ideal world, I'd try and brainwash every single fighter to make them think they are the best in the world. That way they'd all have the confidence to fight each other. When you get two people who genuinely believe they are good, they will fight each other, no matter how many political hurdles they have to overcome to do so. When you get one fighter who believes he's the best, and the other's just in it for the money, it kills the sport. I'd give all fighters the confidence that I've got, then we'd start getting somewhere.'

With the Thompson contest now rubber-stamped, I often listened to Haye and wondered whether his ambition and impatience would eventually lead to his downfall. His mantras, boasts and plans made me dizzy and scared, as he ridiculed rivals and refused to entertain the idea of hanging around or following the conventional path.

'If you put me in with Kelvin Davis, the IBF world champion, in November, I'd beat him,' said Haye. 'In my mind, there's absolutely no way that Davis or the WBA champion Jean-Marc Mormeck can beat me. Both are under six foot tall, both are natural light-heavyweights and both are limited. I've never actually seen the WBC champion Wayne Braithwaite fight, but I'm told he's the most dangerous of the three, not that that particularly bothers me.'

All the time Haye talked, he sat there squeezing his fist and rubbing his deformed knuckles, as though revving his engine ahead of an impending drag race. His idle boasts registered with the rest of his body, and he reached a state of boxing arousal, prepped for battle and ready to thump somebody. It was then that I held up a dartboard with the face of Swansea's WBU cruiserweight champion Enzo Maccarinelli plastered across it.

'That whole thing is a joke,' said Haye. 'We've wanted to do a fight with Maccarinelli for a while now, but all we hear back from them is that it's better to wait eighteen months and build the contest up. Do you think I'm prepared to wait a year and a half to fight Maccarinelli? I'm not prepared to fight him when he's already been beaten a few times, which is always a possibility when a delay like that happens. If it's a good enough fight today, and the fans want it, why bother waiting until tomorrow?'

Once it finally arrived at the table, Haye devoured his food with the same fervour and speed he promised to exhibit against any one of the world champions he verbally crucified that afternoon. Deep in thought, at least for a minute, Haye chewed with intent.

'Oh, shit, take a look at that,' he then abruptly said, pointing with his mouth full. His finger was directed outside the window at a leggy blonde with a portfolio in hand. 'Now *that's* a solid nine.'

The perfect ten rating was reserved for one woman and one woman only in Haye's life. He dished out scores to strangers as though chucking crusts to ducks, but never delivered highest honours to anyone but his girlfriend, Natasha. A hairdresser from East Grinstead, brunette Natasha Davis was now living with Haye in a Clapham apartment and doing her utmost to ensure he stayed on track, ate, washed, slept and woke early each morning.

Haye and I moved on from the café that July afternoon and caught up with Natasha at a local Sainsbury's car park. Wearing a baseball cap and jogging outfit, Natasha hauled a trolley full of shopping bags towards her car as the pair of us belatedly went to help out. Rather than bemoan the fact she had to lug her shopping trolley around alone, Natasha offered only a warm and welcoming grin as we approached.

'How was training?' she asked.

'Good,' mumbled Haye.

'How do you feel?'

'Fine. A little tired, that's all.'

'I got that salmon you like . . .'

This was the first time I'd properly met and been introduced to Natasha, having previously seen her dotted around ringside at David's fights. While it was a given that she clocked a ten in the looks department, what truly struck me was how Natasha seemed to boast the same score in the personality and likeability stakes, too. I'd never expected Haye to have any difficulty capturing a ten as far as physical requirements go, but had anticipated and feared he'd fall for the vapid type commonly found staggering out of West End nightclubs in eight-inch heels through an orange mask of whore paint.

Such fears were eradicated as soon as I set eyes on Natasha in the oh-so-glamorous setting of a Sainsbury's parking bay, however. Instead of meeting on Oxford Street with designer shopping bags clinging to every finger, we convened in the grounds of a supermarket, Natasha diligently working through her chores in glorified pyjamas. There were no airs or graces about her and she seemed to genuinely care for Haye and his well-being. Satisfaction was derived from seeing her boyfriend achieve his dream, as opposed to any byproduct of increased fame she could score along the way.

Also, despite clearly being beautiful, it was almost as if Natasha was blind to her looks. She strolled through life as though she had never encountered a mirror before or been paid a compliment. In truth, David had chased Natasha through many of London's premier nightclubs in order to eventually catch his prey.

'I didn't even want to go out with him to begin with,' said Natasha, as she drove the three of us to their apartment. 'He was used to having all the girls fall weak at the knees and gather around him everywhere he went. I wasn't like that, though. I didn't see his appeal right away. I made him work really hard for it and knocked him back more times than I can remember.'

'No you didn't,' interrupted Haye, embarrassed by his inability to conquer an opponent. 'I knew you wanted me from the beginning. You were just messing around. You knew you'd always end up with me.'

'That's not how it was at all. I remember you following me from club to club, hoping that I'd give you the time of day. I only caved in because I thought that would be the only way to get you to stop. I didn't know who you were or what you did, and didn't care, either. I think you mentioned that you were a boxer a few times, but I forgot about it each time we met. I wasn't really a boxing fan or anything.'

'Yeah, right,' said Haye with a sigh. 'All I'm saying is, look where we are now. Look what's happened. I got you in the end, so who would you say won?'

David had heard enough stories of humiliation in a field he claimed to be an expert in. Hearing Natasha dish the dirt on his dating inadequacies was akin to listening to a fighter recall how he'd once beaten him up in a sparring session. For once, someone else was rating Haye out of ten.

'Have you seen many of my amateur fights?' asked Haye, as we parked the shopping bags back at his swanky apartment, a pad complete with wooden floors, leather couches and two plasma screens, one for the first-level kitchen and one for the upstairs living area. It reminded me of Tom Hanks' kidulthood hang-out in *Big*, minus oversized trampolines and fruit machines, though I hoped – nay, assumed – the boxer was eagerly working on that. 'I'll show you some of them,' continued Haye, as he dumped the shopping and fled, like a kid bailing on homework and running from his mother's protests. Natasha attempted to thwart his idle plans, but the plea naturally fell on preoccupied ears.

After emptying the required number of shopping bags downstairs, I eventually succumbed to the calls from above and slumped down on the leather three-piece as Haye readied his on-screen masterpiece. Blurred visuals of him slugging away recklessly and knocking out other teenagers were soon the order of the day. Competing mainly in venues that resembled unoccupied scout huts, the fights all seemed to follow the same pattern of Haye starting fast, rushing his opponent wildly, fading, becoming sloppy and hittable, and then ending matters just in the nick of time.

'I was so out of shape for this one,' said Haye, moments before landing a right-handed zinger on the unsuspecting face of a young foe. 'I never trained very well at the best of times, but I'd done *nothing* for this fight. I wasn't actually supposed to be fighting. Someone dropped out and Mick Carney at the Lodge called me up and asked me to fill in. I was actually in the process of banging some girl at the time, and went straight from her house to the fight. I had nothing in my legs. Thankfully, I knocked the guy out in the first round.'

Right on cue, the opponent fell, and we moved on to a 1997 amateur bout with Peter Haymer, a talented fighter who'd later carve a solid professional career himself and claim an English light-heavyweight belt. Haye was sixteen at the time he met Haymer and was already known in amateur circles as 'The Assassin'. He'd garnered a reputation as a vicious and merciless banger, and was the kind of boy mothers wanted their sons to steer clear of when the time came to draw lots.

Needless to say, within seconds of the first round, Haymer tasted a flush right hand and went limp, flopping down to ground level in an instant. Exhausted and relieved, Haye raised his arms high above his head as medical staff scrambled to put Haymer in the recovery position. The broken fighter's mother watched on from ringside, one hand placed over her mouth, tears running down her face, and Haye's celebrations were short-lived once he realised the impact his right fist had had on both Haymer and his distraught mum. Even watching the spectacle back many years later, knowing full well Haymer would climb to his feet, Haye was quick to turn it off.

The next slaying on screen again pitched Haye in the role of heavy-handed bully and, this time, ABA champion Courtney Fry as hapless victim. A significant underdog heading into the bout at Bethnal Green's York Hall, Haye, unable to miss with his right hand, blitzed Fry inside two rounds to conclusively settle a simmering rivalry between the London pair. Despite the manner of the victory, however, Haye found himself pipped by Fry to a place on Britain's 2000 Olympic Games squad.

'That pissed me off at the time,' said Haye. 'I'd beaten Fry and yet the selectors just completely overlooked it. The thing is, if we're working on form lines, they probably should have sent Jim Twite anyway. Jim beat me after the Fry fight, so maybe he should have gone ahead of both of us.'

We fell silent for a moment as Haye sifted through more tapes. Then he hit me with it.

'Have you ever actually seen the Jim Twite fight?' asked David.

'No,' I replied. 'Never.'

'Do you want to watch it now?'

Haye held up the tape and waved it around invitingly. I then shrugged, a gesture which inadvertently offered all the incentive Haye needed to cue up the fight. My shrug was nothing like a declaration of positivity, but was duly interpreted as such. To be honest, despite my natural curiosity, the idea of sitting alongside Haye and preparing to watch the most devastating and infamous knockout defeat of his boxing life so far was incredibly unnerving.

I already knew the plot by now, of course, and such prior knowledge only made the situation worse. The incident in question occurred at the ABA semi-finals of 1999, when Coventry southpaw Twite, eight years Haye's senior at twenty-seven, shockingly knocked out the brash upstart with a booming left cross inside York Hall.

Far from being overjoyed, Haye was nevertheless keen to gauge my reaction to the severity of his defeat. There was the sense that he wanted, perhaps even *needed* me to watch this particular episode in order to fully understand the making of the man. That first-round loss to Twite was every bit as vital to his subsequent progress as the many knockout wins he'd taken great pleasure in showing me that afternoon. I also believed Haye felt the need to punish himself for sitting back and basking in the plight of so many others on film. He was never once arrogant or malicious when reliving past glories, yet couldn't help but sometimes get caught up in the crunch of a punch and the smoothness of the inevitable fall.

'Ready?' asked Haye.

I nodded, then sniggered uncomfortably, as though not yet sure whether I should somehow relish this moment or shut my eyes. Chances are, Haye didn't care how I reacted to it. He just wanted me to familiarise myself with it and realise he no longer had any fear of confronting reality or past demons. I couldn't help but feel Haye displayed a certain strength in showcasing his most glaring weakness.

So, as planned, we sat and watched the fight play out in silence, both primed and ready for what was soon to unfold. Although I'd never before seen the footage, I knew the story and I was aware of approximately how long it took for the dramatic climax to reveal itself. Rest assured, we weren't in for the long haul. Despite knowing the eventual twist, though, I still experienced much of the same tension and anxiety one normally associates with watching a live fight. I knew the big alien lurked around the corner, but wasn't sure just how grotesque it would be.

As it turned out, this alien was of the three-headed and eight-legged variety. A shuddering southpaw left-hand cracked Haye's chin and sent him sprawling across the ring canvas on shattered limbs. The youngster then hauled himself up on what must have felt like eight legs, each one offering a conflicting navigational opinion. Though he bravely made it to his feet, Haye's limbs were conversing in different languages and the referee wisely waved the contest over.

Sitting beside me on the edge of his seat, Haye merely chuckled to himself as the bout ended. He watched himself get nailed, dumped and stopped, and yet passed it all off with a sly grin and a dispirited shake of the head, as though witnessing a random opponent suffer the same fate.

'That was a massive shot,' I said, keen to break the uncomfortable post-fight silence that had crept up on us. 'I can see how it happened now.'

'Yeah, it *felt* massive, too,' replied Haye, as he switched off his video camera and headed towards the bathroom. 'Are you glad you saw it, though?'

'No, not really,' I said.

'If I can watch it, you can watch it,' said Haye. 'It ain't happening again anyway.'

The door then slammed shut, signalling an end to the boxer's swollen bladder and to the concept and memory of defeat.

CHAPTER SIX

BLUE BALLS

My suitcase was the obese lovechild of Boots and JJB Sports, and yet, when I finally met David Haye at Bournemouth's Tralee Hotel on a scorching Friday in August 2004, it suddenly felt worryingly light. I'd seemingly packed for the wrong trip.

'Remind me how old you are again?' said Haye, as he sat at a dining table in the hotel.

'Seventeen,' I replied, bags still in hand and yet to be shown my room. 'I'm eighteen next week, though.'

'Shit. That's not good.'

'Why?'

'You can pass for an eighteen-year-old, though, right? What do you all think?'

Providing a second opinion that day were American heavyweight Vaughn Bean and British-based lumps Michael Sprott and Roman Greenberg. Each was on hand to supply sparring for Haye that month, as well as to apparently sit around a dinner table and pass judgement on my boyish features.

'I've got some shoes with heels you can wear,' said Haye. 'Either that or you can wear one of my hats. It won't put hair on your chin, but it might make you look a bit older.'

I frowned, still unsure where this was heading or, more

importantly, where *we* were heading. Within thirty seconds, a black bowler hat was thrown on my head. Much to the obvious delight of those at the table, I'd been transformed into one of the kids from *Bugsy Malone*, minus splurge gun and New York drawl.

'There are a couple of places we've got to go tonight, and you need to somehow get in,' said Haye, as he repositioned the hat on my head and manipulated my posture. 'A couple of strip clubs, that's all. You'll love it, so long as we can get you in. Have you got a fake ID or anything?'

No driving licence, top hat, Cuban heels, pumps, stilts or whiskers on my chin. I'd failed to pack any of the above. I removed the fedora from my head and still couldn't decipher whether Haye was genuinely serious about his escapades later that night. I'd been invited to training camp, and wasn't entirely sure grinding and gyrating were deemed acceptable alternatives to press-ups and crunches.

My sole source of sanity, Adam Booth, was not present at the impromptu lunch meeting, so I found it hard to gauge the level of sincerity at the table. Eventually, the trainer met me in the dining room and walked me first to my hotel room and then his, filling me in on David's progress along the way. Still three weeks out from the fight, Booth appeared content with what he'd seen, but was soon heading home to Bromley to spend time with his two young daughters. I was told that after the day's sparring session was complete, David would effectively be given time off over the weekend and then resume hard training on Monday, the day of Booth's return.

On the trainer's bedside table that afternoon was a copy of *Boxing News*, dated 13 August 2004 and containing my first published article in the trade magazine. The feature was, of course, Haye-related, and the piece ran as a four-page spread, accompanied by a picture of Haye and world middleweight champion Bernard Hopkins, taken by the boxer himself during time spent in Miami.

'Hopkins really impressed me out there,' David had told me. 'We were hanging out one day, it was getting late, and I asked Bernard what he was doing later that night, as I wanted to party with him. He then told me that he goes to bed no later than nine o'clock in the evening and that the only thing on his agenda that night was to sleep. He then gets up at something like four o'clock and goes running. It's crazy. The guy is nearly forty years of age and still the most dedicated professional in the game. He then asked me what I was doing that night, and I suddenly felt really embarrassed. I lied and told him I was also heading to bed.'

Booth's radar had also switched to slumber and the comforts of home by the time I arrived in Bournemouth. His two young daughters, Keira and Ashton, were sitting in his room watching a DVD of *Austin Powers in Goldmember* as we entered. Adam sat on the edge of his bed, sighed, and appeared to prefer discussing the acting chops of Beyoncé Knowles, as opposed to the lefts and rights of Carl Thompson. He seemed mentally exhausted by the constant pontificating, arranging, ordering and worrying that preceded a crucial title clash.

Despite this self-imposed ban, in the quiet moments we shared that afternoon, watching Mike Myers act the fool on the screen, one could tell Booth, when laughing at a butchered British accent, was always picturing a certain champion from Bolton. He was constantly on his mind, no matter how hard he tried to postpone the thought of battle. We held the pretence for as long as we could, before conversation inevitably turned to Thompson, Haye, the ensuing battle and then, somehow, 'Marvelous' Marvin Hagler. Presumably, if Haye was Thomas Hearns, Thompson was Hagler.

'Have you seen Hagler's fight with John "The Beast" Mugabi?' asked Adam.

Ready to revoke my boxing fan licence, I shook my head in shame and, before I could offer a feeble excuse, Adam punctured his boxing-free zone bliss and hit stop on the television remote control. His daughters spun their heads around in disgust.

'March 10th, 1986,' muttered Booth, while in the process of switching DVDs and then proudly backing away, as though he'd just completed an ice sculpture.

'This fight happened the year I was born,' I said.

Adam froze, amazed by my revelation. 'I keep forgetting how young you are,' said the trainer, as he hit play on the remote control, dimmed the lights and lit a sole candle in the middle of the room. A strange humming sound then started to emanate from his soul, as we sat and watched the first nine and a half rounds of a gruesome slugfest, packed with more twists, turns and ghastly scenes than a Tarantino picture. It was the kind of fight Haye had yet to experience, and one we hoped he'd forever be shielded from. As round ten got underway, Booth checked his watch, hit pause on the remote control and stood up.

'Are you coming downstairs to watch him train?' he asked. 'You've got a choice between that, Hagler–Mugabi or the rest of *Austin Powers*.'

Neither Hagler nor Mugabi resided downstairs, but all the other key boxing components were present, including a ring, heavy bags, fighters and now Booth. Yet I couldn't help but feel, upon entering the ballroom – yes, *ballroom* – that there was a considerable lack of noise. A stereo played loud soul music on the far stage, but the place seemed hollow and soulless despite this. Chandeliers hung from the ceiling, large windows allowed tanned tourists a glimpse from outside, and the comfy carpet enticed me to take my shoes off and roll around like a flea-infested pooch. It was as if a wealthy patriarch had surprised his family with a brand-new boxing ring by the fireplace and grand piano. Waiters and waitresses even passed through the room with drinks and canapés, en route to the kitchen or restaurant, checking the carpet for specks of blood as they walked.

As much as I was disturbed by the lack of screams, pain, sweat and fear, Haye thrived on being his own man, and not having to share space with others. He worked on his own time schedule and meticulously prepared for the session ahead, spending a moment on everything, from song selection and stretches, to skipping and light strolls around the room. *Nothing* was rushed or forced.

His playmates that afternoon – Bean, Sprott and Greenberg – prepared mostly alone and alternated between stretching, working various bags and waiting. Lots of waiting. After about an hour of prep time, it was clear that most in the room, from the fighters to the few yawning spectators at ringside, were ready for some kind of pay-off. The trio of sparring partners were by now squeezed into headguards and gloved up, yet Haye was still at the bandaging stage of his preparation, singing along cheerfully to the strains of 'Step in the Name of Love' by R. Kelly.

Now, I could never stomach R. Kelly at the best of times, but his music became significantly more grating as the soundtrack to Haye's leisurely foreplay. The song had already shuffled to the top of the fighter's playlist at least three times by this point, and it was three times too many for my liking. Having worked with the boxer since the age of sixteen, Booth was familiar with the nature of the beast and knew that, while other fighters in the room were ready for battle long ago, Haye was only going to crack heads when he felt inspired to do so.

As my belly rumbled and my fuse shortened, Haye finally signalled it was time to work, and Booth, taking the cue, arranged the order of duty for Bean, Sprott and Greenberg. The idea was for each heavyweight to spend two rounds in Haye's company and then jump out and allow the next one in, thus maintaining the fresh-ness of all involved. The sparring partners each enjoyed a significant weight advantage on Haye and were expected to push, shove, throw and manoeuvre the cruiserweight around, making every excess pound and inch count.

Bean was first to walk the line and shouted loudest that day. He attempted to push the pace and shoot right hands over Haye's low-held left hand, and then, once the pair grew close, Bean would wail away with both fists at the Englishman's midriff. Despite this whiff of mayhem, however, Haye remained calm, in control and able to stand his ground. Bean was a strong heavyweight, accustomed to bullying bigger men, and yet Haye was more than capable of fending off his two-fisted attacks.

Next up was Sprott, who presented Haye with a respite and Booth with a headache. Working with all he knew, the mild-mannered stylist decided to stick at mid-range and reluctantly offer timid jabs and right hands, much to everybody's frustration. Though clearly skilled, Sprott was not designed to force the pace or work the more intimate moments of a ring. He liked distance and space to think, and preferred straight shots to explosive hooks. So while the comparatively brutish Bean replicated Thompson to some extent, Sprott stood off comparing jabs with Haye for two rounds.

'I need you to throw that right hand, Michael,' shouted a desperate Booth from ringside. 'Let it go. Don't hold back.'

Sprott let it go. He rushed forward blindly behind a wayward right hand, only to be nailed by an incoming Haye counter-hook off the ropes. The pair exchanged furiously on the bell, but it was two rounds too late for Booth's liking. Although his T-shirt told a different story, Haye had yet to break sweat in a fighting sense. Bean got him twitchy, yet Sprott simply allowed him two rounds to recover and mime along to the next R. Kelly track.

'I need that right hand landing,' pleaded Adam, as an exhausted Sprott made his way down the steps. 'Why aren't you throwing it?'

'I'm sorry,' said Sprott. 'I'll throw it. I'm just waiting too much.'

'Don't wait,' said Booth. 'Just go for it. We need you to do this. You're useless to us if you don't throw your right hand.'

Sprott's symptoms seemed contagious, as Greenberg was next to step between the ropes and administer the same affectionate glances in Haye's direction. Drilled to fight on the back foot and carefully pick his shots, Haye wasn't about to force the pace, either, so what occurred was a stand-off situation, where both fighters waited to counterpunch. Neither committed to anything more than pesky jabs and, while the ballet was admittedly pretty to watch, there wasn't a great deal of learning or earning being done.

Haye sparred ten rounds in total and thanked each sparring partner at the conclusion – Bean for having a go, and Sprott and Greenberg for taking it easy on him. As bizarre as it sounds, Booth still required someone to enter the ring and beat his man up, to exert the kind of heat Thompson would undoubtedly generate on 10 September.

Brain frazzled and voice hoarse, Booth immediately set off home with his two daughters in tow, keen to escape the rigorous demands of watching over a talent as mercurial as Haye. Jamie Sawyer, Haye's personal masseur and number three guy in the corner on fight night, also broke from camp that day, but not before handing me a portion of responsibility on his way out.

'I need you to make sure David uses this on a daily basis while we're away,' said Sawyer, as he held a blue rubber ball, too tiny for cricket, yet too big for squash, and proceeded to manipulate it in his palm. 'It basically works on his grip strength. He's got no boxing training to do while we're gone, but he needs to use this.'

Sawyer handed me the blue ball and I slipped it inside my trouser pocket, safe in the knowledge that I'd been given a vital task to carry out. This could be the difference between winning and losing, I thought to myself. Everybody was leaving and I was suddenly alone and somewhat exposed. What if I failed my mission and Haye entered his September duel with Thompson limp-wristed and unable to form a fist? With great power comes great responsibility, and I was now presented with the task of ensuring David's money-making and mind-altering tools were ready for war.

Two hours later, Haye's mind was a million miles away from combat, and his attention was now solely focused on a ballyhooed night out in Bournemouth's city centre, a certain strip club representing first port of call. He buzzed my hotel room later that evening and signalled for me to head to his. Doing as I was told, I ventured to Haye's suite, blue ball in pocket, and unwilling to wear a top hat, irrespective of how much taller it made me.

'What did you think of the sparring earlier?' asked Haye, as he riffled through his closet for some baggy shirts and size-eleven shoes.

'Erm, it was good,' I said, weakly. 'That's the first time I've seen you spar.'

'Yeah, I know, but what did you *think* of it?'

'You did well,' I said, not particularly lying or telling the truth, just dithering in that middle ground of uncertainty and terror. I'd only just got here. They'd only recently allowed me inside the circle. I wasn't about to jeopardise that.

In truth, I hadn't seen enough and didn't know enough at this point to pass judgement on whether Haye looked a million bucks or not. Having never witnessed a fighter's training camp before, I had no perception of time or progress, and was unsure of how Haye was *supposed* to have looked that day. Not wanting to throw the first shot and allow Haye to viciously counter, I remained silent and nervously played with my blue rubber sphere, the item momentarily acting as a stress ball.

'Give that here,' said Haye, as he clocked my idle fidgeting.

'Jamie said you need to use it every day,' came the meek command from my lips.

'Yeah, I know,' sighed the fighter, as he reached for the object and then chucked it inside a bedside cabinet.

'I think you should do it before you go out tonight,' was my pathetic final plea.

'I will,' said Haye, his voice now slightly raised. 'Now try this shirt on.'

Mind preoccupied by the night's more pressing matters, I knew Haye was unlikely to do as he was told now or at any other interval that evening. I wondered whether I should have nabbed the blue ball back and returned it to my room, that way maintaining control and power over the situation. Instead, I'd merely allowed him to hide it away in his drawer and, consequently, Haye had now stolen the initiative. Moreover, when left to his own devices, I figured the prospect of squeezing a blue piece of rubber would be way down his list of priorities. I had been given the task because Haye couldn't be trusted to do it himself and needed his strings pulled from time to time. Alas, I'd merely acquiesced and let the puppet flop to the floor.

His size-eleven loafers were slightly tight, but I didn't tell him. I didn't mention the blue ball again, either. I knew the object would remain in that bedside cabinet all weekend and was simply too afraid to do anything about it. Haye had removed the problem from my mind and, while guilt had now replaced it, I simply accepted and hoped that the boxer probably knew best.

With boxing off the agenda for at least the next forty-eight hours, I joined Haye, training partner Anthony Small and close friend Kamran Naqvi, as the trio traipsed into Bournemouth's city centre and headed towards a strip club with an alarming sense of urgency, the sort absent from Haye's sparring session earlier that day. Haye led the troops into the heart of the city, bypassing drunken revellers, before stopping outside For Your Eyes Only, a strip club and favoured hang-out of a young boxer on the cusp of presumed greatness.

I'd wrongly assumed this was the first time Haye had visited the haunt. However, from the moment we entered to the moment we left, everybody seemed all too familiar with the fighter as he shook hands with passers-by, high-fived bouncers and hollered at the female cash-hounds working poles. It brought to mind Burt Reynolds swaggering through Hot Traxx nightclub in the opening scene of *Boogie Nights*, minus only flared trousers and The Emotions' backing track. Boxer rather than porn director, Haye was nevertheless in demand. I came to the conclusion that only a select few in the club actually knew what his occupation was and the rest were simply attracted to the convincing face and strut. Haye walked, talked, dressed and breathed like a celebrity. Yet to win a meaningful professional title and barely out of boxing diapers, he could have already been heavyweight champion of the world for all anyone cared. We didn't walk into the club that night, we were carried in on invisible thrones. So much for age concerns. Tonight I was eighteen years of age, and not one person inside or outside the club dared question me.

The four of us were ushered to our table and instantly greeted by Roller-girl, who arrived complete with silicone tits and a wardrobe of hang-ups and insecurities. She kissed Haye on both cheeks, groped his bulging muscles and then timidly waved at the rest of us. Other working girls looked on with envy as Roller-girl engaged in shallow conversation with the king. After five minutes of verbal vanity, Haye ordered drinks and further attention.

'I've been pretending to be the heavyweight champion of the world since I was a kid,' said Haye, as he drank from a glass of cranberry juice. 'I used to tell all the girls at school that I'd be heavyweight champion of the world one day and that they'd be stupid not to get with me while they had the chance. Even when I was boxing as an amateur, I'd go to all the best clubs in London and buy the flashiest clothes. I didn't have a pot to piss in and yet didn't mind risking it all to look good. I knew I'd get it all back eventually.'

Unsure of strip club etiquette, I squirmed uncomfortably in my seat and scanned the dimly lit room for a set of guidelines or rules. I half expected to see one of those swimming pool plaques, complete with dos and don'ts and the prohibition of heavy petting and diving. If I had trouble searching out the manual, the next best option was simply to consult its author and, coincidentally, the very man sat beside me. Money in hand, Haye was already setting his GPS for the evening. He knew stage names, real names, middle names and pet names of all the performers, and was able to attract women to the table with a snap of the fingers or a cursory glance.

'Tell me which one you like,' said Haye, as I scanned the floor like a judge at Crufts, attempting to work out my type in a swamp of smiling, synthetic sameness. The girls were more android than human, each blessed with bottle hair, plastic chest, and enough spirit in their hearts and alcohol in their bloodstreams to perform designated roles with aplomb. Now seasoned enough to spot subtle nuances amid so much similarity, Haye, the head judge, had already compiled his own league table of the joint's very best dancers.

'I'm going to get you Destiny,' he said, gesturing to a black-haired dancer in a minuscule red bikini. Kiss, hug, corny dialogue and breakneck negotiation ensued, and suddenly I was assailed by the writhing limbs of Destiny, apparently the number-one-ranked stripper in all of Bournemouth. I'm sure her rosette sat proudly on her parents' mantelpiece, wedged neatly between a netball trophy and spelling bee certificate. The dance cost ten English pounds and, strangely deriving more satisfaction from it than I did, Haye coughed up the stripper's entrance fee.

'This is the first time he's ever been to a strip club,' narrated Haye. 'I told him you were the best, so you've got to make this one extra special for him, okay?'

Destiny nodded in agreement and apparently continued her offensive for a few more minutes out of sympathy, though, without any kind of reference point, I took David's word for it that she was the best of the bunch.

I was in awe at how playful and ridiculous Haye could make the whole encounter, as he'd trash-talk the strippers, ask them inane questions and make their jobs tougher by fiendishly placing obstacles such as chairs, tables and glasses in their way. He seemed to genuinely get a kick out of the process, and was certainly having more fun now than he'd had at the boxing ballroom earlier in the day.

While Haye was in his element being yanked left, right and centre by his new friends, the rest of us were less enamoured of a three-hour stint in a strip club. Still, we all accepted Haye's venture as a form of therapy, and on balance I considered it perhaps his reward for a hard week's work. I told myself it wasn't an everyday occurrence, and that Haye was only messing around in a sober state, switching the game on women who could normally play their punters so expertly.

Three hours came and went in the flash of a g-string and, with an exasperated Small leading the pack, we marched on to a regular nightclub adjacent to the strip club. Small was excited by the prospect of real people, while Haye dragged his feet and moaned for the very same reason. The reality of a nightclub shattered the illusion and fantasy he was able to create at his favourite hotspot.

It was 2 a.m. and this seventeen-year-old was just happy to be let inside again without the humiliation of pretending I'd left my wallet and driving licence at the hotel. 'They're all with me,' commanded Haye, as he bypassed the queue and slapped hands with the bouncers, just like in the movies.

Vaughn Bean stayed in his hotel room that evening, eager to recuperate from his spar earlier in the day. He went for a jog along Bournemouth pier and then slid into bed for an early night. Bean was only twenty-nine years of age, but spoke, acted and appeared older and wiser than his years. The soft-spoken pug made more noise inside the ropes than he did outside, yet preached with an integrity and knowledge that forced one to listen whenever he decided to part his lips. The American had once shared canvas space with such boxing luminaries as Evander Holyfield, Michael Moorer and Vitali Klitschko, and sparred like a man who'd been in with bigger and better.

Bean dropped a majority decision to Moorer in March 1997 and then, by September '98, had also taken Holyfield the full twelve rounds in a losing WBA and IBF world heavyweight title effort. The results remained noteworthy on Bean's record, yet he always felt he could have done more.

'Don't get me wrong, I'm happy to say I went the distance with those guys,' he said. 'The thing is, I know I had more to give. I just didn't have the belief to bring it all out. Boxing is ninety per cent mental and ten per cent physical, and I've always had problems with that ninety per cent. Everybody said I was going to get knocked out in one round by Holyfield, and it was hard for me. I told myself I ain't getting knocked out in one round and I did all I could to make sure that wouldn't be the case. I never believed that I was going to win that fight, though. I was just happy to prove people wrong and not get blown away.'

Since losing to Klitschko in 2002, Bean had beaten up two losers in Indiana and was in the process of rebuilding his shattered confidence. His spell in boxing rehab would continue on 11 September, one day after the comparatively flamboyant Haye's bout with Thompson.

'Me and David are totally different animals, man,' said Bean. 'I can't be out all night like he is and then go to the gym the next day and kick ass. Don't get me wrong, I used to be like that. I used to be like David back in the day, but man, I'm nearly thirty years old now, and I've got to put things in perspective. Boxing is my life right now and I've got to make it work. I've got a family back home, and all the money I get from stuff like this [sparring] goes straight to my family.'

Bean smiled at each mention of Haye, as though envious of his cavalier approach and his complete faith in his God-given ability. While Haye had to be coaxed down from his elevated pedestal, the unsure Chicagoan was yet to find his.

'I look at David sometimes and think to myself, damn, why couldn't I believe in myself like that son-of-a-bitch?' said Bean. 'He won't go into fights scared of the opponent, and sometimes that can be a bad thing. That guy's just flat-out confident. That prescription's fine in small doses, but you've got to be careful of ODing, man.'

Bean was as wise as he was wide, and I enjoyed both watching him fight and listening to him speak. Unlike me, he'd been around and seen things and was, therefore, able to analyse progress far better than I could.

'Oh man, David can go to the moon and back if he truly wants it,' reassured Bean. 'He can be the champion of the world over in America and can dominate the division for a while. He's a big, powerful guy at that weight, and I don't see many of the top American cruiserweights standing up to him once they feel his hard right hand and fast combinations. Not only that, but, looking beyond cruiserweight, David definitely has the power and smarts to move up to heavyweight if there's money to be made there. First things first, though, right?'

Right.

Haye didn't need to be told about the danger he faced on 10 September and, for the next two days, most certainly wasn't. Days consisted of strolls into the town centre for food, walks along the beach for sun and then evenings at the strip club for sightseeing. Even when ploughing through Bournemouth during daylight hours, Haye struggled to keep away from his favourite playground, and would often dally in front of For Your Eyes Only for a catch-up chat with Phil, a malnourished doorman who patrolled the club from opening time to closing time seven days a week.

'I'm here from eight o'clock in the morning until four o'clock in the morning the next day,' said Phil, as we paid the club a brief and surreal mid-afternoon visit.

'That's crazy,' said Haye, eyes wide in disbelief. 'Why do you work so many hours?'

'I don't have to,' said Phil. 'It's my choice. I don't even get paid extra for it. I choose to do it because it keeps me active and I enjoy it. What else am I going to do with my nights? Sit at home with a can of Foster's watching crap on television? No, thanks. I've been there and it wasn't nice.'

Perhaps unsurprisingly, Phil looked like a man who spent too much time hanging out in strip clubs. His hair was greasy and thin and his skin was blotchy, with lines that told a thousand stories. He'd clearly turned some controversial chapters in his life and yet, despite his problems and presumed tiredness, Phil's positivity was strangely contagious.

'We've got space for you every night, David,' he said. 'Listen, this guy's been coming here non-stop for the last two weeks now. I keep telling people he's a boxer, but they won't believe me. They think

I'm joking. It's a tricky situation for me, because I love you coming down, but I also know you probably shouldn't.'

'It's all right,' said Haye. 'I've got a couple of days off, that's all. I'll be back in training on Monday. Then I'll have to stop popping down for a while. At least until next weekend.'

'Win next month and you're welcome to visit whenever you want,' said Phil. 'I can't make the same promise if you lose, though.'

'I won't lose,' promised Haye, stretching out in the middle of the pavement. 'Training's going really well.'

'I know you won't lose, David,' said the doorman. 'Thompson's getting on a bit anyway, isn't he? I remember watching his fights with Chris Eubank years ago. It's incredible to think he's still going these days. He's got to be an old man now. Take it from me, there are certain things you can't do when you reach a certain age. No matter how hard you try, it just won't happen.'

It wasn't much fun being seventeen years of age, either, as I found out later that evening. Deserted by the main attraction, three of yesterday's four amigos again made their way towards the cul-de-sac of clubs in Bournemouth's city centre. Haye had beaten us there, of course, and was already ensconced at his favourite strip joint. Rightly assuming the fighter preferred to be left alone, the three stragglers continued on regardless, choosing to return to yesterday's nightclub, rather than wake Haye from his dream.

Advised to 'say you're twenty-two' as I approached the bouncer on the door, we soon discovered the benefits of being attached to a man expertly masquerading as the world heavyweight champion. Without identification or a prayer, I was rejected at the door to the very same club we'd nonchalantly bowled into the night before. This author was, after all, only seventeen.

I raced home that night, keen to hit my bed free of alcohol and with both a clear head and conscience. I jogged along the pier, passing by two strung-out junkies screwing under a bridge, and was back at the hotel within ten minutes. Homebody Bean was stood alone outside, sweating in a Chicago Bulls basketball jersey and swigging from a water bottle.

'What happened to you?' asked Bean, as we shook hands.

'I got turned away for being under age,' I said.

'Man, that sucks,' said Bean, impressively halting a potential guffaw. 'You know, it ain't so bad. You won't have the headache or nothing tomorrow, if that's any consolation. Shit, I'd do anything to be seventeen again.'

'I'm eighteen next week. Have you been running?'

'Yep,' said Bean, rubbing his stomach as though a genie might appear. 'I'm down to, like, 230lbs now. I feel pretty good.'

'What are you doing now then?'

'Going to bed. We're training again Monday, right?'

We were. Booth and Sawyer did, indeed, arrive back in Bournemouth that Monday, armed with fresh ideas and impetus and keen to remove Haye from the strip club and avert his gaze back to the ballroom. The fighter had enjoyed plenty of down-time over the weekend and it told on his first session back, too, as he struggled to accomplish standard tasks that would once have come so easily to him. Booth led a basic circuit session, and had Haye and Small undertake it side-by-side in an attempt to drive both towards their respective goals. Instead, the combination merely fuelled idle chatter, and allowed Haye an outlet when the going inevitably got tough. He fell way short of the targets set by Booth, and flunked everything from sit-ups and press-ups to squats and lunges. Haye, of course, nonchalantly laughed off his failings, chalked it down to time off and assured everyone it would all eventually work out, but his strain and pain, even through the most basic of drills, was somewhat disconcerting.

'Has David been using that thing I gave you when I left?' whispered Sawyer, as we both looked on.

'Erm, I don't know,' I said. 'I think so.'

'What do you mean?'

'Well, he took it off me.'

'I told you to make sure he did it each day.'

'I know,' I said. 'He took it off me, though.'

Jamie shook his head. He knew exactly what had occurred and why it had happened. Grown men lacked the gumption and gonads to speak up to Haye, so it was little surprise that a seventeen-year-old kid turned away from a nightclub the previous night had struggled to make his voice heard.

Ultimately, though, regardless of how insignificant the task may have seemed in the bigger picture, I'd had the chance to make Haye do something against his will and failed miserably to do so. I'd been given an opportunity to hit the pause and consider buttons on a training camp that, to the eyes of this naïve newcomer, appeared to be spiralling towards an uncertain destination. Conversely, I'd allowed my thoughts and fears to be hidden inside a bedside cabinet. 'I trusted him to do it,' I pleaded, pathetically. 'He said he was going to.'

CHAPTER SEVEN

BRAIN DAMAGE

David Haye was never scared of Carl Thompson, but was unquestionably afraid of what his own ambition and fists could do to the proud forty-year-old. For Haye, the image of Thompson in gloves was one associated with a childhood spent watching the fighter on television with parents Jane and Deron, as well as siblings James and Louisa, at their family home on Gatehouse Square in south-east London.

They all felt a warm affection for Thompson, and that never wavered for Haye, even when agreeing to fight him as a twenty-three-year-old man with dreams of his own. Haye required Thompson's shopworn body to aid his own career progress, but felt dirty and disloyal as a result. So, when the time came to go head-to-head with Thompson at the pair's pre-fight press conference, the younger man trod carefully and appeared almost apologetic about the veteran's inevitable plight.

'I've trained for twelve hard rounds, so don't think I'm going to just go out there and try to blast him out early,' said Haye, two days before battle. 'I know Carl can knock me out cold at any stage, and that's why I have a lot of respect for his skills. I've had to train extremely hard for this fight, and have definitely trained harder than I've ever done before in my boxing life. I know Carl can do damage if I'm not on it.'

Haye reiterated this line at numerous intervals that Wednesday afternoon, as though establishing a clear respect for the champion he was about to banish. It was all in the name of competition, he'd promise. Nothing personal, just business.

'I haven't disrespected Carl in any way and I wouldn't even think about doing so,' said the challenger. 'He may have felt insulted when I first called him out, which would be understandable given how experienced he is, but there was no disrespect intended. I just wanted to test myself as soon as possible. I feel it is now my time to show I belong and prove that I'm the best cruiserweight in the world, even at this early stage in my career.'

If Haye spoke like a political candidate, embracing the power of the podium, Thompson apologised for his comparative blandness and instead drawled like an old bluesman, sat on the stoop making noise with a slide guitar.

'Everybody knows I don't like talking, but I just want to give David maximum respect for taking the fight,' said Thompson. 'Not many people would come and challenge me the way he has done. David reminds me of myself a bit, really. He's got a true fighter's heart, and he comes to fight and comes to win. I've had all the same attributes throughout my career and I still have them now. People have criticised David for taking this fight and have said that he's trying to steal a title from an old man, but that's all just cheap words. I'm sure David hasn't taken me for granted, because believe me, this guy sat here is not an old man.'

Thompson had scored thirty-two wins to date and was fresh – well, *relatively* fresh – off the biggest performance of his career. However, en route to a ninth-round stoppage of Sebastian Rothmann to claim his IBO belt, the Bolton fighter withstood a frightful beating, the sort that indicated retirement, even in shock victory, was perhaps on the horizon.

'I always fake being hurt in fights, and people now don't know whether I'm faking it or whether I'm really hurt,' said Thompson, when quizzed on his painful last showing. 'What people don't understand is that I've got great powers of recovery. I can get hit with big shots and recover extremely quickly. That's always been the case throughout my career.

'I've got no doubt David is going to rock me and hurt me at some point in this fight, because I'm going to be in his face. That's where I'll always be. I've already accepted the fact that I'm going to get hit, and the question is now whether I can withstand the punches. If I get hit, hurt and dropped, I'll still get up and bring it back to him just as hard. When you hurt me, I'm going to hurt you.'

Thompson's declaration of inevitable punishment instilled tangible fear in my mind for the first time ahead of the fight. While Haye spoke like a homecoming king, Thompson recited passages from the street-fighting handbook. You couldn't shake or surprise granddad. At forty, he knew exactly what his body could and couldn't do, and relied on sheer stubbornness to carry him through. When one expects punishment, it makes it far easier to then digest.

'I don't expect him to try and outbox me, because he's not that silly,' added Haye. 'He'll look to work my body, slow me down and take me into the later rounds. I haven't been past four rounds yet, so, for all he knows, I may have no stamina beyond a certain point. He might think I'll blow a gasket after four rounds and he'll then be able to knock me out.

'What I've done to counter this is push myself to the limit in sparring and training. It's been the hardest training camp of my life, but I feel it's all been worthwhile. If the fight does go into the eighth or ninth round, I feel I'll have the engine to cope with it.'

The day after his impassioned speech to the nation's media, Haye defied Sonny Corleone and took business to the dinner table. He fled Wembley Arena on Thursday afternoon, friends and associates in tow, and sought a hearty meal to reward his body for making the 200lbs (14st 4lbs) cruiserweight limit with 2¼lbs to spare. As expected, Haye had looked a picture of health, athleticism and fitness on the scales earlier that afternoon, while Thompson barely flexed or raised an arm in anger.

Minutes after stepping off the scales, Haye rounded up the pack and drove to the nearest pub-restaurant on the outskirts of Wembley. Once inside, he ordered anything they allowed him to, including chicken breasts, ribs, rice, potatoes and a plateful of steamed vegetables. When the food ran dry, the fighter simply ordered more, or stole leftovers from the dishes of others.

'Carl kept saying he was sparring with a guy named Tony something, but couldn't remember his surname,' said Haye, a toothpick dangling from his mouth. 'I was actually praying he wasn't going to say Tony Moran, but then he said it. *Tony Moran*. He said he'd sparred with Tony Moran and Mark Krence. Shit, does he really think that's ideal sparring for someone like me? I kind of felt sorry for him. He really doesn't know what's coming to him.'

When talking about Thompson, Haye was able to alternate between statements of sympathy and respect and declarations of disdain and violence. He admired the veteran's career and character, but, with the fight now quickly approaching, showed no hesitation in sweet-talking him towards the ledge.

'Carl actually said he was prepared to take punches in the face and that he was expecting me to hurt and drop him,' added Haye. 'I couldn't believe that when he said it. Does he think he'll just be able to keep fighting on as I'm smashing his face with punches? It doesn't work like that. If I hit and hurt him, he's getting knocked the fuck out.'

Everybody at the table was in agreement and nodded along with Haye's savage intent, while simultaneously scoffing at Thompson's attempted bravery. Fight agent Frank Joseph held a mobile phone to his ear and relayed betting odds; he later explained to me how he knew of at least half a dozen people who had lumped significant five-figure sums on Haye winning inside the first round.

The opinion was popular at the table, too, as each person took it in turn to offer their own brief and unapologetically biased breakdown of how they expected the fight to unfold. Content to eat and grab food from wherever he could find it, Haye was oblivious to most of the throwaway opinions offered. Calls of first- and second-round knockout victories were rife, before the parcel was then handed to me and the music abruptly stopped. The spotlight shifted above me and I watched as Haye's head rose up from his plate and his eyes fixed on mine. Suddenly he seemed to care. He dropped his fork by the side of the plate and chewed his food, previously uninterested eyes and ears now awaiting my verdict. Here was my moment, I thought to myself, as I wiped my forehead with the back of my hand, inhaled deeply and awkwardly manoeuvred a stray slice of carrot around my plate with a butter knife.

'I think you will stop him in the first round,' I said, analysing Haye's blank response in the process. 'Thompson will just be too easy to hit, too slow, and won't be able to avoid what's coming. I can't see him getting through the first three minutes.'

I felt like a low-ranking mob soldier being interrogated by the capo on suspicion of flipping to the FBI. I could feel Haye's eyes burning a number into my forehead, brainwashing me in a manner I was unable to stop. He was the Thought Police and I was uttering sentiments he wanted me to think.

Truth be told, I wasn't deliberately massaging Haye's ears with a sweet sonnet of early victory that afternoon. I wanted to break the mould – believe me, I did – but simply couldn't. I genuinely believed Haye would overwhelm Thompson early, and that there was nothing Carl's weary bones and mind could do about it. I respected Thompson far more than most at the table, but still saw no way the champion could conquer a younger, fresher, quicker and more powerful hitter. Confidence at an all-time high, David never offered his own opinion that day, nor was he ever asked for one, but he clearly nodded and winked after I'd delivered my own prognosis. I saw it. It was true. I was now part of the problem.

At some point during the evening of 10 September 2004, Carl Thompson jogged to Wembley Arena. Refusing to catch a lift, whether by promoter's transport or taxi, Thompson and coach Maurice 'Hard' Core instead opted to run the mile-and-a-half distance from their hotel to the fight venue. Unsure whether this was the truth or merely a piece of pre-fight mythology, I'd heard the story mentioned by a variety of people around ringside on the night of the event. Not only that, rumours were also rife that Thompson and Core had been barking military-style commands and chants along the Wembley pavements en route to the arena. People stood, stared and naturally wondered what these two black men were hollering about at that hour of the evening. Perhaps it was only an urban legend after all, but whispers soon grew to shouts, and the peculiar scene appeared to be in keeping with what I'd grown to expect from Thompson. The behaviour seemed to fit. There was nothing pampered, manicured or smooth about the way Carl functioned. What choice had he but to run and make his own way into battle?

Wembley Arena was only partially full that September night, yet it felt like *everybody* was there. There was no escaping the scrutiny. Even my father and two younger brothers had snared floor tickets to watch the continuing ascent of our fighting family mascot. From my seat on press row, I'd continually glance across at my family, only too aware of the expectation, both on Haye's shoulders and on my supposed words of wisdom. I got the sense that if Haye flopped, it would be just as much my fault as his.

In the short interlude before the evening's main event, I gratefully experienced a much needed moment of clarity. I learnt that it was sometimes perfectly acceptable just to assume the best and use blind naïvety as a coping method. This was evidently the tactic employed by Natasha, Haye's girlfriend, as she made her way towards me in a show-stopping green dress. Oblivious to the potential for designer damage, Natasha battled her way through press row, treading on toes and egos in the process, before momentarily occupying the empty seat beside me.

'I take it you'll be coming to the after-fight party,' she said, while handing me a fetching purple wristband. 'You're eighteen now, right?'

'Yes,' I replied, 'but I'm heading back with my dad and brothers in the car.'

'Oh, I see,' said Natasha. 'Well, if you do decide to come along, just tag on to me or David and we'll show you the way.'

'I can't even think about celebrations yet,' I said, shaking out the nerves that had accumulated in my hands and legs.

'Yeah, I know what you mean. He'll be fine, though. He's trained really hard for this fight and I know he will win. He always wins.'

Natasha exhibited the kind of positivity verging on delusion that I only wished I too could experience. She had utter belief in the gifts of her boyfriend, and couldn't conceive of any mortal overcoming him in his domain. No reasons were necessary. On the flipside, I was prone to analysing things far too much, and would often brood on Haye's shortcomings while exaggerating the plus points of opponents.

Whatever my concerns, none were shared by Haye himself that September night. Accompanied by gurning glamour model Jodie Marsh, the challenger entered the ring wearing a white T-shirt with the sleeves sliced off, revealing his perfectly sculpted weapons, and swaying along to the R. Kelly track 'Happy People', a song I'd first heard while receiving a lap dance in a Bournemouth strip club.

In stark contrast, and with all the subtlety of an AK-47, Thompson charged towards the ring, backed by the familiar chorus of 'Eye of the Tiger'. Rather than mime the words, he instead acted them out and stared forcefully up ahead at the challenger in the ring. The intensity was terrifying and palpable to all at ringside. Either Thompson's growl was the last stand in a great career, or he was deadly serious about what he planned to do to Haye once the talking stopped.

Although he was far too courteous ever to admit it, I'd always believed Thompson felt slightly offended and disrespected by the way Haye had called him out and chased the fight. The hunter had only acted in the manner of an ambitious young pro, of course, yet Thompson was a proud fighter, and was aware of the fact that Haye was only being pushed towards an early title shot on the assumption that he, the champion, might be tottering on a slippery slope. Thompson would never have said as much, but it must have preyed on his mind, especially given the way he scowled, shook his head and grunted at Haye as the pair finally stood in the Wembley ring together. Thompson stared his young challenger up and down and almost smirked at the sight of Haye in a pretentious bandana and T-shirt with his ring moniker emblazoned across both. The marketable Haye represented everything Thompson wasn't, and it both hurt and disgusted the champion. The quick-witted challenger was being fast-tracked on the road to stardom after only ten professional fights, whereas Thompson had had to endure years in the wilderness, taking short change for long slogs and participating in epic shoot-outs watched by only a handful of anoraks.

If Thompson needed to inflame the situation, Haye remained calm and was a picture of cold-hearted composure during the referee's pre-fight instructions. Terry O'Connor brought the two title contestants together at centre ring, and Haye refused to look at or even acknowledge the presence of Thompson. Standing side on with his head tilted to the floor, Haye chose instead to briefly visualise the violence he was about to unleash on a family hero.

Now, under normal circumstances, most boxers would be overjoyed with first-round statistics that indicated they had thrown over one hundred punches and landed a healthy percentage on the skull of their bewildered opponent. Such numbers would ordinarily reveal a certain dominance. Indeed, on 10 September 2004, David Haye launched a bombardment of 105 punches in the general direction of Carl Thompson in the first three minutes of their IBO title encounter. The challenger tossed jabs, right crosses, slashing hooks and wild uppercuts towards the chops of the champion, missing some, but landing many more. There would be no let-up or room to hide. Thompson needed a bunker. A rampant Haye would frequently step back, draw Thompson in and then, as if bored or embarrassed by a potential lull, bite down on his gumshield and churn out reckless combinations, alternating haphazardly between the left and right fist. Haye attempted to hit anything in sight, and would slug Thompson's head, face, neck, shoulder, chest, stomach and back in an effort to bring about a premature conclusion to the bout.

With barely a minute to go in the opener, Thompson was blown back to the ropes and Haye flurried desperately, eager to overwhelm the champion and beckon the referee into stopping the bout. The challenger wasn't landing anything clean or particularly meaningful, yet was sufficiently on top and seemingly on the verge of duping the referee into halting proceedings. I leapt from my ringside seat and pleaded with O'Connor to stop the fight, not out of concern for Thompson's well-being, but, bizarrely given the circumstances, out of fear for Haye's long-term prospects in the contest. Having gambled and invested so much in this head-scratching first-round salvo, I knew Haye was hell-bent on securing his desired result. He emptied his brain and body in an attempt to remove Thompson in the first round. I recognised that Thompson wasn't about to budge and that a stoppage would have been woefully premature, yet couldn't help but hope O'Connor would take the bait and end matters. Haye was facing a short window of opportunity and, having chanced everything he had on it, would never be the same after it had slammed shut.

The young bully slumped down on his stool at the round's conclusion, having just produced more power-punches in one round than he'd thrown in his entire ten-bout career. It was also approximately one hundred more than I'd seen him manage in ten rounds of sparring in Bournemouth. Suddenly, the cautious and slick counterpuncher had reverted back to his old amateur ways, those of the heavy-hooking, all-or-nothing slugger. Under stress, anticipation and expectancy, Haye had reverted to type.

Despite the inauspicious nature of Haye's early investment, he still managed to sweep the first round conclusively on all three judges' scorecards. He also snatched the second round, building on a dominant start with more desperate pile-drivers and hooks launched from his hip, thigh or above his head.

Although he was landing more scoring shots than Thompson, none of the punches were causing any decisive damage and, more critically, Haye's work became sloppier, wider and weaker as the second round progressed. By the session's mid-point, his pace had dropped alarmingly and his punch output jammed up. Far more accustomed to this situation than Haye was, the forty-year-old champion on the receiving end was simply happy to survive and make deposits. By scoring occasional blows whenever Haye stopped punching, Thompson was effectively laying the foundations for a projected takeover later in the contest.

It was a strange spectacle to behold, as Haye stole the first three rounds decisively, landing numerous heavy whacks in the process, but seemed to be edging further towards a losing position. We could all sense it. I glanced over at my family in between rounds three and four and vividly recall my father shaking his head and pretending to bite his nails. Our man was three rounds up and in control of the scorecards, yet we all knew the judges would probably be deemed unnecessary. This wasn't going the distance. Haye had already made sure of that.

As round four commenced, we watched the challenger bounce on his toes at centre ring, as if trying to kickstart some movement and zest in his limbs. He frowned and sighed, unsure why Thompson was still hanging around, and confused as to why his picture-perfect body couldn't operate the way it was supposed to.

Momentum shifted and Thompson fed off the severity of the beating he'd sustained in the first three rounds to mount the first genuine signs of a comeback in the fourth. He landed hard jabs and overhand rights on Haye, who was now backing away with his hands down, no longer rapid enough to escape Carl's brave retorts. I watched as Haye shook his head in shame each time a Thompson shot rudely clipped him. There was a look of acceptance on his face and, while he wasn't getting particularly hurt by Thompson's punches, the challenger now realised he could no longer budge the champion and was stuck in first gear with a tank ticking on empty.

Worryingly immune to any notion of defeat, Thompson soaked up Haye's best and was now visibly overtaking the younger man, a reality which left Haye broken and forlorn on his stool at the end of the round. Carl had comfortably pocketed the round on the scorecards and, in finally turning losing rounds into a winning one, had made a significant statement.

It came as no surprise, therefore, that Haye's plight only worsened in the seminal fifth round, as Thompson increased his work-rate and forced the challenger into retreat mode. Haye made one final attempt to rally back, landing a right hand in a neutral corner, but was unable to offer any sequel to his success. Instead, Thompson covered up, waited for Haye to throw and then, when realising nothing was coming back from his spent opponent, sprang off the ropes and dropped the younger man with a right cross to the top of the head.

Haye paused on one knee, listened to the frantic advice of Booth, and then used the ropes to rise on the referee's count of six. He nodded to the referee, pressed his gloves together and appeared in a rush to foolishly get back to trading debilitating punches with Thompson.

Of course, having encountered this situation countless times before, Thompson knew exactly how to go about ending matters. As routine for him as brushing his teeth, the champion increased the tempo and started banging vicious left hooks and right hands into Haye's exposed head. With thirty seconds left in the round, Haye lazily lurched forward, both arms pumping out, like an extra from a George A. Romero zombie flick. It was a disturbing image of a fighter sucked dry of energy, stamina and life, now functioning purely on instinct and pride.

Seventeen seconds remained in the fifth round when Thompson bounced on his toes and unleashed a huge right hand to Haye's temple. Instead of slumping to the floor as many by now expected, the younger man froze and swayed back woozily to a neutral corner. He was done. Arriving on the scene a moment after Thompson was referee O'Connor who, like the rest of us, knew Haye's time was up. Two manic right hands and a white towel of surrender signalled the end for the beaten gunslinger, who was bravely still firing back with right hands of his own at the time of the stoppage.

More fatigued than hurt, Haye was rescued by both his corner and the referee, and returned to his stool on unsteady stilts. He was quickly administered an oxygen mask and, even amid extreme fatigue and possible concussion, appeared reluctant to smudge his immaculate image.

Too tired to lift his arms, an equally spent Thompson was pushed and pulled around the ring by his excitable cornermen. His chief trainer, Maurice Core, could be heard exclaiming, 'He's just a boy. Ain't nothing but a little boy,' as he danced merrily around the four corners of the ring.

I too felt like a little boy at that moment, and one in need of a motherly hug. It sounds ridiculous and perhaps heartless given the barbaric nature of the sport, but I never feared for Haye's health or well-being during those four-and-three-quarter rounds of psychological (for me) and physical (for him) torture. Nobody ever wants to see a boxer hurt in the ring, especially one they know and care for, but the idea of Haye being physically damaged never crossed my mind. I wasn't nervous or scared for that reason. I wasn't upset because my friend had been punched in the head repeatedly, bruised and concussed by countless blows to the brain. No, the most distressing factor for me was simply witnessing Haye's inability to fulfil his dream. This man's dream wasn't to beat Carl Thompson or even win the IBO cruiserweight title. It was far more than that. Haye dreamed of winning and unifying the world cruiserweight belts and then doing the same as an undersized heavyweight. Instead, he'd tripped and collapsed at the very first hurdle and now faced up to the realisation that his ultimate goal was further away than any of us envisaged.

It was tough watching Haye get beaten up physically, of course, but far worse seeing him disrobe mentally. The humiliation was worse than the punishment, from where I was sitting. Whether that made me a sadist or not, I don't know, but, in the space of twenty minutes, I'd gone from hanging on and believing Haye's every word to doubting everything, from the legitimacy of his training camp and tactics to the choice of opponent and spelling of his own name. Haye's cape had ripped while attempting to soar prematurely through skyscrapers.

I stuck around and kept my father and brothers waiting in the car that evening, not knowing whether I'd even get to see Haye by the time of wrap-up. It was nearing midnight, and I was both hungry and depressed, a horrible combination at the best of times. My father bombarded my phone with missed calls from the Wembley Arena car park, presumably wondering when I'd finally grace them with my teary-eyed presence.

Sensing it was best just to make a move, I worked my way through the back corridors towards the dressing rooms, where both Haye and Thompson had earlier prepared for war. I bypassed the sounds of jubilation emerging from Carl's room and continued on through to the improvised wake held in Haye's. Booth caught me at the door and beckoned me in.

Once inside, I saw Haye sat up on a bench, legs stretched out in front of him and a doctor nearby filling in forms. The beaten fighter was surrounded by loved ones, including Natasha, whose purple wristband ultimately proved redundant that night. Nobody was getting carried away with advice or blame and Haye, yet to be given the chance to formulate an explanation or excuse, was content just to smile and shrug.

'How's it going?' asked the wounded fighter as I approached. It seemed a ridiculous question in the circumstances, but was a sign of how Haye was able, on the surface at least, to brush off defeat and pretend Friday was Thursday.

'Forget *me*,' I said. 'How are you?'

'Fine. I've just got a massive fucking headache, that's all,' replied Haye. In fact, he'd used the headache as reason to prematurely leave the post-fight press conference. 'It's probably the worst headache I've ever had. It feels like someone's attacking my brain with an axe. It's killing me.'

On the doctor's advice, Haye took his headache to the hospital for tests. I watched him clutch his head and neck in pain as he was led out, and told him I'd call the following day to check on how he was doing.

I walked round the back of the arena that evening, through the deserted car park and towards my father's car, hoping – nay, praying – my family wouldn't mention anything about the fight for the duration of our journey or, indeed, the remainder of that year. The last thing I wanted to do was talk about what I'd just witnessed. Boxing doesn't do tear-ducts, but I wished it did that night.

Sticking to my promise, I called the beaten boxer early on Saturday afternoon, giving him just enough time to rise and shake off the cobwebs from the night before. The decision to call him was a no-brainer for me, as I kept harking back to old movie tales of defeated sportsmen waking up the day after a crushing loss and discovering their entourage reduced by ninety per cent, old friends and followers no longer interested in a piece of a withered former champion. I knew this attitude was commonplace in boxing, too, and I wasn't about to succumb to it. Besides, I still believed in Haye, even if that belief was significantly weaker than it had been twenty-four hours before. More than that, though, I now cared for him as a person.

So the phone rang and, thankfully, the fighter picked up. He was out of hospital and being driven home by Natasha at the time.

'I just felt like shit in there,' recalled David, as he finally removed his media bandana and got down to the nitty-gritty of what actually went wrong. 'My legs were the problem. They just felt so heavy and slow. I couldn't lift them at all by the third round. I had no life, energy or bounce in them. As soon as my legs went, I couldn't get in position to throw my shots. I was never hurt in the fight, though. I just felt really tired and exhausted and my legs wouldn't move. I tried getting on my bike and outboxing him, but it wouldn't happen.'

He hadn't yet found his answers, but was getting warmer. A couple of days later I discovered that Haye was, indeed, getting warmer and had, in fact, gone on holiday to Gran Canaria. He'd travelled out there alone and told me he was going to 'sit by the pool and think for a week or two'. Although I didn't necessarily buy into his proposed itinerary, I liked the image of him reflecting on his mishap poolside with a rueful frown, notebook and pen.

A week later and an unexpected email arrived in my inbox with an attachment. The accompanying document was titled 'Statement' and it contained 3,000 words meditating on the fighter's first professional defeat. It was unquestionably the longest and most heartfelt piece of writing Haye had ever devoted to any one subject.

Engrossed as I was by the unvarnished account of his first professional setback, a concluding poem impressed me above anything else. Haye's poem remains the most poignant, candid and distressing testimony I've ever read or heard from a fighter. It also offers an insight into the psyche of a humbled man coming to terms with the stark demands of his profession.

Boxing is a sport,
Sports are there for us to play.
Playing should make us happy,
Happiness is a chemical reaction in the brain.
Boxing damages the brain.

PART THREE

Lessons learnt and focus realigned, David Haye becomes 'The Hayemaker' and embarks on a lengthy winning streak.

CHAPTER EIGHT
HAPPY PEOPLE

The fallen fighter couldn't stomach watching the entire drama, so he fast-forwarded the tape his uncle Donovan kindly provided him with and hit pause at the start of the fourth round. By this time the image on screen was one of desperation, panic and inevitable defeat. Hysterical commentators prepared the epitaph. The BBC's poster boy and future star was hitting the self-destruct button on his biggest stage to date and we could only watch helplessly.

It couldn't have been easy for David Haye to rewind and scrutinise footage of his public dressing down. I remembered how he'd once shown me a video of the night he was knocked out in the amateur ranks by a Jim Twite left cross, but time had healed that particular trauma. It was comparatively easy to look back and smirk. After all, since that defeat in 1999, Haye had gone on to excel as both an international amateur and fledgling professional, whereas tiler Twite flunked as a pro and returned to the grout-spreader and spirit level not long after.

Rewinding the Carl Thompson debacle was a different proposition altogether. Haye was still living the defeat, as opposed to looking back and recalling it from a higher plateau. He still felt the headaches, heartache and battered pride. Despite a seemingly unshakeable self-belief, even he wasn't sure whether everything would be rosy up ahead. None of us knew how he would respond to the setback. Nobody knew whether defeat to Thompson would act as the impetus to embark on something special, or instead be seen as an impassable speed hump in a career rattling along too fast for its own good.

So, with question marks still swirling round his aching head, Haye sat down in the living room of his apartment and hit the play button on his remote control. As was always the case whenever I observed him watching fights, he began in a relaxed posture, arms up and over the side of the sofa, while his legs were hoisted up and stretched out on a leather pouffe. Gradually he would bite his nails and rip the skin from his fingers and knuckles, as a frown of concentration swept across his forehead.

As seconds and minutes passed, Haye's demeanour would become more agitated and rigid, as he'd fidget, dodge, weave and deflect imaginary blows with a shake of the head or a whip of the hand. I could never tell whether he was aware of these mannerisms, but I interpreted them as the uncontrollable reflexes of a man programmed to fight. It was, in essence, a form of fistic Tourette's. Haye would watch boxing in a trance and would always play himself. He'd wince or moan whenever he witnessed his on-screen self cop a wayward shot in the mouth, and he'd shake his head despondently when falling short with punches of his own. Rather than merely watch it, Haye relived it in slacks.

On that late-September day, the fighter didn't have much to rewind or reward himself for. Instead there was a lot of groaning and grimacing as he watched an anonymous 23-year-old cruiserweight – someone he may have once known – stumble around the ring and receive a harsh lesson from a physically inferior, yet infinitely wiser champion.

Haye watched the footage for no more than six minutes. He started at the bell to welcome round four and ended the tape when referee Terry O'Connor crossed his arms in a signal of defeat. He couldn't watch any longer, and didn't require the benefit of replays or alternative angles. Haye already knew why and how he lost, and wasn't turning to the tape for proof. Perhaps he only decided to consult the video that day to remind himself of the fact that so many others would have seen it too.

Admittedly, it always confused me how Haye could only watch the final two rounds and skim through the first three entirely. To the casual eye, it appeared that he had done his best work, if one could call it that, in the opening segments of the fight. The collapse and subsequent images of despair played out in the fourth and fifth rounds, the pair combining to make nearly six minutes Haye would presumably have wanted to forget.

'I didn't need to see what I did wrong at the start,' explained Haye. 'I know why I was fighting like I did at the end, and I couldn't put myself through watching that bullshit at the start. The first few rounds were terrible, even if I was winning them. That's when all the damage was done. I'd rather see myself get beaten up and stopped in the last round, than watch me act like an idiot for the first three and still win them. I don't know if I'll ever be able to watch the first few rounds.'

He never did. Moreover, the road back for Haye was a humiliating one. He returned to modest slots on leisure-centre shows and spanked opponents he was supposed to beat at earlier junctures in his career. The humbled fighter refused to braid his untamed Afro for a one-round demolition of Valery Semishkur in December and then nearly forgot to turn up altogether for a hollow January win over Garry Delaney. Haye would eventually stop the West Ham heavyweight in three rounds, but, travelling alone on the tube that night, he left his apartment late and arrived at the fight venue an hour after he was supposed to. Still, at least he made the effort to tighten and smarten up his hair for comeback bout number two.

Ukrainian walkover Semishkur had, of course, originally been lined up to face Haye on the amateur star's professional debut. Delaney, likewise, was slated to defend his Southern Area cruiserweight title against Haye in November 2003. By the time he actually did face David in January 2005, Delaney was a bloated heavyweight version of his former self, and all semblance of ambition and pride had vacated his tubby loins. Since losing to Thompson, the go-getting Haye had been forced back to the future and treated the exercises with the disdain he felt they deserved. He craved immediate challenges, the chance to put the record straight, yet the establishment, and boxing protocol, advised him to remain patient and rebuild. Though the tape warned him against it, Haye once again craved Carl Thompson.

'I'm going to school you,' the boxer said to me on the eve of his January date with Delaney, as he shuffled through a box of old records and compact discs. He pulled out Leon Ware's *Musical Massage* LP and a George Benson hits collection. Perhaps I was old beyond my years, but I was elated on first discovering Haye had more of an affinity with my parents' record collection than he did with the hip-hop-dominated sounds of most inner-city boxing gyms. Haye's musical library was organic, classic, old-school, and contained the work of musicians, as opposed to computer programmers or hype men. It represented a scattershot insight into his childhood and his diverse upbringing, offering samples of the best of both black and white musicians from the past forty years. There was Marvin Gaye, Stevie Wonder, Earth, Wind & Fire, Prince, Michael Jackson, George Michael, Billy Joel and James Taylor. I treated the library as an education, the chance to pull up old records and familiarise myself with cover art I'd never seen before.

'So, who is the best then?' I asked.

'Singer?' said Haye. 'That's tough. Personally, I can't look past Marvin.'

'Really?' I replied. 'I've always preferred Stevie to Marvin. He has a bigger range, and can also do so much more than just sing. He is a virtuoso with many instruments and wrote, arranged and played on all his best albums.'

'I know,' said Haye. 'None of that matters, though, when it comes down to attitude and delivery. Marvin just delivered on every level, both on albums and when singing live. He was *the man*. Stevie was a child genius and was manufactured to be great, whereas Marvin had to live a bit and hustle. That dude had to work hard and experience shit to get where he was. He was a *bad* man. He had that swagger and attitude that Stevie always lacked.'

'Yeah, but I'm talking about classic albums and songs, and I think Stevie has more. *Songs in the Key of Life, Innervisions, Talking Book, Fulfillingness' First Finale* . . .'

'What about "Here, My Dear" and "What's Going On"? Marvin had just as many great songs and albums. Listen, I'm a massive fan of both and love all their stuff. I'm just saying, Marvin was a lot more interesting and fascinating as a person and performer.'

'But Stevie is blind. He can't exactly get up and dance.'

'I'm aware of that. You can't fake what Marvin had, though. You either have the story and the charisma, or you don't. Maybe I just prefer bad guys with rough edges. I mean, Marvin was shot dead by his own father. He wasn't just singing about boys chasing girls. The guy had some serious issues and problems that he wanted to discuss. That's what elevates him to that next level for me. Stevie is great, too, but he has a bit more of a cheese-factor going for him. I prefer my singers to talk about death, drugs and divorce and live on the edge a little.'

Minutes after defeating Garry Delaney in Brentwood, the giddy victor revealed a wish to challenge reigning European cruiser-weight champion Alexander Gurov by the end of 2005. The veteran southpaw Ukrainian was six feet six inches tall and had notched thirty-three of his thirty-eight professional victories by knockout. Hardly an ideal prescription for a man supposedly overcoming the after-effects of a crushing first loss, yet David Haye wouldn't have it any other way.

It wasn't a conversation about boxing that finally crystallised Haye's character in my mind. It was a debate on music. I had by now realised David wasn't the type to do things in half-measures, and he was right – dallying in mediocrity was dangerous. Having at least attempted to adhere to the traditional rebuilding process, Haye was now two fights in and reaching for the trigger again. He was determined to go back to doing things his way, for better or worse.

I was a natural pessimist, someone content to travel the tried and tested route, but Haye was a different animal altogether. He was an emotional, visceral and volatile gambler, dice in one hand, shotgun in the other. Rather than sustained and glorious, his period of potential greatness would be swift and emphatic. He was Marvin Gaye.

"What's Going On" would have to wait, of course, but as 2005 stretched its legs, Haye began to score the kind of victories that would, ultimately, lead to both redemption and a title shot. He blitzed Australia's former world light-heavyweight title challenger Glen Kelly in two rounds in March, and then, by October, repeated the dose on Italian Vincenzo Rossitto. Both men were ranked within the top ten by the World Boxing Council (WBC) and therefore considered legitimate tests of Haye's post-Thompson blues. Appearing to have turned a corner, the Londoner barely put a foot wrong or received a blow in return against either. He even managed to halt Kelly five rounds quicker than it had taken our hero Roy Jones Jr to do the deed in 2003.

Whether in words or actions, it was clear that Haye's biggest threat in 2005 was his own impatience. Unwilling to take stock, slow down or ease off the throttle upon losing to Thompson, he now performed at breakneck speed and, for the first time in his career, began to glance over his shoulder.

'What was Sugar Ray Leonard doing at twenty-five years old?' Haye asked on the day of his own twenty-fifth birthday. The date was 13 October and the cruiserweight was en route to Huddersfield at the time, sitting in the passenger seat of his Range Rover beside designated driver and Leonard encyclopaedia Adam Booth. I lurked behind the pair for the duration of the journey and occasionally poked my head through the crack between the seats, keen to discover why Haye had suddenly become so enamoured of Leonard, a clear favourite of Booth, yet never someone for whom Haye had previously displayed any particular fondness.

'Let me think,' pondered Booth, clearly enthused by his pupil's sudden desire to discuss his all-time favourite subject. 'If I've got my dates right, he was knocking out Thomas Hearns in the fourteenth round of a world welterweight title fight at Caesars Palace. Yeah, Leonard beat Hearns on September 16th, 1981 and he was born on May 17th, 1956. So that would make Leonard twenty-five the night he beat Hearns.'

His stats were never in doubt, of course, and the realisation that Leonard was only twenty-five the night he scored his career-best professional victory surprised us all, even Booth, who knew all there was to know about the multi-weight world champion.

'That's amazing, isn't it?' said Haye. 'You couldn't imagine a fighter nowadays being involved in that type of fight at that age. Most boxers in Britain don't relinquish their British titles until they're thirty.'

'It's nonsense,' said Booth. 'Leonard beat an undefeated Wilfred Benitez for his first world title when he was only twenty-three.

Leonard was obviously a special talent, but there's no reason to hang around if you're good enough.'

Haye was clearly bothered by the reality of turning twenty-five and, to date, being without a world title of any shape or form. He laughed off Leonard's freakish achievements that day, but I could tell the magnitude of Sugar Ray's career highlight shook Haye, a fighter who, though investing all he had in a race against time, could never surpass what the likes of Leonard had achieved at a younger age.

I liked to call it the 'Orson Welles effect'. Welles, of course, famously wrote, directed and starred in *Citizen Kane* at the tender age of twenty-five. The film would later be regarded as the greatest movie of all time. Seriously, what hope do the rest of us have? Just as I would never write or direct anything resembling *Citizen Kane* by the time I was twenty-five, Haye also knew there was little point moulding his career on the templates of bona fide boxing geniuses. He remained confident of one day hitting those kinds of heights, but you got the sense Haye now realised success was no longer a given, and that he was blessed with only a short shelf-life within which to achieve the goals he'd bragged about since the age of ten.

I take great satisfaction in highlighting the fact R. Kelly was no Marvin Gaye, either. Furthermore, the moment an R. Kelly song wormed its way through the speakers of our car radio was often a prompt to switch stations. Save for his sterling work on the 1996 *Space Jam* soundtrack, an unlikely staple of my childhood, I'd yet to find anything from the man that so much as passed my ears as a pleasant or tolerable din. One of his more recent efforts, 'Happy People', represented a far greater level of evil in my mind and ears, as the song had been used by David Haye as walk-in music ahead of his first professional loss to Carl Thompson in September 2004.

So, when the opening beats to R. Kelly's hit found their way into the speakers of our family vehicle on a cold, wet December evening in 2005, I knew what our next plan of action needed to be.

'Can we switch stations?' I asked Mum, before leaning over and toggling the dial on her car radio.

'What was wrong with that one?' went the inquisition.

'Just superstition,' I said. 'That was the song David walked out to against Carl Thompson. Talk about a bad omen.'

Now, on a normal December day, I'd probably have let the song slide and used powers of mind control to block out any unfortunate memories attached to it. However, that day in December was the sixteenth, and was also the evening Haye would attempt to wrest the European cruiserweight title from Alexander Gurov. In fact, 'Happy People' kicked in just as we reached the halfway point on our journey to the Bracknell Leisure Centre, the scene of the organised and regulated crime Haye sought to commit later that night. Thankfully, unlike previous Haye hangouts Rotherham and Huddersfield, Bracknell was a mere twenty-minute drive from our family home and, rather than having to bunk lifts or endure lengthy coach and train rides, my mother was on hand to chaperone me towards one of the closest leisure centres in the area.

I laughed when Haye phoned me up with news of the venue and proceeded to bark down the earpiece about how it was 'in the middle of fucking nowhere' and that 'nobody would bother turning up for anything in Bracknell'. The choice of venue was ideal for me, of course, yet was anything but for a star in the making, desperate to increase both his fan base and his collection of belts. This was a major fight for Haye and also British boxing and yet, despite the high-stakes nature of the match, only a few hundred people would pass through the turnstiles. It was hard not to sympathise with Haye, as his three most important fights post-Thompson had all taken place in minuscule venues, often leisure centres, and all based many miles from his London headquarters. Alas, there was no fan base to speak of and, just as in any great chicken-and-egg scenario, it wasn't exactly clear whose fault it was. The promoters blamed Haye's inability to sell tickets, while the boxer condemned their inability to book venues closer to home, thus denying him the chance to nurture and expand a potential following. Whatever the reasoning, the forgotten challenger arrived in Bracknell that December night with very few fans on hand to witness his most testing assignment to date. He'd have to go it alone.

Of course, the consensus view going into the European title fight was that whichever puncher landed first would remain upright, and the fighter foolish enough to cop one on the chin would be staring up at the lights. That much was a given. Haye whacked hard with his right hand and Gurov generated similar force with his left, thrown from a rigid and upright southpaw stance. Neither man was deemed to possess the greatest chin or punch resistance, though I always felt Gurov was the more fragile and susceptible, especially mentally. He'd been stopped in each of his four professional losses and had been halted three times within the first three rounds. He started bouts slowly and took a while to simmer. Case in point: Britain's Terry Dunstan famously wrecked Gurov inside a round back in 1998, when he caught the cagey Ukrainian cold and early with merely seconds gone in the fight.

The champion was now thirty-four and, though he'd yet to show too many signs of wear and tear, I nevertheless had the feeling he was again ripe for a quick finish. His reaction times had slowed, his ability to withstand pain had diminished and his all-round game operated at a fraction of the speed he managed in his twenties. However, I was also aware that Haye needed to exploit all these possible failings before he himself got clipped on the chin and sent spiralling south.

Veteran Gurov had won thirty-eight of forty-three professional bouts the night he met Haye, and boasted a staggering thirty-three knockouts to his name. Yet such small print soon counted for very little. On his way to the ring, the ice-cold champion had resembled a farmer witnessing a UFO land in the middle of an Iowa crop field, and less than a minute later, he was *convinced* he'd seen little green aliens.

Circling, watching and plotting, a coiled Haye snapped and immediately stepped in with a hard right cross from out of range, catapulting the punch against the exposed chin of Gurov with less than a minute gone on the clock. The southpaw champion, stunned by the velocity of the assault, could do nothing but swallow the shot flush and collapse backwards onto the ring canvas, eyes debating the merits of staying open, and legs isolated in all sorts of unnatural positions. With eyes and legs in dispute, it was hard to see a way back for Gurov and, sensing his predicament would only worsen should the fight continue, referee Guido Cavalleri called a halt to the bout in the very first round.

In the blink of an eye and thwack of a right hand, Haye had become European cruiserweight champion. It was easier and quicker than even he said it would be. Though behind schedule, Haye was now twenty-five and reasonably happy. It took him a year to start forgetting the traumas of *that* September night, but only forty-five seconds to catch up.

CHAPTER NINE
EYES AND EARS

'Dave ... Dave ... Dave ...' It was often easier to penetrate David Haye's defence with punches than it was to successfully penetrate his ears with information. If in doubt, ask Natasha Davis. Shielded behind his MacBook Pro computer or BlackBerry phone, or submerged under waves of reality-based nonsense spewed from the television set, 'Dave' was normally dormant and in need of social lubrication. He wouldn't ignore his girlfriend out of spite or lack of interest, but more habit and an inability to multi-task. When Haye's mind was focused on something, nobody, not even his girlfriend, had the tools or ability to deflect his attention. By now, saintly Natasha had become accustomed to the invisible wall and, while some might have given up hope after the first holler of 'Dave', she was experienced enough to persevere in her attempts to flip the engaged sign.

When it came time for the roles to be reversed, of course, Haye demanded an immediate response.

'Where is my charger?' barked the boyfriend, as he stomped his feet and scoured the room for his laptop's juice boost. 'Have you seen it *anywhere*?'

Hidden behind a copy of *Heat* magazine, Natasha would peer round, acknowledge David's question, and then offer advice, even if, ultimately, it failed to help solve the conundrum.

'Yeah, *but where is it?*' Haye would continue, temperature soaring and patience shortening by the second. I often wondered how the prowling champion would react if his girlfriend had replicated his own stance on interrogation and merely waved her hand in a silent code to call back later.

In truth, Natasha was far too civil to ever deliberately blank out her partner's predicament. Yet it wasn't enough to simply attempt to help; only a conclusive response would satisfy Haye. If Natasha didn't have the answer, then it was clearly her fault and she must have hidden the object as a test of both David's patience and his orienteering skills. Having watched both scenarios unfold on numerous occasions by now, I still wasn't sure which one made me squirm more.

I spent three weeks at the pair's Clapham apartment in January 2006, and the arrangement allowed me a clear path into Cannon Street, home of *Boxing News*, who'd generously handed me a work-experience stint as part of my journalism degree. It was hard to know whether my presence inside the walls of no sound was a help or hindrance, as sometimes I felt like a useful aid and reluctant shrink, and other times represented a further distraction. Haye used me as a source for all the conversations he couldn't have with his girlfriend, while Natasha utilised time spent away from her boyfriend to discuss his good and bad points with me.

'I've had to learn to accept the way he is,' she told me one January afternoon, with Haye away training in London's West End. 'He's used to having people do a lot for him, so he pretty much expects it. Once you realise what kind of person he is, though, it's easier to deal with the moods. Usually after his fights, when we go away on holiday, he's great. He only becomes awkward when he's preparing for a fight or is particularly busy.'

Time spent in one another's company often dwindled as fight time approached, and Natasha would see little of Haye during the week of the fight and on the day itself. Some better halves may have pushed their influence on an emotionally unbalanced boxer, yet Natasha knew her man better than most and wasn't concerned with locating the limelight.

'I'm not one of these girls who hang on to someone because it might help them become famous,' said Natasha. 'I would never want to be famous anyway. I'm only interested in seeing David accomplish his goals and achieve the things I know he can. I don't even think about my role in the whole process. Even though he might not always show it, I know David appreciates what I do for him and that he likes having me around. He always tells me that he'd have struggled to carry on against Lolenga Mock if it hadn't been for me, and it's nice to hear stuff like that.'

As much as I enjoyed spending time in their company, preferably one at a time, the idea of temporarily living in the pair's spare room was somewhat daunting. In addition to acting as open-all-hours advice line, my presence in the basement also allowed me an early insight into preparations for Haye's next bout and first European title defence, tentatively scheduled for March 2006.

While manager Adam Booth took care of the immediate future and scoured the European Boxing Union's top-fifteen rankings in pursuit of a first title challenger, Haye and I dreamed bigger and turned our attention to the mammoth world cruiserweight title battle between WBC and WBA champion Jean-Marc Mormeck and IBF king O'Neil Bell on 7 January in Madison Square Garden, New York.

I'd kept it to myself up to this point, but, yes, it was true, Mormeck and I had history. In fact, I'd fallen head over heels for the rugged Frenchman ever since watching him beat WBC world champion Wayne Braithwaite in April 2005. Knowing these men were the ultimate templates by which to gauge Haye's progress, I stayed awake all night, jumping on any internet feed of the fight I could find, eager to discover just how good the two champions at the top of the tree were.

The hard-hitting Braithwaite was the boxer with considerable hype, generated by a substantial knockout ratio and wild, hazardous fighting style, which combined hands-down switch-hitting with all-out slugging. Mormeck, on the other hand, was a comparatively modest thirty-two-year-old of Antillean descent who'd spent the early portion of his career fighting on Eurosport to little fanfare or adulation. He'd improved as the years had passed, but Mormeck lacked the explosiveness, punch power and star appeal with which Braithwaite teased the moribund cruiser-weight division.

How wrong we all were. Taking the fight to Braithwaite from the get-go, relentless Mormeck chugged after the WBC champion and slung hooks and uppercuts into his opponent's head and body with a bitterness and ferocity that belied his mild manner. So often used to being the aggressor, Braithwaite was dumbstruck by Mormeck's front-foot tactics and could only retreat to the ropes and attempt to parry Jean-Marc's loud and hurtful swings.

For eight rounds in April, Mormeck was a one-man marching band. He dropped Braithwaite in the fourth round, hurt him on countless other occasions, and showed the kind of intensity and come-forward fire that Joe Frazier would, incredibly, summon each time he faced Muhammad Ali. The tank-like Mormeck didn't hook as forcefully as Smokin' Joe, of course, but clearly possessed the same kind of hard-nosed work ethic and spirit.

The vaunted punch power of Braithwaite failed to get him out of trouble and, as the bout wore on, Mormeck changed tactics somewhat and decided simply to box the final four rounds, abandoning previous attempts to engage in a close-quarter battle. Even when deciding to move and dance on the back foot, however,

Mormeck did so effortlessly and with a grace that contradicted his bruiser build.

To my eyes at least, Mormeck appeared capable of doing it all that night. He brawled better than any brawler I'd seen in years, and counterpunched better than most counterpunchers. He made Braithwaite look about as dangerous as a child with a plastic spoon, and did so by fighting inside and outside, giving 'Big Truck' every chance to land his patented power punches.

By the time Mormeck was awarded the unanimous decision at the bout's conclusion, my head was in a spin. I couldn't have been more impressed by the new double world cruiserweight champion and couldn't have been more worried for Haye's projected climb towards the victor's lair. As much as I rooted for Haye in any bout, I failed to see a way past the versatile and talented Frenchman. Not only was he gifted as both a slugger and counterpuncher, Mormeck also seemed tough, durable and stubborn in all the ways Carl Thompson was. He was Thompson with talent, a dangerous proposition for anyone, let alone Haye.

Nine months on and I was still telling Haye how great Mormeck was and how he'd unequivocally destroy IBF champion Bell that January morning. The fight had already taken place in America, of course, but neither Haye nor I knew the result by the time we huddled around his laptop on the morning of 8 January. We both picked Mormeck to win, but I could sense Haye saw more potential in Bell's fists than I did.

It all started positively enough for Mormeck. Technically astute and by far the crisper puncher of the two, Jean-Marc stole many early rounds from Bell on sheer aggression and hustle. However, as the bout wore on, Mormeck's intense work-rate dropped and Bell, shoulders relaxed and fists tight, began to score success with his dense right hand. By the time the tenth round greeted us, both men were physically exhausted, but Bell had a better knack of disguising it. We both sensed what was coming.

Slinging heavy leather at the Frenchman's body, Bell took the fight to the street and began to simply beat Mormeck up. Suddenly, my hero swayed back to the ropes in exhaustion, a shadow of the fighter I'd fallen in love with in 2005. Mormeck looked lost, his eyes those of a young boy struggling to locate irresponsible parents in a supermarket.

As Bell bullied Mormeck and drilled him with consecutive right crosses, we both knew the end was near. Haye leapt in anticipation, while I held my head in my hands, knowing full well I was about to witness the collapse of one of my favourite fighters. Mormeck's mouthpiece was knocked out by a Bell blow, and further right hands crashed into the champion's skull as he stood prone in a neutral corner. Bell was unforgiving in his attempts to finish, and Mormeck, seemingly out on his feet, could only cover up, sag to his haunches and then keel over in a fatigued and battered mess. The favourite fell in stages and ended up positioned on the canvas like a man praying to a greater God for some form of forgiveness. Nobody could help him. Mormeck was knocked out for the first time in his career.

'Oh my God,' roared Haye as the bout ended. 'That was fucking brutal! I can't believe it ended like that!'

Unable to add any colour to Haye's commentary, I simply sat and endured the replays, most of which again highlighted the copious amounts of leather Mormeck received to the head in those closing seconds. 'I never expected to see Mormeck get destroyed like that,' added Haye.

Within minutes, David was on the phone to Adam Booth, informing him of what he'd just watched and pleading with him to chase up a potential fight with Bell. He insisted the fight could be made for March or April and that Bell would be interested in taking the fight as 'he'd see me as an easy tune-up'. Haye played down his own hopes in the fight and banked on the possibility that Bell underestimated his threat and would fall into the trap. I listened in on the conversation and, though openly petrified, was full of admiration for Haye's ballsy bluster. We'd both watched the same O'Neil Bell emphatically club Jean-Marc Mormeck to within an inch of his life, and yet I wasn't on the phone to a boxing manager in the hope of confronting the victor anytime soon. Even through a scratchy internet stream, I could see, feel and hear the power, and I wasn't about to volunteer to be on the receiving end of it. Cut from an entirely different cloth, however, Haye wanted Bell and he wanted him now. The erratic Jamaican featured in Haye's dreams and my nightmares from that day on.

I spent every night of my January stay in Haye's spare room, save for one particular night, when both he and I were thrown out of his home, due mainly to a mix of carelessness and the evil web of deceit known as social messaging websites. In short, Haye left his cherished laptop open in the living room, only for a curious girl-friend to take a peek and stumble upon certain messages and photographs she'd rather never have found. Much shouting and pleading ensued, as Natasha launched accusations David's way, and the boxer appeared unable to slip them in the way he could so effortlessly evade punches. In the end, with me in the middle, or, more accurately, downstairs hiding in the kitchen, Haye relented and moved away from the fire, taking me with him.

We spent the next few hours riding across eggshells in his hefty Range Rover, stopping off for food at Nando's, me unsure of the true problem and Haye fumbling for a way out. Insisting there was no real harm done and that Natasha had no reason to be upset or concerned, Haye sounded part desperado and part magician, as he attempted to erase the evidence in *his* mind, at the very least. I couldn't be sure whether he was genuinely in control or whether he'd slipped into a state of delusion and was now kidding himself that all was bliss and Natasha's rage was merely a result of optical illusion. Having heard what I'd heard, and been aware of Haye's weakness for instant messaging sites, I knew Natasha wasn't play-acting or exaggerating the pain of a paper cut. Whether she'd truly discovered damning evidence, or merely tripped over a deceptive snap of a bimbo in a two-piece, I couldn't be certain. Either way, we both bore the brunt of miscommunication.

'My contact lenses are back at your house,' I said to the boxer as we crossed town in his Range Rover.

'Can you do without them for one day?' asked Haye. 'We can't go back there tonight.'

With eyes drying out by the second, I made do with my final disposable pair for another hour and then tossed them away into the night, rendering me blind and angry, though substantially less than Natasha probably was. Like two suspended schoolboys preparing for the told-you-so wrath of parents, a reflective Haye and I ventured through London towards Bromley, home of go-to sage Adam Booth, on call to offer a sympathetic ear and a sofa to sleep on.

Through partly cloudy eyes, I then made my way back to Haye's apartment in the morning, eager to get my hands on a new pair of lenses. For Haye, meanwhile, driving in pensive silence for perhaps the first time ever, there were far bigger stakes up ahead. This was the most nervous and insecure I'd ever known him, and it was by now clear Natasha presented a greater threat than any of his previous gloved opponents.

'Wait here,' said Haye, as we parked up outside his apartment. 'I'll get your bags.'

'Don't forget my lenses,' I pleaded. 'They're in the bathroom.'

Haye nodded, paused for a second, composed himself behind the wheel and then finally made his move. He opened the driver's door and reluctantly climbed out, the cogs still turning inside his head. Normally a decisive and spontaneous individual, Haye now seemed calculated and scared to the point of malfunction. He tried half-heartedly to laugh off the episode as he pivoted to leave, but I knew this was serious. Nobody, not Carl Thompson, Alexander Gurov or any of the world cruiserweight champions could instil this level of concentration, anxiety and fear within Haye.

I waited alone in the Range Rover for approximately half an hour, before Haye, thankfully carrying my bags, not his, made his way back to the driver's seat. He climbed in, and duly released a monumental sigh of relief.

'Everything sorted?' I asked.

'Yeah, I think so,' said Haye. 'She's a lot calmer today. I've still got some work to do, though.'

With that, he put his foot down on the accelerator and I attempted to place a rubbery contact lens on my eyeball, without the aid of a mirror, soap or water. It wasn't clean, it wasn't accurate, but I could now see clearly, and that's all that mattered. I think that made two of us that morning.

A week later, Haye departed for South Beach, Miami, to begin preparations ahead of his first European title defence against the unbeaten Dane Lasse Johansen in March. Adam Booth would later join him, but, for the first two weeks of camp, Haye played the part of roaming warrior, gumshield and gloves in tow, challenging all-comers in various Latino-flavoured Miami gyms. He was alone again.

I briefly provided company on fight night as the fighter spotted me lingering outside York Hall in Bethnal Green, hit the brakes on his Range Rover and waited long enough for me to climb aboard. Once inside, Haye jammed his foot down on the accelerator and made the right turn down the side of the famous East End fight venue.

'How is it going?' asked the driver, as he flicked through the tracks on his car stereo and then pumped up the volume to eleven.

'Fine, thanks,' I replied, shouting to be heard and wiping spots of rain from my jacket. 'How about you?'

'Good,' said Haye.

I knew enough by now to realise he felt uncomfortable under questioning, especially when so close to a fight. He didn't like being asked how he felt, and preferred loose and meaningless conversations, as opposed to feeling like the interviewer's subject.

'Have you heard this version of the song?' he continued.

'No,' I replied. 'This is Marvin Gaye, though, right?'

'Yeah,' added Haye. 'This is his version of the song.'

The song playing that night was "I Wanna Be Where You Are", originally written by Leon Ware and Arthur Ross, recorded by a young Michael Jackson, but that night sung by Marvin Gaye, a man who owed much of his 1976 *I Want You* album to Ware's pen.

'I actually prefer the Leon Ware version,' said Haye, who seemed to play Ware's take on the song at least once every time I sat shotgun in his Range Rover. 'As much as I love Marvin, you can't beat the strings in the original. That's what makes the song for me.'

Haye was a sucker for soul strings and, with that final analysis, the boxer spun another right and entered the car park at the back of York Hall. Once parked up, he made his way inside the venue and pulled out his BlackBerry phone to scroll through good luck messages and desperate final pleas for ringside tickets. The phone provided Haye with an excuse to ignore pesky passers-by upon entering the venue and also seemed to represent some kind of necessary distraction for a mind gearing itself up for war. I wasn't sure how wise it was for Haye to be concerning himself with text messages so close to a fight, but assumed he knew what he was doing and that this final connection with the world at large was something he felt necessary.

'Can you do me a favour?' Haye asked me, as we entered his designated changing room for the evening. 'Go and check that these two names are down on the guest-list out front. I can't remember whether I put them down or not, and they both need tickets.'

Haye turned his phone towards me to reveal the names and signalled for me to hurry. Clocking the situation with a concerned eye, Adam Booth followed me out of the room, shut the door behind us and then curtailed my mission.

'Whatever he just asked you to do, don't do it,' said Booth. 'His mind is completely wrong right now and all *this* is not helping. I need to get everybody away from him and I need to completely empty his mind and get him to focus.

'This is the worst he's been before a fight – his head is all over the place. He's had problems with Natasha and they've split up. He's not thinking about the fight right now, and I need him to. So, whatever he just told you to do, forget it.'

This latest development had flown way over my head and forced me into a panicked sprint away from the drama. Booth seemed as worried and paranoid as I'd ever seen him and, it goes without saying, two guests likely didn't get in that Friday night. More disturbing than this portal into Haye's scatty mind, however, was the revelation that he'd split, either temporarily or permanently, from Natasha, better known as muse, mother, maid and mate.

As if still in denial, I checked around inside the main floor space of York Hall, hoping Booth was just dramatising events and that Natasha was actually present, occupying her usual ringside seat alongside David's sister, Louisa. To my horror, I soon realised Natasha hadn't in fact shown and that her seat would remain unoccupied for the duration of the fight. She would instead watch the show on Sky Sports at the London flat she shared with her brother.

For a moment I pondered how Natasha must have felt watching her boyfriend put his life on the line through the tube. I wasn't sure whether the artificial nature of a television set would make the fight easier or tougher to endure. Perhaps it would have been better to watch Haye on television, away from the overwhelming sounds, smells and wayward sweat and blood of ringside. Then again, there was a certain helplessness to being stuck in front of a black box and, knowing Natasha as I did by now, I realised she was nothing if not helpful and caring. Whether in glorious victory or painful defeat, she'd have wanted to be there to comfort Haye at the end of it all.

There would be no quick resolution that night, either, despite Haye's hard-hitting and impatient reputation. The stiff and sturdy Lasse Johansen was more durable than most expected, and Haye was forced to abandon a proposed swift exit and leave the taxi meter running in order to outbox the Dane on the back foot.

This switch-up was not for want of trying, I hasten to add. In fact, Haye blasted Johansen early with any number of jabs and trademark rights, including one which nearly sent the Dane's head flying into Natasha's vacant ringside seat, but, despite the success, Johansen remained annoyingly upright and smiling. Ominously, the challenger, unbeaten in fourteen bouts, also seemed to grow numb to Haye's power as the bout progressed into the middle rounds.

Soon Haye was asked to travel beyond the fifth round for the first time as a professional, and the mental scars of previous traumas were evident in both his body language and his plummeting work-rate. History told us that when Haye couldn't abruptly ice an opponent, he'd usually start breathing heavily, tighten up, become sketchy with his punches and eventually come unstuck. With bated breath, we anticipated the inevitable slump. The champion was winning the bout on the cards, yet there remained a sense that passing time and the hubris of Johansen could still have the final say. Crucially, Johansen also sensed this, and began coming on strong as the sixth round passed and the second half of the bout introduced itself.

Sucking up big gulps of air, Haye was clearly feeling the pace, yet encouragingly remained sharp and snappy with his work. Determined not to be overwhelmed by Johansen's increased tempo, the Londoner stepped into the centre of the ring and slung hard hooks to the Dane's body, reddening his stomach and rib area with immediate effect. The champion was no longer willing to step back or be outmanoeuvred by Johansen.

As the eighth round started to sing, Haye stamped down hard on the throttle and put together a smorgasbord of finishing blows which had Johansen reeling and the referee on edge. The brave challenger, now partially sighted through a swollen mask of claret, was unsteady on his legs and on the receiving end of a series of vicious right hands. Investing everything in roundhouse right hooks, Haye chipped away at Johansen's body and resolve, eventually trapping him on the ropes and forcing the referee to scamper closer to the action. Moments later, with one telling shake of the head, Johansen signalled defeat and referee Guido Cavalleri made the intervention, jumping between the two fighters to call a halt to proceedings.

In a clear nod to growing maturity and inner strength, Haye rode out a mini-crisis, stopped Johansen in the eighth round and exhibited the kind of heart and resilience many believed he lacked. He'd been in a fight, not a shoot-out. He'd boxed, brawled, overcome a temporary brain-freeze and then turned the tables in spectacular fashion. In facing and toppling Johansen, the victorious champion had confronted demons from 2004 and successfully flushed them to the back of his mind.

Back in the changing room afterwards, Haye wanted to scarper away quickly, but was frustratingly held back by an inability to supply the waiting doctor with a substantial enough sample of urine for the post-fight doping test. He sat for over an hour drinking countless bottles of water, before finally summoning the effort the doctor required.

Haye accelerated away quicker than usual that night, as though he had somewhere else to be or something else to do. I sat alongside him in the passenger seat and, before we could even begin to discuss what had just taken place inside the ring, he once again pulled out his mobile phone, though this time for a far worthier cause.

'How are you?' Haye said on the phone. 'Did you watch it? Yeah, I'm fine. My knuckle's a little bit swollen, but I'm all right.'

It didn't take long to decipher it was Natasha on the other end, and that Haye had found the thing he was in such a rush to locate that night.

'He was a tough bastard,' added Haye. 'I hit him with everything I could, but he just wouldn't go down. No, I wasn't really tired, I just waited for my second wind to kick in. Were you worried?'

I imagined Natasha at home, perched in front of the television set, perhaps peering over a pillow, as Haye devilishly toyed with the emotions of the crowd during those perilous middle rounds. I also thought about how much Haye would have valued the sight of Natasha in her ringside seat, just to the side of his corner, as he trudged back to his stool.

'I missed you,' he said. 'It didn't feel the same without you being there.'

After that, the call ended and the pair remained unsure of where they stood with each other. If Natasha was as impressed as I was with Haye's display of guts, passion and heart that night, I could only foresee one possible outcome. Then again, I was also now fully aware that the mechanics of a left jab and right cross had little to do with the workings of an adult relationship.

CHAPTER TEN
CAT AND MOUSE

Most felt Carl 'The Cat' Thompson had used the last of his nine lives in 2004, and that the king's ransom he'd received in beating David Haye would usher him comfortably towards the retirement most advised him to embrace. Yet I spoke to the venerable Carl a little less than a year after he'd defeated Haye and, rather than open the door to impending retirement, the ageing warrior talked about dragging his old carcass to the well at least two or three more times before the game was up. He'd been inactive for nearly a year since the Haye victory on account of niggling injuries, but remained hopeful of defending his IBO cruiserweight title before the year was out, with money still, of course, the deciding factor.

'If I don't get paid what I deserve, then I won't fight, and it's as simple as that. It's not a case of me running or being greedy,' Thompson told me. 'I've been involved in this sport for a very long time and yet I haven't really made a good amount of money from it. People say to me, "Why don't you finish on top, Carl?" Well I'd love to do that, but who's going to pay the bills for me? I'd love to get out now, but I still have bills to pay. There are journeymen up and down the country losing every week to support their family. I haven't lost a fight since 2001 and people still tell me to quit. Pay my bills for me and I will.'

When I spoke to Thompson about the prospect of bin-diving for leftovers in a sport he owed little, the fighter seemed split between regret and despair. A realisation that his body was slowing down clouded any possible happiness he could extract from something that once so thrilled him. The Bolton hero was never paid what he deserved for memorable nights of entertainment and was now reluctantly hanging around for loose change, content to put his body and brain on the line for whoever decided to pay enough cash to warrant the risk. Suddenly Thompson was a different man entirely from the all-conquering champion who had taken and mocked Haye's best last September.

'I just wanted to live a normal life and make some money, but it doesn't happen that way,' said Thompson. 'I'm not naturally outspoken, but I feel as though I have to be to get people to notice me and pay the bills. I'm not going to change now, because that would be phoney, but if I knew that from the beginning, I would have opened my mouth more. I just don't understand why you should have to disrespect other hard-working boxers to make money and get people to sit up and listen to you.'

Thompson did eventually reappear in 2005, when he defeated Frenchman Frédéric Serrat over ten rounds to take a contentious decision victory in November. At the bout's conclusion, the crowd booed the 98–93 verdict loudly and perhaps unfairly given Thompson's history, as Serrat slipped away despondently. The Frenchman maintained a consistent and impressive pace and appeared to outwork Thompson through the majority of the ten rounds.

'I was very unhappy with my performance that night,' Thompson told Anthony Evans of secondsout.com. 'I felt very ring-rusty. I actually thought I'd lost it, but then I spoke to Serrat afterwards and he thought he'd lost it, too. It was one of those fights. People will write me off yet again, but it will be different when I am fighting someone like David Haye.'

Thompson's mention of Haye was a sign of the increased attention the European cruiserweight champion had received since defeating Alexander Gurov in December. As Thompson struggled to secure a foothold against Serrat for ten punishing rounds in a non-title bout, Haye instead swept everything under the carpet with a forty-five-second demolition of a European champion. Having served up Haye's only pro defeat, Thompson was confused as to how it had all come to this.

'People are actually asking me how I managed to take Haye's punches,' said Thompson. 'Are their memories really that short? I took his shots for five rounds last year and didn't go down once. Haye hasn't proved anything to me this year. I know he looks very good when he is hitting people, but how good did he look when I was hitting him back? He's only been hit back by me, and look what happened.

'David beat a good fighter [Gurov] impressively and he did the job very well, but it annoys me that people get so carried away with it. I've held the European title twice and never lost it in the ring. David did the job, but it was the same job Terry Dunstan did on Gurov eight years ago. I then knocked out Terry Dunstan. So, while I give David credit, I am not getting carried away with what he did, simply because it was done eight years ago.'

Not long after he watched Haye lift his first meaningful professional title in Bracknell, Thompson was then robbed of his own, a belt he never lost in the ring. Thompson failed to defend his IBO title in 2005 for a number of reasons, some related to injury, some to money and some due to Sky Sports' sudden refusal to televise and bankroll fringe 'world' title contests. After many years of trying to flog WBU, WBF and various intercontinental and international baubles as legitimate championships to bemused viewers, Sky Sports decided to significantly up their quality control midway through 2005, and subsequently the IBO, as well as many other alphabet organisations, became victims of the blackout. The likes of Thompson, Jawaid Khaliq and Damaen Kelly were then all stripped of their IBO titles, through no fault of their own.

If the IBO title was judged the only potential reward for beating Thompson, the Bolton fighter now found himself even further in the wilderness. Very few fighters would voluntarily become entangled with Thompson in a relatively meaningless non-title affair. The money would not be attractive enough and the risk would still be too great.

The only man crazy enough to entertain such a proposition in 2006 was David Haye. Aware of Thompson's recent plight, Haye and manager Adam Booth looked on like concerned carers, all the while waiting for their moment to spoon-feed the ex-champion his poison.

'We want to do the Thompson fight,' Booth told me the day after Haye's gruelling win over Lasse Johansen in March.

While the story was easily written, I wondered whether many, including Sky Sports, would buy into it. I knew how much Haye craved the chance to settle the score with Thompson, but most people, especially those exposed to Thompson's lacklustre showing in November, could no longer see a reason for bout number two. They pointed to Haye's swift rise to the top of the European rankings as proof that he'd matured and improved. Thompson, on the other hand, had only boxed once since beating Haye and appeared old, creaky and as uninspired as he'd looked for years. It no longer seemed like a fair, competitive or even worthwhile contest.

'We could big him up massively in the build-up and say it's my biggest test yet,' said Haye. 'Carl would say that I've proved nothing since beating him and that I need to avenge the defeat in order to call myself the best in Britain. He'd say my European title means nothing until I've beaten him.

'The first fight was a war and a fight-of-the-year contender, so

I can't see how people wouldn't lap it up and want to see a rematch. Carl hasn't lost a fight since we met, so we can still sell the fight with that angle.'

Booth and Haye were determined to make the fight appear feasible, but were also aware of the fact they'd struggle to offer Thompson enough cash to act as bait. Having been paid £100,000 for the privilege of stopping Haye first time round, Thompson was unlikely to accept much less for risking it all in a sequel. He wasn't about to sell his soul for half price on an empty promise. Carl realised the end was near and that the possibility of defeat was far greater than first time round.

Unfortunately, while Haye and Booth were bolstered by cash from the BBC in September 2004, the money on the table from Sky Sports for a rematch was drastically less appealing to both fighters. Of course, Haye was able to soften the blow of a reduced pay-day with the lure of gaining revenge, but it was unlikely Thompson had enough reasons to accept a payment which would have been a fraction of what he received in 2004.

Regardless, Booth urged me to ring Thompson and wave a £45,000 offer beneath his nose. Fighter and trainer waited by their respective phones as I sat by mine and pondered the right moment to contact Thompson and offer him a final pension packet containing less than half the money he'd received for the pair's first clash. This was the first time I'd ever been this close to the business end of a major fight and it was nerve-racking to think I'd soon be negotiating figures with Carl Thompson, a personal hero of mine.

I wanted to see Haye gain revenge over a man who'd haunted us both, but still didn't like being in a position where I'd have to haggle with a former champion who needed money, a supportive hug and an honest opinion above anything else. Rather than offer any of the three, I could only explain how Sky Sports didn't have the capacity to produce the kind of pay-day the BBC had once brazenly thrown his way. I'd advise him to accept the £45,000 offer and persuade him the amount represented bumper pay in 2006. I was a fan of the fighter and the man, and it depressed me to think that, within half an hour of putting down the phone with Booth, I'd potentially be bartering with one of boxing's true gentlemen.

'David's always been keen to fight you again, Carl,' I later said over the phone, playing on Thompson's competitiveness, and finally creeping nearer the big question. 'I don't think he'll feel completely satisfied until he's beaten you in a rematch.'

'Exactly,' said Thompson, as though he finally now understood. 'That's exactly how he *should* feel. Why doesn't he talk about that more? That's the attitude all fighters should have. I'm glad David feels like that. That makes me feel better. People keep talking about how great he is, but he must know that he needs to beat me first before he can properly move on.'

'Oh, he does. Some people reckon it would be a step backwards for him now, though.'

'Rubbish. I've been a European champion twice and I never lost the belt in the ring. I'm better than the guys Haye has beaten at that level. I'll always be ready to fight David. Look, once I've beaten somebody the first time, I *know* I can always beat them again. I know I can beat him again.'

'Okay then,' I said, cracking my knuckles in anticipation. 'How would you feel about boxing David again this year?'

'That sounds great,' replied Thompson. 'The sooner the better. They know where to find me and they know how easy I am to deal with. If they come up with the right money, I'll do the fight.'

So here it was – the big offer. I fluffed my lines, hesitated momentarily, and then blurted out the reduced figure, all zeros emphasised for effect.

'I couldn't do it for that,' said Carl. 'That's a lot less than what I got for the first fight. What did I do wrong to get a fraction of what I made for the first fight? The money should go up, if anything.'

'I think it's due to the television situation,' I said. 'Sky Sports can't offer the same sort of money the BBC could. Also, this fight wouldn't be for a title or anything. It would just be a non-title twelve-rounder.'

'I'd happily fight David in a twelve-rounder for no title, but I can't accept an offer that low,' said Thompson. 'I've got bills to pay and a future to look after, and I don't know how many fights I've got left. A fight with David Haye would be massive in this country and I need to get paid what I'm worth. Like I always say, I'll be the guy making the fight and taking the punches to my head.'

I paused and decided to call off my attack. Thompson was right. How could I possibly debate with a man as passionate, likeable and deserving as Carl? He never once grew irritated with my probing, never screamed or shouted his disgust and never blamed me for the inability to rustle up more cash. Instead, he merely outlined his current situation, expressed a clear wish to box Haye again, and seemed as disappointed with the inevitable stalemate as I was.

'Look, I got one hundred grand for the first fight and, although I appreciate the situation, I still need to be paid near that figure to make it worthwhile,' explained Carl. 'If they come back with eighty-five, we might have a deal. That's the sort of figure I have in mind anyway, and that's nearly twice as much as what they're offering.'

Eighty-five never arrived and, instead, Thompson decided to announce his retirement from the sport during the first week in May. In the end, he would go without a vital pay-day and Haye would wave goodbye to the chance to scratch an itch that had been festering since September 2004.

Unable to accept Thompson's retirement as a legitimate reason why the fight could no longer happen, Haye went into denial and explained to me how his nemesis would leap back into the gym the moment he was offered a substantial amount of money for the rematch. Haye was convinced they'd come up with the cash somehow, whether in a month's time, a year's time or five years down the line. No matter how inactive and stubborn Thompson became, Haye would always keep half an eye on the Bolton brawler, counting the pennies in his pocket and wondering whether the time was right to toss them in Carl's path. Alas, with money the primary issue, Haye always retained a position of power over Thompson, despite the fact he'd lost to the man in 2004. They both had something the other wanted, yet Haye was the only one who could do something about it.

Picture the scene. A baying mosh pit awaits the first sinister chord of their favourite thrash metal song, and then Barry Manilow waltzes out on stage with an apology and the opening lines to 'Mandy'. I witnessed David Haye experience the boxing equivalent in the summer of 2005.

Belgian cruiserweight Ismail Abdoul was soft, harmless and vanilla in all the ways 'Mandy' was and all the ways Carl Thompson wasn't. The 29-year-old globetrotter was the ultimate safety harness, a fighter designed to tuck up, protect himself and ultimately lose fights over the twelve-round distance. He beat sub-par foes, lost to ambitious ones and dazzled against nobody. He offered little offensively and even less defensively, appearing at times like a woodlouse with gloves. Durable and predictable, Abdoul was the antithesis to both Haye and Thompson, but, with a ranking of fourteen, landed a European title shot against the Englishman on 21 July 2005 in Altrincham.

'I just need to come out of this fight unscathed,' Haye told me before heading to South Beach, Miami, to work with Booth and Cuban trainer Jorge Rubio. 'Abdoul doesn't offer anything to hit but his head, and it's very easy to break your hands on somebody's forehead or the top of their head. To be honest, that's the only risk for me in this fight.'

It's fair to say Haye wouldn't come close to breaking his hands, nor a sweat. The champion threw only twenty jabs, one right cross and one left hook in the first round against Abdoul that long July night in Altrincham. Barely anything landed. Coming back the other way were twenty attempted jabs from Abdoul's feeble left hand and two right crosses, all of which clipped either thin air or Haye's gloves. Abdoul was petrified of opening up, and Haye was either unable or unwilling to prise open his foe's watertight shield. Bone dry, Haye stood upright between rounds and never bothered to sit on his stool or even convey the image of a fighter in the midst of an epic battle. He knew he wasn't.

The crowd inside the humid and sticky Altrincham Leisure Centre soon became agitated and upset by the course the bout seemed to be taking, as each round resembled the last and offered nothing in the way of excitement or progress. If you'd seen round one, you'd seen them all. Rinse and repeat. Most in the venue had left by the midway point in the bout, and I'd failed to attend altogether. Other commitments forced me to stay home and watch – endure – the fight on Sky Sports, thus signalling the first major Haye fight I'd been absent from ringside for. Thankfully, back at ringside was Natasha, who'd since patched things up with her fighting fellow.

By the time the final symphonic bell rang out, I counted one pretty right hand and an uppercut as the only two meaningful punches landed by the casual champion in the entire twelve rounds. That was two more than Abdoul managed, of course. By the time the judges were nudged awake, they handed Haye a unanimous decision victory via scores of 120–108 across the board. In reaching that goal, Haye landed only seventy-one punches, some sixty-nine more than I cared to remember. Abdoul, on the other hand, could claim only a paltry nineteen. All in all, the entire 36-minute spectacle was about as enthralling as watching someone else watch paint dry.

He'd only been been retired for a matter of months, yet I sensed Haye and the rest of us, for entirely different reasons, already missed a certain someone. Save us, Carl Thompson.

CHAPTER ELEVEN
KINGPIN

In four rounds and eight minutes of action, David Haye was told he landed only one punch. He remembered landing many more. The nineteen-year-old English amateur boxer had outboxed, outfoxed and seemingly outlanded Italian opponent Giacobbe Fragomeni in Halle, Germany, but boasted neither the punch stats nor victory to prove it. Instead, Haye met Fragomeni in a vital Olympic Games qualifier in 1999 and walked away with a shattered dream and an 11–1 scorecard. Yes, that meant that, in 480 seconds of combat, Haye landed just *one* punch. Even our mutual friend Stevie, singer of Motown fame, counted two.

Nevertheless, thirty-year-old Fragomeni, a battle-hardened former European champion and bronze medallist at the 1997 World Amateur Championships, benefited from the ineptitude of partially sighted judges and nabbed Haye's ticket to the 2000 Olympic Games in Sydney. Competing in the light-heavyweight division, Fragomeni would ultimately lose to Cuban Isael Alvarez in the first round of the Games, while Haye watched the entire event at home. Fragomeni then turned professional in May 2001, and Haye, having pocketed a silver medal at the World Amateur Championships, followed suit nineteen months later.

Seven years on from their first encounter, Haye and Fragomeni were conveniently positioned as the number one and two professional cruiserweights in Europe. Haye had added the European title to his name and Fragomeni had successfully hustled his way into the spot of mandatory challenger. Operating primarily in Italy, Fragomeni, then thirty-seven, promptly motored to 21–0 and was being hurried towards title opportunities on account of advancing age and hair loss.

By the end of 2006, the old amateur rivals were paired in a European title clash, with Haye as champion and Fragomeni as the number one ranked challenger, this time as pros. The title contest was scheduled for 17 November in London and would also double as an official eliminator for O'Neil Bell's WBC world cruiserweight title. More than that, though, victory over Fragomeni would grant the Englishman the revenge he'd craved since 1999.

If Haye was ever concerned with what was at stake that November night, he had a funny way of showing it. In an added coup, or distraction, depending on your stance, Haye had decided to audition a number of potential ring-card girls for his pivotal clash with Fragomeni, and intended to whittle down the considerable list to four lucky females. One early frontrunner sat around a table with us – Haye, Adam Booth and me – at Ask restaurant in Piccadilly Circus, merely days before the next fight and, as if to reassure us, insisted Haye's latest pursuit was to be expected.

'I think for David it's all about a particular image he is trying to create,' she said. 'It's obviously not normal for a boxer to choose his own ring-card girls, but David has an image that the public see and he has to live up to it. People almost expect this kind of thing from him now.'

I still hoped high-calibre ring-card girls were just beneath concussive knockouts in his list of priorities, yet sensed the two were drawing ever closer as this particular fight approached. Now rejoicing in his position as capital headliner, Haye was immersing himself in all manner of pre-fight distractions, the kind trainers curse and showmen embrace.

'This after-party's going to be brilliant,' said Haye over lunch, as the ring-card girl received her barely-there fight uniform, and kill-joys Adam Booth and I shook our heads disapprovingly. 'Have you ever been to Gilgamesh before?'

Before anyone could answer, Haye pulled out a wad of invitations from his bag and dumped them on the table in front of us. Professionally designed and arresting to look at, the invitations impressed each of us, though I couldn't quite bring myself to admit it.

'Jesus,' I sighed, 'shouldn't you be worrying about winning the fight first?'

'Of course I'll win it,' went the fighter's reply. 'What shall I do? Sit in the corner of my bedroom and not speak to anyone for two days? That's just anti-social. I've been fighting for sixteen years now and am used to all this. Fighting's what I do. Organising an after-party is far more of a challenge.'

Although I had my reservations – not of the table or booth variety – I couldn't help but be impressed by Haye's enthusiasm for organising such an event. The prospect of another painful defeat made his efforts all the more laudable. I remembered the cancelled after-party in September 2004 and became wary of his boundless enthusiasm for popping champagne before there was just cause for celebration. As if sensing my uncertainty, Booth leaned over and nudged my arm, before switching the subject entirely.

'So how should David go about beating Fragomeni then?' asked the trainer, as he dropped back into his seat and crossed his arms.

'I think he just needs to stay outside the danger zone', I said, vaguely. 'What I mean is, Fragomeni is pretty basic in what he does, but he's very effective if you let him fight his kind of fight. He can't fight at range or from the outside, and he can't fight going backwards. But he's very dangerous up close, in his type of range.'

I scanned Booth's face for clues. His piercing stare remained fixed on me, and only a sharp nod and widening of the eyes revealed any indication that I should continue with my forecast.

'David probably has the power to hurt him at any point in the fight, but it's important not to just assume Fragomeni will go down from one shot, like most of the others have,' I added. 'This guy has probably got one of the best chins you'll ever hit, so it's likely he'll remain upright for a while. Also, just because you don't blast him out with your hardest punch, doesn't mean you won't be hurting him or chopping down his resolve. Think of it like a health bar on a computer game. You see the health bar in the top corner of the screen, and you watch it gradually decrease the more you hit the guy. Nobody's head is designed to take punches, so every shot that connects is doing something.'

Little did I know, but those throwaway comments would go some way to foreshadowing Friday's European title fight, and a long way to defining my relationship with the hard-hitting champion.

For the time being, though, that lunchtime breakdown over pizza would be the last time we spoke of Fragomeni or game plans until the day of the fight. When reality became a little too overwhelming, Haye, like so many others, would retreat, shrink and hide in a realm of fantasy and fiction. Situated behind an impressive sliding door in his Clapham apartment, Haye's portal to escapism was a video library catering for all manner of diversion. There were Oscar-winners, cult classics, B-movies, martial arts flicks and many of his own fights on archaic VHS tapes. His favourite films were *Pulp Fiction* and *Alien*, but he also had a soft spot for the 1987 teen flick *Some Kind of Wonderful*.

'That was my first favourite film,' said Haye, eyes misty with nostalgia. 'That was the first movie that made me cry. I watched that thing so many times as a kid.'

As I skimmed the video rack on that grim Wednesday evening, Haye noticed I was holding a copy of *Kingpin* in my hand, and immediately jumped to his feet.

'Please tell me you've seen *Kingpin*,' he said.

'Erm, no,' I replied, terrified by the consequences.

Haye theatrically put his palm to his forehead, as though about to faint, grabbed the DVD from me and trekked across to the player in the corner of the room.

'You *have* to watch it,' he said. 'It's probably one of the funniest films I've ever seen, if not *the* funniest. Bill Murray kills it in it. Are you ready to watch the funniest film you'll ever see?'

We did and it wasn't, yet Haye was convinced my life would reach a standstill if I didn't familiarise myself with the life and times of Ernie McCracken and his overgrown pubic hairpiece. Despite having seen it countless times before, Haye still laughed and enjoyed himself more than I did and, in truth, that merely confirmed that watching the film was a wise idea. After all, Haye was the guy who had to fight in less than twenty-four hours – not me.

On the eve of the fight, Haye's brain turned back to Bill Murray, as he introduced me to *The Man Who Knew Too Little*, another of the few Murray movies I hadn't seen. Girlfriend Natasha retreated to bed halfway through the action, only to return when it ended, begging Haye to rest his eyes and mind. He did, after all, have the small matter of a championship fight the next day. It was now midnight and Haye was still wide awake, distractions aplenty and brain racing. Not content to just settle for a single serving of Murray, however, he now contemplated watching another film, much to his girlfriend's disapproval. Reluctantly conceding ground, Natasha again highlighted the fact she was turning in and demanded her boyfriend turn the volume down if he wished to remain defiant and presumably in a relationship. Haye nodded and waved her to bed, not wanting to be disturbed as he plucked a *Marx Brothers* box-set from his collection.

'I remember you saying you'd never seen the *Marx Brothers'* films, right?' Haye asked me. 'Well, tonight's the night.'

Starting with *Duck Soup* and ending with *Animal Crackers*, Haye and I sat and watched Groucho, Chico and Harpo act the fool into the early hours of the morning, both relying on the DVD's essential subtitles option to help fully appreciate the rapid-fire wisecracks, while also allowing us to set the volume to sleeping-girlfriend-friendly.

I looked across at Haye from time to time, often mid-cackle, and wondered how he'd manage to go from rib-tickling laughter to bone-crunching maliciousness in a matter of twenty-four hours. It seemed perverse to think that the joker sitting alongside me would be the same man looking to disconnect a title challenger from his senses the following evening. I also questioned how Haye would even go about plotting and executing his slumber when the time finally came to get his head down. How can anyone possibly rock themselves to sleep with the threat of war on the horizon? What would he think about? How would he switch off?

'I'm never a great sleeper,' Haye admitted, as he switched television for laptop at the conclusion of *Animal Crackers*. 'It's best just to go to bed when you can't keep your eyes open any longer. Otherwise, you'll just lie there for hours, waiting for something to happen.'

Haye spent most of Friday away from Natasha, as both knew the pre-fight protocol by now. Natasha busied herself shopping and visiting her brother Matthew across town, while Haye and I walked into Clapham to find a local hairdresser willing to braid his hair for the Sky Sports television cameras later that night. At the hairdresser's, specialists in styles for black men, Haye was told to return in an hour. So, in order to kill time, we walked around Clapham Common and read the latest edition of *Time Out* magazine, in which Haye had a question-and-answer feature on the back page. Contained within the article was enough profanity and crudeness to shatter my mum's clean-cut image of the boxer for ever. His inspiration for boxing? 'Pussy.' Needless to say, I hid the magazine inside my coat, in the hope that neither Natasha nor my mother ever set eyes on it.

'What can Fragomeni actually do tonight?' asked Haye out of the blue, as we sat down on a park bench on Clapham Common and devoured a polystyrene box of rice, peas and West Indian chicken.

'What do you mean?' I replied, taken aback by Haye's sudden desire to discuss the fight. I'd been so used to talking about everything *but* the fight, that I'd half-forgotten the man beside me would later defend his belt that evening.

'For example, if you were him, how would you approach the fight?' he rephrased.

'He'll get close and make you work at a pace you don't like working at,' I said, remixing the kind of sentiments I'd offered two days before. 'He has to get close to throw punches.'

David contemplated my answer for a moment and nodded his head, mouth full of food. He finished chewing and then turned to me and muttered, 'I never really thought about that thing you said the other day.'

'What was that?' I replied.

'When you said to not get deterred when hitting someone with your best shot. I never really thought about the fact that a guy might be able to take your power to begin with, but then it may eventually catch up with him and he'll fold. I've never seen it like that. I've always thought that if a guy could take my best shot, then I'd have to panic and do something different. I've always been so used to hitting and hurting people that it's almost scary to imagine someone walking through my punches. You're right, though, nobody is built to take punches to the brain.'

Suddenly I felt vindicated, and my presence around Haye seemed meaningful and important. There would be no 'thank you' per se, but I didn't need one. This was the first time he'd ever truly acknowledged anything I'd said, and it made me content to know he was listening and valued my advice. It was a heartening moment, and one which allowed me to think that, although I'd never boxed competitively, there were still words I could offer this high-achieving prizefighter. With new-found power came a greater sense of responsibility, though, and I now felt worryingly accountable for what would occur later that evening.

Back home, only an hour or so before he was due to leave for Bethnal Green's York Hall, the mood remained relaxed and Haye sorted out his kitbag to the sounds of classic soul music blaring from his laptop.

'Are you taking your iPod?' asked Haye.

'Maybe,' I replied. 'Why?'

'Well I'm taking mine, that's all,' he said. 'I'm not the greatest conversationalist on the way to a fight. I'm just warning you.'

Our taxi arrived at a shade past seven o'clock. Natasha would leave moments later in a separate taxi shared by friends. True to his word, the fighter offered little in the way of words or wise-cracks from that point on as he climbed inside the black taxi, greeted the driver and then promptly inserted his ear-buds.

'What are you going to listen to?' I asked, as I sat down beside him in the back seat. Haye shrugged and whizzed his index finger around the circular face of his iPod. 'A little bit of everything,' he said. 'Something happy.'

Haye had no idea, but, although heeding his advice, I'd only listen to my songs on a low volume that night, so keen was I to gain an insight into the sort of tunes a prizefighter blasts on the way to battle. Expecting tales of blood, guts and impending doom, I pictured Haye gritting his teeth in violent anticipation, as riffs from the likes of Slayer or Megadeth lined his lobes. Instead, and much to my surprise, Haye bobbed his head cheerfully, occasionally air-drumming and soloing at an imaginary keyboard, to the sounds of 'Can't Take My Eyes off of You' by Frankie Valli, 'My Cherie Amour' by Stevie Wonder and Earth, Wind & Fire's 'I'll Write a Song for You', as well as a smattering of upbeat material by early Motown girl groups. Yes, I repeat, this man was on the way to a *fight*. Haye was in his zone all right, but it was one consisting of neon lights, flared trousers and cocktail waitresses on skates. There was a seventies disco going on inside his head and Haye was the only invited guest. Everybody, including Giacobbe Fragomeni and me, were barred for the next forty-five minutes, as Haye listened to songs that reminded him of childhood and, perhaps, happier times.

It felt odd to be this close to Haye for so long and not hear his voice. Although I'd always felt that the man was naturally a far quieter person than most imagined, he was still far from taciturn, and was someone who liked to fill silence with words. He would always have something to say and a unique way of saying it. It surprised me, therefore, to learn that Haye didn't want much in the way of dialogue en route to this particular fight. I didn't blame him, of course, as, put in his shoes, I'd have still been locked inside a bathroom back at the house. However, I'd been so used to seeing Haye project a relaxed and carefree exterior in recent days that I'd half-expected him to break out a game of snakes and ladders on the back seat. Though never exactly cantankerous, there was a growing sense that, by the time Valli had finished his encore, and rain lashed down heavily against his window, Haye was becoming short on patience and high on the thought of combat. Rush-hour traffic only heightened this simmering agitation, too, as the boxer occasionally stopped his music to offer shortcuts to the cab driver, only to then run into further gridlock.

Haye's uplifting playlist had run its course twice by the time we eventually approached York Hall. Once we pulled up alongside the venue, he tapped on the window and then jogged my arm.

'Look who it is,' he said. 'Seems as though we weren't late, after all.'

Walking towards the front entrance of the venue was challenger Fragomeni, accompanied by four members of his team, each kitted out in matching Team Fragomeni-emblazoned orange and white tracksuits and baseball caps. They never saw us, but we saw them.

'I wonder where they're walking from,' said Haye, as we continued to spy on the opposition.

There was something surreal, eerie and disturbing about the whole idea of peering at the enemy before leading them to slaughter. It was hard to ascertain how Haye felt about the situation, but there was a peeping-Tom aspect to it that both thrilled and frightened me. We watched the crew of Italians march in silence, both of us thinking the same thoughts and hoping for the same outcome at the end of the night. I had nothing against Fragomeni or his band of loyal followers, yet couldn't help but wish for them to be defeated and devastated, crestfallen following a failed attempt to dethrone the man sitting alongside me in the black cab. I hoped and prayed for it, but never said it. If anything, I was ashamed to forecast and visualise the downfall of a human being I had no connection or relationship with. Fragomeni was a humble family man with children, yet such minor details meant little to us in this mutual pursuit of violence and success. The enemy needed to be beaten up and his zero extracted. Neither of us expressed our thoughts that night, but through palpable tension Haye and I were no doubt experiencing the same mixed emotions. Ultimately, while I could only watch and hope, the man beside me was the one equipped to do something about it.

Once inside, York Hall was as hectic as I'd ever known it. Fight fans were crammed in everywhere, from the balconies to the floor. A hundred or so Italian supporters were stored on the upper level and draped flags and banners over the edge. They wore football shirts and waved flags bearing emblems of Italy's greatest clubs, including Juventus, Internazionale and Fragomeni's personal favourite, AC Milan. Sometimes I'd double-check to make sure it was only flags being flung over the edge, not olive-skinned bodies. There were also mutterings of hundreds of disgruntled fight fans being turned away at the door, as the venue frantically bolted the gates shut in a late attempt to avoid disaster. It had taken the Londoner nearly four years of fruitless touring, but, finally, there was a sense that Haye was home and popular at last.

The vast number of people crammed within the four walls concerned me, yet energised both champion and challenger, who appeared hell-bent on delivering the kind of fight they'd spent weeks promoting and promising. The fighting styles married perfectly and the pair's differences combined to create the desired dynamic.

The odd couple traded blows furiously through the opening quarter of the bout, as Haye attempted to stick from the outside and catch Fragomeni with jabs and crosses coming in, and the stocky Italian pressed forward with purpose. As predictable as his tattoos were illegible, Fragomeni motored characteristically from the off, bobbing from side to side as though avoiding an incoming swarm of bees. He twitched and fidgeted his way inside Haye's range, often running into trouble en route.

Haye was in control early, and benefited greatly from his quicker hands and feet, yet it was clear already that Fragomeni was a cut above previous title challengers. Plenty landed on the challenger's chin, nose and temple, but little shook or hurt the squat aggressor.

The first five rounds were competitive, but mostly belonged to Haye, who landed the cleaner blows and created the more dramatic flashpoints along the way. Then, as if to underline this early dominance, Haye visibly hurt his challenger for the first time in the sixth round with a stunning one-two combination. The granite-jawed Fragomeni copped both shots on the buzzer and was sent stumbling into the ropes, a scene which triggered the crowd to leap to its feet in unison, convinced Haye was finally about to make his power tell and close the show.

As expected, the champion did everything possible to end matters and chucked any number of hooks and uppercuts at the spinning head of Fragomeni. With Carl Thompson still hopelessly imprinted on my memory, however, I couldn't help but think Haye's impetuous attempts to finish Fragomeni would again somehow lead to his downfall. Although hurt and shaken, Fragomeni wasn't *yet* ready to go. Thankfully, Haye figured out the situation himself and wisely backed away from the wounded animal, following an initial flurry of childish exuberance. Within seconds, Fragomeni's head was clear and the challenger was back on the front foot, making Haye work for every escape, move and punch.

Having survived the biggest scare of the bout so far, Fragomeni's intensity only increased in the seventh, as he now figured he'd taken Haye's best and was through the worst of it. Barely a minute of the round had passed when Haye found himself backed up to the ropes with Fragomeni in hot pursuit. The champion became slack with his defence, allowed Fragomeni to slip a punch combination through the guard and, suddenly, blood began to pour from a slice above Haye's left eye. Ringsiders gasped in horror at the sight of his chiselled features drenched in claret. While some fighters appeared suited to a little bit of complementary combat sauce, Haye wasn't the type to get trapped in the kind of dogfight that would yield a potential cut or gash. In fact, it was the first time Haye had ever suffered a cut, either as an amateur or as a pro, and we all feared the worst. It was hard not to. Haye was deep into one of the most arduous and punishing wars of his career, against a challenger all wrong for him stylistically, and was now facing the handicap of his first ever wound.

Fragomeni was still likely down on the cards, of course, but, with the way the colour was flowing, most assumed the judges' scores were now unnecessary. Moreover, Haye's work became sloppy and desperate in the aftermath, as he tried with all his might to battle through a jet-stream of blood. David was no longer sure whether to continue trying to outbox his marauding foe or to simply invest everything in his punch power and attempt to end matters in a potentially damaging tear-up. He was now embroiled in a slugfest, the kind he'd never before experienced or anticipated being involved in.

Amid the blood and sloppiness, and the onrushing threat of Fragomeni, Haye somehow managed to relax and clear his mind in the ninth round. In contrast, Fragomeni, having given so much in the previous two rounds, now appeared suddenly hamstrung, and was unable to throw either hand with the same frequency or intensity he'd once displayed.

The Italian was gasping hard for breath and was led around the ring on tired legs as Haye retreated on stronger pins and bounced a loose combination off his opponent's bald noggin. A left hook to the body followed from Haye, which forced Fragomeni to dip his arms and suck up more air. Realising he had his man hurt, the champion doubled up his body attack and then rattled Fragomeni with a clubbing right hook to the back of his head. In an instant, and from seemingly out of nowhere, Haye had made a major breakthrough and shaken Fragomeni to his very foundations. Unable to hide, fire back or posture up, Fragomeni hunched over, wobbled backwards and sought a trap-door by the ropes. Haye tore after him, unwilling to allow the challenger either a moment's respite or a place to hide. He landed three further wild right hands, including one which deflected off Fragomeni's head as he dropped to his haunches by the ropes.

It had taken eight and a half rounds of chipping away, but Haye had finally knocked a significant lump out of Fragomeni's resolve. The Italian was down, stunned and exhausted. As referee Daniel Van De Wiele crowded over the challenger and administered the count, I watched in delight as the Italian's corner took matters into their own hands. Former WBA world light-welterweight champion Patrizio Oliva, perhaps the most respected fighter in the room that night, grabbed the white towel, climbed the steps and waved the symbolic piece of cloth over the top rope. He'd seen enough. Although he'd by now climbed to his feet, Fragomeni had yet to return to his senses and didn't complain. If trainer Oliva said it was over, it was over.

As a party threatened to break out in the congested York Hall aisles, Haye was backstage getting stitched up and looking forward to a celebration of his own. I entered his changing room after the fight and found Haye stretched out on a table as a doctor hovered over him and carefully applied stitches to the first cut of his boxing life. The champion's right hand was red raw and a rapidly rising welt was visible on his centre knuckle. The fist was swollen and fit to burst, like a giant blood blister.

Natasha and best friend Karlton Bryan were by his side, and Haye looked as exhausted and mangled as I'd ever seen him after a fight. Gone was the motor-mouth of previous fights, as he spoke slowly and wearily and made a conscious effort to save his words.

He realised the magnitude of what he'd just achieved, but wasn't yet able to explain it.

'What did you think?' asked Haye, moments after I'd entered the room.

'You looked like a Jamaican Arturo Gatti in there,' I replied. Haye burst out laughing, and I was warned by the doctor to not make the fighter strain. 'I don't know whether that's a good or bad thing, though.'

'What was the fight like on the scorecards?' said Haye, now piecing together a version of the fight via the snippets and recollections of others.

'You won all the rounds, no doubt,' said Karlton, sold on his best friend's superiority.

'I don't know, I think it was pretty close,' I said. 'You won the first few, but then it became closer. Fragomeni may have won a few of those middle rounds. I think you were probably one or two ahead in the ninth.'

'I couldn't even remember how the rounds went,' said Haye. 'I remember I hurt him early in the fight, but the rest is pretty much a blur.'

'Did it feel like a hard fight when you were in there?'

'Yeah, I knew it was hard. It definitely felt like we were going at a hard pace. I could feel it. Did it look like a quick pace?'

'Yes. It was definitely the most entertaining fight you've ever had.'

'Great. The fans sounded amazing out there. I hope it looked as exciting as it felt on television. I don't mind having fights like that, so long as the fans enjoy it.'

I watched the doctor apply eight stitches to Haye's eye, and couldn't help but feel his patchwork was sealing the young champion's membership into a special club. It's a perverse thought, but often a boxer won't feel like they truly belong until they've tasted their own blood in the smouldering heat of battle. Haye sipped his own blood that November evening and came out the other side, belt and rankings still intact. 'It sounds sick, but I actually enjoyed getting cut,' Haye would tell me later that night. For a fighter who once prided himself on appearing immaculate, both in appearance and in fighting style, Haye now found much to admire on the tougher side of town. He liked strutting around in Dolce & Gabbana shades for days after the fight and, though it pained him at the time, enjoyed being viewed as a walking billboard for his demanding profession. Mere occupational hazards, perhaps, but Haye now boasted a busted hand and slashed eye that no model, accountant or stockbroker could ever rock so suavely.

PART FOUR

Likeminded trailblazers, David Haye and trainer/manager Adam Booth have remained a strict two-man team for the duration of their incredible boxing journey.

CHAPTER TWELVE
WARM UP, WARM DOWN

Now, admittedly, geography had never been a strong point. Two days before leaving for the Turkish Republic of Northern Cyprus, I'd wrongly assumed south was preferable to north and that €500 would tide me over for the duration of ten days. Unbeknown to me at the time, the more commercialised south of the island – popular with British expatriates and pill-popping clubbers – would be left untouched that summer. I was heading to the northern side and a region that dealt in Turkish lire, as opposed to euros. I blamed it on miscommunication.

A teenage David Haye had spent many summer months losing himself in the bars and clubs of Ayia Napa, but now found himself in Ozankoy – a sparse, quiet and desolate region on the northern side of the island. Now twenty-seven, and preparing for the biggest fight of his life, Haye was all grown up.

A newcomer to both the north and south, I left for Cyprus on 16 September 2007, having been invited to watch Haye prepare for his first world title fight. I'd pictured a paradise of a southern variety, but the Turkish Republic of Northern Cyprus was instead a sinister, dusty and foreboding sight in the middle of the night, reminiscent of a scene from a Cormac McCarthy novel. I was unnerved by the surroundings, spoke no Turkish, boasted the complexion of a man held captive in a wardrobe, and didn't exactly merge into the backdrop, even in the dim anonymity of night.

Thankfully, the darker-skinned Adam Booth travelled over with me that September night. He owned property on the island, and his knowledge of local politics was enough to ease my mind and shake the fear of being entangled in any *Midnight Express*-type escapades throughout the course of my residence there. Born to a Turkish-Cypriot father, Booth was as immersed in the culture as an Englishman from Carshalton could possibly be, and had recently discovered a love for the picturesque island.

He introduced his young boxing star to the beauty of Northern Cyprus in 2007, and David Haye was also quick to fall head over heels for the land's rustic qualities and sense of isolation. Haye and Booth sought a change of scenery, in both a training and a lifestyle sense, and Northern Cyprus was a world apart from the intoxicating crowds and fumes of central London. Though they still remained residents of the United Kingdom, the pair rented a villa in Ozankoy and spent many summer months of 2007 amid the dust and sand, savouring the silence and solace. With nobody to turn to but each other, fighter and trainer geared up mentally and physically for the toughest test of their respective careers.

Fresh off a March revenge victory over rival O'Neil Bell, the latest world cruiserweight champion Jean-Marc Mormeck would await the Englishmen in November, presenting the kind of challenge that required extreme adaptation and sacrifice. An original date of 28 September in Levallois, near Paris, was given for the proposed meeting of Haye and the new WBC and WBA world cruiserweight champion, only to be changed to 10 November. In the end, Haye's shot would arrive nearly twelve months after he'd earned the right to it. Not content to sit idle for that length of time, a 215lb Haye cameoed in the heavyweight division in April, swatting Poland's Tomasz Bonin inside 105 seconds of the first round at London's Wembley Arena.

Though short on rounds, the fighter was now back among the cruiserweights and high on ambition.

'Mormeck won't last three rounds with me,' declared a typically antagonistic Haye. 'This is going to be just like when George Foreman fought Joe Frazier. It's going to be *that* one-sided. I'm going to travel to his back garden and beat Mormeck like Rodney King.'

The idea of finishing Mormeck quickly in all-out warfare became something of a mantra that summer as Haye looked to hammer home the message whenever he could. The challenger made it his mission to tap-dance provocatively on Mormeck's last nerve and reiterate a desire to start fast, push for the early knockout and engage in a slugfest. Of course, while publicly making such brave proclamations, Haye and strategist Booth were quietly tucked away, first in London and then Northern Cyprus, plotting the kind of game plan that contradicted every word the media heard from them. It was a secret plot, full of deception and double-crosses, and I was the third man in on it. I treated Mormeck like a subject at school and, whenever I could spare the time, would press play on the next DVD, reach for a pad and pen and meticulously take notes. I wasn't sure yet whether Haye would ever see the scribbles or, indeed, even care, but I enjoyed watching Mormeck in action, and the subsequent note-taking soothed my own fears. The more I saw of Mormeck, the more I understood him, and the more hope I had of Haye eventually dethroning him. Although I had no ring experience myself, I tackled Mormeck from the perspective of a student and painstakingly analysed everything I saw. I couldn't relate to emotions felt, but my distance from the sport allowed me to view things coldly and clinically in a way that perhaps even Haye and Booth couldn't.

'So, come on then, tell me what he's going to do and what's going to happen,' Booth had said, as we sat together on the plane to Cyprus. The trainer had a notebook of his own at hand, and his rapid grabbing of a pen told me he was serious and that my views were appreciated.

In total, we traded riffs on Mormeck's strengths and weaknesses for approximately four hours of the five-hour flight. It all seemed so easy to the pair of us. Research and analysis was, after all, the simple part, and neither Booth nor I would have to physically interpret our scathing observations. With my volume button suddenly turned up, though, I felt more responsible and powerful than ever before. Here I was, just turned twenty-one, and now in a position to pass judgement on the strategy of a challenger looking to dethrone a champion in a world title fight. My words were deemed important and the hours of research I'd undertaken appeared worthwhile. I knew I'd seen more of Mormeck than most, but had never expected anyone, let alone Booth and Haye, to heed or care about my opinions. It would have seemed unbelievable, if it wasn't so damn scary.

Booth and I arrived in Cyprus twelve days before Haye was first supposed to face Mormeck, and seven weeks before the rearranged date. David, meanwhile, had remained on the island with girlfriend Natasha, and busied himself during slow afternoons with a spot of painting and decorating and the occasional training session. Fully burying himself in the culture around him, Haye employed a team of local workers to help realise a pet project he and Booth had been working on for much of the summer. Within hours of touching down on the island, an excitable Haye picked Booth and me up in his Range Rover and proceeded to drive us down an old beaten track, on past the signs to Ozankoy, soaring through dust clouds kicked up by the tyres, and then parked outside what appeared to be a derelict warehouse.

'A month ago this place was completely run down and out of use,' explained Haye, as he walked us towards the makeshift entrance. The cruiserweight used all his muscle and might to yank back the iron door at the front of the warehouse, and beckoned us inside with a curled index finger.

'I liked this place from the moment I saw it,' he continued. 'I have everything I need out here now. There's a boxing ring, punch bags, mirrors, weights, a big tyre to hit, skipping ropes, the lot. You won't find many better gyms than this in England.'

Upon entering the rusty gymnasium, we were instantly greeted not only with red bags and Grant punching gloves, but also throwaway scraps of metal and various pictures of November's opponent Mormeck. Head shots, action shots and caricature portraits. Like a hormonal teenage girl's bedroom shrine to a boy band, the pictures were *everywhere*. There were images of Mormeck scrapping with rival O'Neil Bell plastered on mirrors, and pictures from press conferences attached to walls. The champion's impressive career record had even been printed off and sat menacingly in paper form on the ring canvas.

'This tells me his mind is getting on the fight,' said Booth. 'I couldn't be happier with what I'm seeing right now.'

It was the trainer's own work of art that caught my eye, however. Before he'd left for home earlier that summer, the surprisingly artistic Booth had drawn a life-sized image of Mormeck onto a red punch bag. Booth slugged it to the body as he brushed past and Haye would do the same at numerous junctures during training camp. Though the Englishman was aware that the living and breathing Mormeck would clearly present a tougher and livelier proposition on fight night, the surrounding portraits helped act as a constant reminder of what lurked just around the corner.

Haye's second revelation that night came moments later, as he parted his eyelids and explained to Booth how a small piece of iron had mysteriously flown into his eye during a light training session.

'I think the iron was on the glove and it caught me,' he said. 'It really hurts when I close it and I haven't been able to get much sleep since it happened. I reckon the lens is scratched.'

Unable to properly spar or train since the incident, Haye was swiftly booked in for an appointment at a local hospital. That minor hiccup delayed his progress, and also made another newcomer on the island feel somewhat redundant for the next couple of days. Former two-time Haye opponent and European title challenger Giacobbe Fragomeni arrived not long after Booth and me, and the rough-and-ready Italian was booked to spar with Haye the following Tuesday. Fragomeni and adviser Christian Cherchi checked in at the Malpas hotel, a mile from where Haye and Booth stayed on the island, and were immediately told of the unfortunate news.

With sparring on hold for the time being, Haye, complete with black eye-patch, heeded the doctor's advice and rested up for twenty-four hours, insisting the minor hurdle would be a blessing rather than a curse. Following the delay to the fight's original date, Haye had seen his weight plummet even quicker than expected, and was now hovering just above the 200lb cruiserweight limit, with weeks to spare and the bulk of training yet to begin.

'Two hundred and fifteen pounds,' shouted Haye, from the bathroom of his Ozankoy villa. 'This is the lowest weight I've ever been six weeks before a cruiserweight fight. I usually have to cut that sort of weight in the last couple of weeks.'

In addition to island humidity and the delay, a key factor in Haye's mission to see 200lbs register on his bathroom scales was the organic cooking of girlfriend Natasha, who sacrificed life back home in London to cater for Haye's needs on a daily basis in deserted Northern Cyprus. Relying mainly on a clean diet of fresh fish, chicken, pasta, rice and steamed vegetables, Haye would have his meals laid on for him three times a day by the outside pool. It was another vital job expertly taken care of and one less problem for the temperamental prizefighter to worry about. Of course, the real masterstroke in all of this was that Natasha was a vegan and had never eaten meat herself. With sacrifice evidently the watchword on the island, a bare-bones crack team of Natasha and Booth's girl-friend, osteopath Claire, ensured bellies were fed, eye drops were applied and wheels kept turning when egos and emotions collided.

The following day, I topped up on factor-fifty sunscreen and joined Haye, Booth, Fragomeni and a stopwatch at the local athletics track on the outskirts of Kyrenia. The 400-metre track surrounded one of the most enticing football pitches I'd ever set eyes on, and was framed by picturesque views of nearby mountains. Haye would occasionally venture into these mountains for long-distance runs, but, for the most part, relied on shorter sprints to help build stamina and retain explosiveness. A recurring problem with shin splints, as well as a dislike of slow jogs, ensured Haye spent more time on track than he did climbing mountains.

A natural sprinter, Haye seemed at ease with short distances, and would eventually use a combination of sprints in order to both strengthen his legs – crucial to the type of game plan Booth had constructed – and top up the necessary cardio for a hard slog. Working on a back-to-back format, Booth would instruct his fighter to sprint one hundred metres inside fifteen seconds, rest for thirty seconds, and then run the one hundred metres back to the starting line. The pair called this unusual activity 'one hundred hundreds' and the idea was for Haye to peak at the right time and be equipped to run one hundred consecutive one-hundred-metre sprints, with just thirty seconds' rest in between each. Although I often feared the worst when Haye neglected conventional long-distance runs, the sight of the boxer compiling one-hundred-metre sprints was something to behold, especially given the quick times and intensity produced. Haye was fast and fit. I should know – one day I foolishly tried keeping up with him.

Those unique back-to-back sprints would be the only activity Giacobbe Fragomeni shirked that week and, by Wednesday, Haye was free to finally spar the patient Italian. Receiving his instructions second-hand via Cherchi, eager Fragomeni was informed the first spar would be mostly technical, as Haye wanted to ease his way back into action and work on a few tactics Booth had devised for him.

'I haven't really done that much proper sparring recently,' warned a shadow-boxing Haye, as he bobbed on his toes to the unmistakable rhythm of Bob Marley's 'Jammin'.

Earlier that day, Haye was surprised to learn, or perhaps be reminded of the fact, that he would have only boxed 105 competitive seconds in the space of a year by the time he stepped into the ring with Mormeck. That was all it had taken for him to disconnect heavyweight Tomasz Bonin from his senses in April. This lack of competitive activity showed in sparring that day, too, as Fragomeni, the beneficiary of a recent twelve-rounder in his homeland, found his rhythm quicker than Haye. Combining patchy moments of the sublime and the ridiculous, Haye mixed periods of sloppy punching and wayward timing with cameos of defensive wizardry and countering. His power and superior speed allowed him the last laugh in most exchanges, but they were exchanges nonetheless.

'That was just me doing my Kelly Pavlik impression for you,' joked Haye, after one less than impressive display of standing in range and getting repeatedly hit in the face. For the sake of context, Ohio slugger Pavlik was a scrappy but effective middleweight contender and a man known for his ability to give and take heavy punches with the world's premier hitters. A comparatively prettier fighting specimen, Haye knew when he screwed up and flattered to deceive, and would often saunter over to a mirror and slug away in frustration at a punch bag, the accompanying grunts becoming those of desperation and disappointment.

Clearly less than impressed by Haye's failure to initiate the agreed-upon set of tactics, Booth revealed his own way of getting through.

'Sometimes I just don't say anything,' the trainer said, as we watched Haye take out his grievances on an unfortunate bag. 'Rather than rant and rave, I'll just look at him and say nothing. He'll get the point. He knows what he did wrong. Then, when I do say something, it tends to stick next time.'

Booth stayed silent for the remainder of that particular session. When he instructed Fragomeni to try and knock his man out, he meant it, too. Despite initial reservations from Fragomeni, the message stuck and Giacobbe tore into Haye like he'd halved his wages. Calm under pressure, Haye coped with it surprisingly well, though the strict taskmaster in the corner still spotted much to improve on.

'I thought he was poor tonight,' said Booth. 'His technique wasn't there, his punches were sloppy, and he was getting hit every time he backed up. If Fragomeni is able to land those sort of punches on him for six rounds, imagine what Mormeck will do. Mormeck is bigger, stronger and hits much harder. David can't sit there taking those kind of shots. I don't know why he does it. I've told him he's got to move and use his legs, yet he stands there and trades.'

The trainer–fighter relationship felt particularly strained that September night, as we made our way from the gym to the villa in Haye's Range Rover. Not one word was spoken the entire journey home. Haye pondered his performance and Booth racked his brains for answers. Fragomeni and Cherchi were due at Haye's villa later that night for a barbecue, and I was thankful for the possibility of authentic kebabs, alternative voices and a lightened mood.

Once the Italians boarded the plane home on the Sunday, Haye and Booth, left with even fewer people to turn to, faced up to the prospect of spending the next week and, indeed, future weeks in one another's company. There would be other sparring partners flying in, of course, but living and training arrangements left little in the way of free space or time alone. The pair would travel to the gym, the track or the mountains together, and would then ride back home in the same manner and in the same car. They'd eat the same food around the same table, watch the same movies to kill the same time, and sleep under the same roof at the end of the day. This arrangement was ideal on the good days, as both clearly enjoyed each other's company, but, when darkness washed over the island in the second week, everybody felt the suffocating claustrophobia and growing tension.

Haye would choose to spend more time on his laptop or watching films than on the track, and Booth would sit and wait in the living room, tapping his watch impatiently, as the fighter waved a hand and signalled he'd rise when he felt inspired to do so. Half an hour later, Haye would begrudgingly drag himself up from the kitchen table and follow Booth, who by now was already in the car, engine started. This pattern of disobedience continued on a daily basis, as Haye increasingly stayed up late, woke up late and skipped training sessions. If he was due to train twice a day, he'd make it once, on account of an injury or issue from the day before. If the pair planned to hit the track at 11.30 a.m., Haye would reschedule and make it 12.30 p.m.

With words used sparingly from that point on, the sudden silence told me all I needed to know about the faltering relationship between student and teacher. Even when sitting alongside each other in the car, banter and light-hearted jabs, the sort both normally specialised in, were non-existent. They drove with a purpose, as if to get matters over with as quickly as possible.

There was no catalyst or turning point for the soured communication, but the strife grew from day to day, and seemed to stem from Haye's inability to carry out Booth's advice in sparring. The trainer was concerned for his fighter and started to doubt whether he was capable of performing the instructions they'd drawn up in previous weeks. More than that, though, and perhaps the real reason for the unsettling silence, was Haye's refusal to train when Booth wanted to, and the fighter's need to hold the power at all times. Often Booth could only sit and gaze in vain at his watch, while Haye meandered through breakfast or searched for humorous videos on YouTube. Gentle nudges or rallying calls didn't work. Haye was clearly his own boss, and in complete control of his future. If he didn't want to train, there was nothing Booth or anybody else could do or say about it.

One day on the track, Haye realised just that and kept on walking. What started as a customary warm-up ended as a one-hour declaration of independence and power, as he paced the athletics track with a slow, methodical and emotionless stroll that infuriatingly went on and on and on.

Meanwhile, Booth sat on a plastic seat in the nearby football stand, one hand on his stopwatch, another on his dampening forehead, and waited for the moment his fighter signalled the warm-up was over. The signal never came. Booth was left to watch Haye walk in long circles, seemingly unwilling to engage or even make eye contact with him. The trainer was reluctant to push or scream, either, so what played out was a passive stand-off, where neither man drew his pistol or claimed victory. Haye walked and Booth watched.

'What is he doing?' I asked Booth, midway through the episode.

'I honestly don't know,' said Booth. 'He's been doing this for over half an hour now. This isn't warming up. If he doesn't want to train, he's better off just telling me and going home. Nothing's going to get done like this.'

'Do you know what's wrong with him?'

'No. I've told him I'll get him a new trainer if he doesn't feel he can listen or learn anything from me any more. I don't have a problem with that. I've already put a few names to him as sugges-tions. If he doesn't see any worth in what I'm telling him, what's the point in sticking around? This is just wasting our time. I could be at home with my daughters now, instead of sitting here watching him walk around a track over and over again.'

I could sympathise with Booth, of course, as he was essentially reduced to spectator status that day, and was clearly missing his family back home in England. He resented Haye for making him stick around on days like these. Booth didn't feel valued or respected, and it was the first time I'd ever known of a rupture in their rela-tionship. It was most definitely the first time I'd heard Booth contem-plate bringing another face into the watertight set-up. Haye and Booth had always been a strict two-man team, and appeared to take pride in the bond and wavelength they shared.

Sensing this mutual sulk had now gone too far, I caught up with Haye on track and paced alongside him, occasionally glancing across to gain an insight into where his mind was. Less talkative than normal, Haye was still nevertheless on decent terms with me.

'When are you going to stop warming up?' I asked on our second lap together.

'In a minute,' Haye said with a heavy sigh.

'Are you all right?'

'Yeah. I've got a couple of things I need to think about, that's all. Don't worry about it.'

'I do worry about it, though.'

'Well, don't. It's not your problem. I'll work it out myself.'

I let him continue on ahead, while Booth rose from his plastic seat and waited in the car with the engine running. Haye's engine never would properly start that day as he walked for forty-five minutes before silently and glumly joining Booth and me in the rented car. Booth would have left of his own accord that day had he brought his own vehicle. I'm sure Haye would have done the same. As it turned out, neither had any choice in the matter. I retreated to the back seat as they sat up front in total and utter silence. Haye refused to explain what had gone on and Booth was now apparently beyond the point of caring. With an average daily temperature of forty degrees, most afternoons were hot in the back seat, but that day felt particularly sizzling. I directed my head out the back window, both as a means of cooling down and escaping the simmering animosity up front.

We arrived back at the villa in time for lunch and, oblivious to what had gone on, other halves Natasha and Claire were all smiles and plastic plates, assuming the fighting pair were content to eat together at the table by the pool. A plan never likely to work, Booth instead took his plate to his bedroom, and Haye carried his laptop outside, thus burying himself in a world away from his upcoming fight and next training session. The twosome were separate entities for the first time since I'd known them, and it was both disturbing and confusing. I still wasn't sure how they'd reached this point. I pressed Haye again as we ate lunch, but he remained as guarded as he'd been on the track.

'I've just got a few things on my mind, that's all,' he said. 'There are a few things that don't feel right and I've got to get my head round it. They're my problems, nobody else's. I know you're concerned, but I'm the only one that can sort this out. Nobody else can. Trust me.'

'I just don't like seeing that happen,' I said, referring to Haye's lengthy walk of shame earlier that day. 'This is the biggest fight of your life and you're in such a great position. Imagine how many other fighters would love to be where you are right now.'

'Yeah, I know,' replied Haye, sighing as though he'd just been reprimanded by his mother for skipping homework. 'You don't need to tell *me* that.'

I knew my half-hearted plea would likely fall on deaf ears, but I needed to say something, if only to show I cared. The non-relationship between Haye and Booth was hardly normal, and everybody bore the brunt of it. It was far from an ideal working set-up and, as a result, there was no work getting done. Sure, Haye still had five weeks left of training to rectify matters, but Booth was as dejected as I'd ever seen him and was now beginning to question whether his champion-in-waiting even had any fight left in him.

'I don't think David believes he can win this fight,' said Booth, as we passed a punctured football back and forth along a forgotten side road the following day. 'Mormeck has always been a nightmare for him stylistically, and I genuinely feel David has tried doing the things he needs to do to win the fight and now realises he can't pull them off. So he's panicking and rethinking things. He's not sure whether I've fucked up by telling him the wrong things or whether he's fucked up by not being able to carry them out.

'David's never worked on his left hand like he should have, because his right hand has always been able to get the job done. He would always win fights with big right hands, so he neglected using his left the way he needed to. Now he's fighting Mormeck and the left hand is going to be even more important than the right.

'The same applies to his legs. David has never liked running and never spent much time strengthening his legs, and now he needs strong legs more than ever. If he can't punch while going backwards, then this fight is only going one way.'

On day three of the drama, Haye and Booth finally spoke. They sat in Haye's parked Range Rover and discussed matters for approximately five minutes, before once again parting. Booth's initial forecast proved correct.

'David told me he no longer thought he could carry out the tactics we had planned and that he wouldn't be able to move and box the way I want him to,' revealed Booth, as we travelled across town to a local football game. 'He said he was physically incapable of doing it and couldn't understand why I was trying to get him to fight like Ray Leonard.'

Booth then asked his fighter what he planned to do as an alternative. 'He said, "I don't know yet – I'll think of something when the time comes",' added the trainer. 'So what do I do now? Do I accept his opinion and come up with another game plan that is geared to his strengths, even if it may prove to be the wrong thing to do? Or do I continue along this path and get *nothing* from him?'

They'd reached an impasse. Distance was seemingly the only remedy, and Booth made the first move, declaring he'd head home to England as soon as a flight could be arranged. Booth needed some time alone for the sake of his own sanity, and Haye, too, would benefit from not being judged.

The exasperated teacher returned to England the very next day and the pupil, now free from scrutiny and expectation, loosened up somewhat and motivated himself for the next two days and nights. I feared the worst when Booth left, and wondered how Haye would summon the enthusiasm to train with nobody present to remind him of its importance. Encouragingly, though, he reacted like a petulant child intent on proving the world wrong. He packed his own bags and headed to his home away from home, the rustic warehouse with a ring. For two nights in a row, Haye and I travelled down to the makeshift gym, where I'd watch the fighter shadow-box to warm up and then slug away at the heavy bag for ten separate three-minute rounds. I was apparently in charge of arranging water bottles, monitoring the stopwatch and praising his efforts at the session's conclusion. There was nothing scientific, clever or particularly impressive about what Haye was doing, but I warmed to the fact he had taken matters into his own destructive hands and was wading into the bag with a sense of damaged pride and determination that had been sorely lacking from previous sessions. Though unwilling to discuss it, Haye clearly felt angered or let down by someone or something, and was now transferring that negative energy into far more positive pursuits. Ten rounds on the heavy bag would never be enough to defeat Mormeck, of course, but it was a sign that Haye's brain was back on boxing and that he was willing to work at something more than walking pace.

I left Cyprus the following Wednesday, and Haye did likewise, booking himself on the same five-hour flight I'd intended to use to help restore perspective and sanity. It was a relief to head home and close my eyes to the prospect of my favourite fighter underachieving on the biggest night of his life. Suffocated by negativity, I saw only darkness ahead.

Haye, on the other hand, was back to being his usual animated self, perhaps still blind to concepts of fear and failure. There was no sign of panic or desperation on his part, as the boxer introduced me to his favourite tunes on his iPod before passing comment on various articles in my copy of *The Ring* magazine. It was while skimming through the self-proclaimed 'Bible of Boxing' that I caught Haye reading a story about Jermain Taylor and instantly felt the urge to pounce.

'Don't you find it strange that Jermain Taylor doesn't even like or follow boxing?' I asked, referring to the fact that the Arkansas-based middleweight champion had frequently cited a lack of interest in the very sport that defined him. Taylor was an unbeaten world middleweight champion at the time, but would lose his belts the following weekend to Kelly Pavlik.

'I don't think you have to particularly like a sport to be good at it,' replied Haye. 'There are plenty of top sportsmen and women over the years that were just born to do something, and may have not even liked what they were doing at the time.'

'Don't you think it's a bad thing if Taylor doesn't love the sport, though?'

'No. So long as he trains hard and keeps winning, what does it matter? His lack of interest in boxing may actually help him. He might be able to switch on when the time is right and not clog his brain up with it all too much.'

'Do *you* love boxing?' I asked, taking my chance.

'Yeah, of course. I love watching fights, and love being involved in them. It's just in my blood, I think. I can't help it.'

'Do you still enjoy it?'

'I wouldn't say any boxer *enjoys* the concept of actually getting in the ring, with all that pressure and expectancy, and then having a fight. There are more fun things to do in life. You don't have time to sit back, relax and enjoy it. I enjoy knocking people out and love the moment when you see a guy rocked and hurt, and you're about to wade in and finish him. *That's* enjoyable.'

'So, if Taylor's love for boxing is at one, where does your love for boxing rate out of ten?'

'It's hard to say. I definitely couldn't live without it, but, then again, it's not like there aren't other things I like or want to pursue. I'd like to be retired by the time I'm thirty, I know that much. Until then, though, I'd definitely say it's my life. I don't go more than a day without thinking about it in some way, shape or form. I'm reading this magazine now, aren't I?'

Yes, he was. But so was I. Unlike Haye, I wouldn't have to whip my body into the best shape of my life to fight WBC and WBA world cruiserweight champion Jean-Marc Mormeck in November. Haye would, and he didn't need anybody reminding him. This was, after all, *his* problem, not mine.

Two weeks later and Haye woke up. He was reunited with Booth in Cyprus and the pair once again lived, ate, breathed and dreamed in shared head space. The first training session was every bit as excruciatingly frosty as the last, however.

'We didn't say a word to each other throughout,' recalled Booth. 'I sat to the side of the warehouse and stayed there the whole time. David had been training on his own for a week or so before I got there, so he'd found a routine and was simply going through the motions in front of me. It was incredibly uncomfortable. I didn't want to give him the satisfaction of saying something, and vice versa.'

The pair rolled up to the same gym on day two and Haye once again led a solo warm-up as Booth sat with his back to the wall. Little was said and cursory glances offered the only form of communication. Haye stepped into the ring to shadow-box and Booth, perceptive even through tired eyes, reacted instinctively to a flaw in Haye's footwork. He leant forward, cleared his throat and said, 'When you move to the right make sure you kick your right leg out.' Perhaps a throwaway comment under normal circumstances, Booth got just two words into the sentence before a suddenly captivated Haye fixed eyes on him. Rather than a look of bitterness, it was one of sheer focus and forgiveness.

'I will always remember the look he gave me,' said Booth. 'It sent a shiver down my spine, and nothing else he did in the gym that day mattered. All I needed was that look. It told me he was now willing to listen. From there the job was easy. We had four weeks together and have never worked better.'

The breakthrough was, of course, inspired by a need to pull

together with time running out, but also came as a result of renewed communication and understanding. Time away had offered the pair a period for reflection, and also helped shed light on the reason for Haye's initial histrionics on the athletics track that frightfully uncomfortable afternoon in September. What was first assumed to be the sulk of a disobedient fighter later transpired to be the contemplative stroll of a man about to become a father for the first time. A secret to the rest of us at the time, Haye's girlfriend Natasha was pregnant with their first child and the young boxer now had someone else to fight for.

CHAPTER THIRTEEN
TRÈS BIEN, MONSIEUR

Hours before the fight, David Haye and Adam Booth dined on spaghetti bolognese at a downtown café in Levallois. Pre-fight tradition often called for a lengthy walk, casual chat and a hearty meal and, though in Paris, both pined for a diversion of the Italian variety. Once plates were cleared, the pair strolled back across the bridge towards their four-star hotel. It was then that Haye, capitalising on silence, decided to stop his march abruptly and turn to face Booth.

'When am I going to feel it?' asked the fighter.

'Feel what?' replied Booth.

'Feel *something*,' said Haye. 'I don't even feel like I'm fighting tonight.'

Booth waited. He wanted to get his response right. It would potentially be the last chunk of advice he'd get to pass Haye's way before the pair later reconvened at the fight venue.

'Maybe,' he said, 'that's just the way it is supposed to be.'

As the fighter and trainer resumed their walk back to the hotel, Booth smiled to himself and recalled a Lloyd Honeyghan interview he'd watched ahead of the Bermondsey fighter's stunning victory over world welterweight champion Don Curry in 1986. When asked how he felt ahead of his monumental task in Atlantic

City, underdog Honeyghan shrugged, looked the reporter in the eye and said, 'It just feels like I'm at home or walking down Walworth Road. I don't feel anything. I'm not coming to piss around, I'm coming to win.'

Just as Booth had contemplated the right words to say on that bridge, I too encountered the very same predicament moments after arriving in Levallois. Speaking over the phone in dry monotone, a tired-sounding Haye, now hidden away in the safe and quiet confines of his hotel room, called me to visit him hours before the first bell of his world title challenge against Jean-Marc Mormeck. He asked if I could help take some rubbish downstairs and then promptly hung up.

Happy to carry out this small and insignificant duty, I walked along to room 501, knocked, waited patiently beside some black bin liners – presumably the aforementioned rubbish – before being beckoned in by Haye, who was sat prodding a chicken and pasta meal alone at his laptop. Stevie Wonder was conversing with him through speakers and Sugar Ray Robinson demonstrated boxing Utopia on screen.

'How are you doing?' I asked, assuming that was the preferred etiquette in such situations.

'Good,' replied Haye, with a mouthful of food and a headful of dreams.

'Did you want me to carry something downstairs for you?' I said, uncomfortable with the idea of sticking around so close to showtime.

'Yeah, just one of my bags over there,' replied Haye, as he pointed to a pile of T-shirts, tracksuits, towels and blank CDs. 'It's all right, though, we've got a bit of time. Take a seat. You make me feel uncomfortable just standing there.'

This was something Haye would often repeat to me when clocking my upright, rigid and uncomfortable stance. Not wanting to impose on any situation, I'd regularly bide my time and wait for the call to relax, before actually sitting and festering. I didn't want to overstay my welcome at the calmest of times, let alone this close to Haye's biggest fight of his career. Nobody else was present in the room, and I could sense this was the challenger's final chance to grab some time alone and possibly even sleep ahead of battle. My mere presence, whether standing or sitting, would prevent both.

'Watch this,' said Haye, swinging the laptop to face me as I took a seat on a nearby chair. 'It's Sugar Ray Robinson against Jake LaMotta. Their fourth and final fight. I've also been watching this great Sugar Ray compilation.'

The boxer munched along excitedly with the punches landing on screen, shook his head in disbelief at some points, punched the air at others and generally seemed in awe of what he was witnessing.

'How *good* was that left hook?' said Haye, as he rewound footage of Robinson taking out Gene Fullmer with one pulverising left. 'I wish I had a left hook like that. Man, can you imagine how many people I'd take out if I could hook like Sugar Ray?'

We watched that Robinson left hook travel back and forth at least ten times that evening, and Haye was absolutely right. As gifted as he was, and as potent as he was with his own debilitating right cross, Haye would never hook like Robinson. Very few would, of course, but such a statement resonated even more on a night like that one, as Haye was made only too aware of how much that particular shot was necessary against a squat slugger like Mormeck. He had, after all, spent days and weeks winging awkward left hooks at punchbags in his lonely gym in Northern Cyprus, desperate to reclaim something he'd neglected many years ago. The concussive puncher had dallied too long perfecting his right cross to ever get close to emulating Robinson's effortless left, and he knew it, too.

Switching between seven separate windows on his laptop, Haye would drift from footage of Robinson and Sugar Shane Mosley, to his email account, iTunes library, boxing websites and forums and social networking sites. His mind was racing, but not in the manner you'd expect of a man merely hours from a world championship fight.

'I used to always think girls sang this song about me,' said Haye, as Jean Carne's 1979 disco hit 'Was That All It Was' played from his laptop speakers. 'It was my ultimate song for banging some piece and then leaving her the next day and ignoring her calls. It was like the soundtrack to my life. I would picture the girls singing it as I ran down the road with my clothes in my hands. I was a mean little bastard back then, and this song has always reminded me of certain girls I left behind.'

Haye's mind had switched to the past, and his shackle-free years as a youth, whereas mine was still occupied by unshakeable doubt and fear of the immediate future. It was a strange contrast in concerns, especially given our differing roles, and I wished my head could be as clear as that of the man about to engage in twelve rounds of heavy-duty action.

'Have you heard my ring entrance music yet?' asked Haye, like an eight-year-old about to unveil his latest Action Man figure.

'No,' I replied. 'What song are you using?'

Haye tapped his nose, spun his laptop towards him and then clicked play on McFadden & Whitehead's 1979 hit 'Ain't No Stoppin' Us Now'. My mind was immediately transported back to watching grainy fight footage of Larry Holmes, the legendary former world heavyweight champion, who used to jog to the ring accompanied by the very same song.

'I think it's going to get everybody jumping around and dancing,' said Haye. 'That's what I like about it. I can't wait to see the crowd out there, man. It's going to be crazy. Do you reckon I'll get booed?'

'No,' I said. 'I don't think the French fans are like that. They're probably more like the German boxing fans, in that they'll just sit and applaud for the most part. I can't see them standing up and chanting football songs like we do back home.'

'Yeah, that's what I thought,' said Haye, almost in perverse disappointment.

There was a clear sense he would have somehow preferred to be booed, heckled and spat on as he entered the ring, as though that would somehow intensify his mood even further. Haye wanted the ultimate foreign boxing experience, to know he'd claimed victory in the most hostile and treacherous of environments.

Unlike me, Haye seemed nonplussed by the threat Mormeck could offer. It wasn't until his ring entrance music kicked in and Haye began to loosen up into a light shadow-boxing effort that any sign of trepidation entered his chiselled frame.

'How do you think he'll start?' asked Haye, in between popping out jabs at thin air in front of me. 'Do you think he'll come out quickly and throw lots of punches?'

'No,' I said, for once fully confident in my answer, but now feeling the pressure of being deemed responsible. 'Mormeck never starts fast. He'll come out, have a look and make you do most of the work.'

'So you reckon he'll just stalk me down and force me to punch?'

'Exactly. He doesn't have the engine to throw hundreds of punches a round, and he knows that. He won't risk emptying his tank. The thing is, he's usually good enough to make people work and make mistakes without actually throwing a punch.'

'Right. So I've just got to stay clean and accurate with what I do, and not fall into his traps. If he doesn't want to throw, I won't throw. Unless I see an opening . . .'

'That's the best way to go about it. He won't start fast, I know that much. He may not even throw many punches at all in the first round. From what I've seen of him, he comes on strongest through rounds two to five. Then he slumps.'

'It's funny how people think this fight boils down to me winning early or him winning late, isn't it? If anything, I see it the other way round. I know I can spark him early or late, but I don't see Mormeck doing *anything* in the second half of this fight.'

'He's never as effective in the second half.'

'Those fights with Fragomeni and Johansen could be important tonight.'

'Definitely.'

'I'm glad I've had them. I now know I can stop guys late on if need be.'

By now, Haye was throwing power punches into the air, no longer feelers with left jabs and prodding rights. He was rehearsing cruel hooks, uppercuts and roundhouses.

'Pound for pound, if you could pair a prime Ray Robinson with Mormeck, what would he do?' asked Haye, doing his utmost not to laugh.

'It wouldn't be pretty,' I said, steadfast in my respect for Mormeck, but, let's be real, nobody's toppling a prime Robinson, regardless of weight.

'What punch would knock him out?'

'Probably his left hook,' I said. 'You know, the punch you don't have.'

Haye chuckled, then unveiled his best attempt at a Robinson left hook, before promising, 'People won't be saying that after tonight'.

With that, Haye stopped shadow-boxing, shook his head free of Mormeck, and paced across the room towards the heap of rubbish forming by his bed. He bent down, separated dirty clothes from their clean counterparts and began folding any reusable items into tidy piles, all the while pontificating on the night ahead.

'There was something not right with him yesterday at the weigh-in,' Haye muttered.

'What do you mean?' I asked.

'It was all in his eyes,' he said. 'Mormeck couldn't look at me. It was like he didn't want to be there. I was trying to get close to him and look into his eyes, but he didn't want to know. Even when we did finally catch each other's eyes, there was an empty and scared look in his. It was as though he wanted to be friends rather than opponents.'

For the next ten minutes, Haye shuffled along, almost in total silence. He swept up rubbish from his bedside cabinet, nearby tables and the floor, and distributed the unwanted items into waste baskets. Dinner trays were parked outside the hotel room door, as were the many empty water bottles that had built up and cluttered his room during the course of the week. It was at this point that I finally decided to avert my eyes from the fighter's laptop and say something.

'Erm, David,' I whispered, 'what exactly are you doing?'

'I'm cleaning my room,' he replied. 'I do this before all my fights, just before I leave my room. I ironed all my clothes earlier, too.'

'Why?'

'I've never really thought about it. I guess I just like to know everything is tidy in my life before I go to war. I like to know it's all taken care of and that there's no mess.'

'So you can then enter a fight with a clean head?'

'Yeah, that's probably it. I just like to have my shit in order. I couldn't care less how tidy my room is the rest of the year, but it suddenly seems really important on the night of a fight. If I'm in a hotel for a fight, I guarantee the room will be immaculate by the time I leave and head to the arena.'

'Do you think it's a superstition?'

'Not really. It just makes me feel good to know my room's tidy.

I actually enjoy the process of cleaning up. It's weird, because usually I'd have nothing to do with cleaning. But when it comes time to fight, it feels great. I'll spend a good couple of hours slowly getting all my shit together. It's never a quick burst. I like to take my time and really enjoy it.'

Sensing this process could drag on longer than I'd first envisaged, I decided to make a break for it. However, before stepping outside to remove Haye's dirty laundry and negative thoughts, I foolishly decided our parting required some sort of exclamation mark or final thought. Racking my brains for an award-winning zinger, I stuttered, choked and instead settled for the ultimate defeatist's mantra. 'Just go out there and do your best tonight,' went the nugget. 'That's all you can do.'

Haye was bent over, lacing a pair of trainers, at this point, and looked up at me with a wide and sympathetic grin.

'Thanks, but that's the talk of a loser,' he said. 'Doing my best isn't good enough. I've got to win, and I'm going to.'

On that note, Haye's rubbish was removed pronto and he was finally alone, a clear head in a clear room.

I wouldn't just watch Haye compete that night as a friend or, indeed, fan. Days before I left for Paris, *Boxing Monthly* editor Glyn Leach contacted me in the hope of cornering someone to cover the WBC and WBA world cruiserweight title bout from ringside. Like much of the British media, *Boxing Monthly* had been denied any credentials for the event, so, aware of my relationship with the challenger, Leach asked whether I'd be willing and able to cover the fight for the magazine. I'd contributed previously to the publication, of course, and had also penned plenty of material on Haye, but never before had I been asked to cover one of his fights and produce an objective report. In fact, I hadn't officially reported on a Haye fight, for magazine or website, since the Londoner defeated 'King' Arthur Williams in May 2004. Suddenly the idea of reviewing Haye's performance seemed somewhat unnerving.

Of course, victory for Haye would have presented me with the alluring prospect of constructing the most gratifying fight report of my brief career to date. I would have gleefully overindulged in explaining the sounds, smells and sensations of the night, and been handed a welcome platform to detail my time spent with Haye in his hotel room hours before the fight. It would be my crowning moment as a wannabe hack and boxing insider. Despite the lure of mutual success, though, I couldn't escape the foreboding stigma of the British loser, especially abroad, and had to prepare my mind for the distinct possibility of crafting Haye's second post-fight obituary.

Once inside the Palais des Sports Marcel Cerdan that Saturday night, however, any illusions of objectivity were well and truly punched to the back of my mind. High on the thin and flaky promise of victory, I was now solely concerned with Haye fulfilling his own dream. I would have sacrificed anything that night, including my own reputation in the profession, to see Haye, a loner in hostile territory, lift the WBC and WBA belts high above his head. Shunned by many of them in the first place, the fighter didn't need a journalist that night. He needed a friend.

As the atmosphere and tension grew inside the arena, shenanigans were plentiful backstage, too. Summoned to a dressing room the size of a matchbox, Haye and Booth immediately demanded a space they could at least both occupy at the same time, and one which allowed them to stretch out their arms. As the French promoters quibbled and delayed, a persistent and, frankly, pissed-off Haye took matters into his own hands. The challenger fled from his designated coop, performed his own impromptu site check of the arena and then kicked in a door, which conveniently led to a basket-ball court.

'This will do,' declared Haye, as he dumped his bags on court and flung both arms out wide. 'I'll get changed in here, if that's all right with you.'

And he did. The idea of overcoming a bully was something Haye would again have to encounter before the night was out, and a minor power squabble beforehand was just the appetiser he required to set his mind right.

Meanwhile, on a nearby ringside table sat a menacing life-sized stone sculpture of Jean-Marc Mormeck's head. No reasons or back-story were offered for its appearance, but, naturally, I viewed its presence as the first bad omen of the evening. To make matters worse, as I settled into my ringside seat I realised the sculpture seemed purposely directed to face me, Mormeck's eyes locked on mine. I zoned out, stared hard at the statue, and, to anyone unaware of my acute anxiety, must have resembled a man in the throes of a hallucinogenic drug trip. I was transfixed by the figure for minutes, before realising I needed to look away. I started to get the feeling Mormeck had winked at me. He was renowned for his solid chin and unbreakable will, and this homage to his toughness was a solemn sign of what Haye and I could expect. It was also one I hoped someone would cover with a blanket before the first bell tolled.

I was relieved to discover that when the first bell did indeed even-tually sound, the real-life Mormeck appeared comparatively normal and soft. Not only that, but this heavy-breathing version was posi-tively relaxed, loose and human in both appearance and flaws. He moved, shielded his head anxiously under attack, and trudged towards Haye with a measured, but almost pedestrian rhythm. Mormeck's mean exterior, the one promised by the ringside statue, seemed to betray him. Many would have been surprised by such a revelation, but not me. As I'd told Haye earlier that evening, I expected Mormeck to start slowly, and with apologetic puppy eyes to boot.

Haye, on the other hand, exchanged an airy bounce for a sinister stare and stance. He was primed to explode, and was working against his better wishes and instincts to hold back and not erupt on Mormeck's inviting dome.

Just as we'd forecast, Mormeck was in a defensive shell and offering little in the first round, save for the top of his skull and the hardened edges of his abdomen. There was a scant scoring target to hit, and Haye sensed it. Fighting temptation, the challenger refused to force any openings and hand Mormeck the opportunity to feed off mistakes.

The first three minutes of the fight were a surreal spectacle to behold, as the whole affair almost seemed easy. The champion Mormeck offered little in the way of threat and Haye, fighting at his own pace, and a comfortable and measured one at that, was able to punch and move whenever he wanted to. Eleven more rounds like that and Haye would have been a lock to take the titles home. Having studied Mormeck for the best part of two years, however, I knew the real storm was just around the corner.

Alas, Mormeck upped his work-rate as the bout progressed, and duly quickened his pace and shortened up his shots. Content to throw in range, Haye was also making investments in the form of vicious lefts and rights aimed at the chiselled Mormeck mid-section. With each slug that landed in the pit of Mormeck's belly, the champion would visibly wince, weaken and gasp for air.

As is the way with momentum swings in boxing, however, just as you start to see a glimpse of light, somebody pulls down the shutters. Early in the fourth round, while retreating to a neutral corner, Haye was caught on the temple by a glancing Mormeck left hook, and was sent scrambling to the floor on unsteady legs, like a first-time ice skater attempting an elaborate pirouette. His legs slid across the ice, his eyes were keeping track of a frantic ping-pong rally, and Haye's head was a mess of shock and sudden doubt.

Wisely, Haye took the full eight-count and then nodded to Booth in the corner. Upon rising, his pins remained shaky, but his eyes and mind appeared to be clear. He registered referee Guido Cavalleri's count and went right at Mormeck from the restart. As always, I expected the worst, and began racking my brain for excuses, reasons and a route back. I could see no U-turn in the fight for Haye, and knew Mormeck was an unforgiving finisher if offered the opportunity to close the show. Hardly a born survivor, I also realised Haye wasn't used to being in this position and that he might now pay for his swashbuckling nature in the face of adversity. Despair had never felt so real. It was now just a matter of time.

Encouragingly, though, Haye was quick to clinch the buoyant champion upon the restart and walk him backwards, a tactic I'd implored him to use in the weeks leading up to the bout, having spotted Mormeck's inability and reluctance to fight out of one. Time and time again Haye would grab Mormeck and march him across the ring, draining the champion's strength reserves and exerting his own alpha male dominance in the ring. As the two fighters split from one particular clinch, Haye slugged Mormeck with a wild right hand to the back of the head, and I watched, almost in a dreamlike haze, as the champion staggered ever so slightly. Referee Cavalleri rightly administered a stern warning to Haye for hitting on the break, but, irrespective of the legality of the shot, I'd noticed a chink in Mormeck's make-up and, perhaps for the first time in the fight, the cruiserweight king had felt Haye's power. Curiously, as the tumultuous fourth round came to a close, there appeared still to be a semblance of hope. Mormeck no longer seemed made of stone.

Aware of the need to make another impression on Mormeck, a rejuvenated Haye started the following round, the fifth, at a brisk pace. He whacked right hooks and left hooks into the head of the champion, and switched attacks downstairs with the kind of seamless sophistication the 'Sugarman' once employed as first a welterweight, and then finally a light-heavyweight.

Mormeck, for his part, didn't go all out, as many had expected. He continued to stalk Haye, offering very little for the challenger to hit, but had seemingly called a momentary time-out on his own advances. A more relaxed Haye also began utilising his left hand more as a jab, hook and uppercut, figuring Mormeck's defence against the right cross was simply too resolute.

This sense of Haye finding his feet was only heightened in the sixth, as he conducted one of the best rounds of his 21-fight professional career. Crossing the t's and dotting the i's on his – up to that point – patchy defence, Haye made Mormeck miss big punches at will throughout the three minutes. He slipped jabs, parried right hands and leaned away from Mormeck's heavy combinations, as though playing pat-a-cake with a young girl. His defensive work on the ropes was improvised, instinctive and inspired at times, much to the satisfaction of my hands, which were now clapping together in unison and positivity for the first time in the bout.

While Mormeck huffed and puffed and pummelled thin air, Haye bravely slammed hard rights and lefts into the gut of the hesitant hometown hero. One left to the body, in particular, had Mormeck non-responsive for a good thirty seconds after it landed, and seemed to spook the normally poker-faced prizefighter.

'Perfect,' was the review from Booth, as Haye slumped to the stool and rested between rounds. 'Thirty-two punches. You're well within.'

Before the contest, Booth had informed me that Haye was averaging eighty-five punches per round at their Ozankoy gym in

Northern Cyprus. This obsession with the maths of the fight simply made Haye aware of how much more he had left in him, and allowed him to navigate his way through the fight in a manner that kept him one step ahead of the similarly economical champion.

Going into the seventh, Mormeck was left only too aware of how much Haye had remaining in the tank. Noticing a critical drop in his opponent's work-rate, Haye upped his own tempo, began planting his feet more and hurled sickeningly heavy shots into Mormeck's head and torso. The sounds of Mormeck getting nailed were like those generated from a bass drum. Boom. Boom. Boom.

A hard left cross, thrown from a momentary southpaw stance, caught Mormeck bang on the chin for the first time in the fight and acted as the beginning of the end for the Frenchman's reign as champion. Remaining patient, Haye landed further right hooks and left uppercuts, as well as a vicious right hand to the body. He then switched to the other side and chucked a left hook and a flush right uppercut at Mormeck's jaw. It was the final right uppercut, however, that disconnected Mormeck from both his senses and his WBC and WBA belts. Landing square on his chin, the almighty punch forced Mormeck to sway back towards the ropes in a groggy state. Unsure whether Haye would follow up high or low, Mormeck instinctively dropped his left arm to protect his body. He guessed wrong. Haye went high and dished out a final, sadistic right hook behind Mormeck's ear, which sent the champion crashing to the floor in a heap.

'He's *gone!*' I yelped from ringside. 'It's over! Wave it off! He's *done!*'

Motionless for a few seconds, and seemingly unsure of his whereabouts, Mormeck eventually rose at the count of eight and tottered around unsteadily in Haye's corner. Cavalleri gave him every opportunity to continue, including a long count and a question, but

Mormeck simply had no answer. He shook his head, eyes still vacant. The referee had no choice but to listen to my advice and wave it off.

Storming the ring in frenzied passion, Booth hoisted his 200lb fighter high above his head and spun him around. They'd done it. Haye had become WBC and WBA world cruiserweight champion and silenced the French crowd in the process. Some had even decided to switch sides, so impressed were they by Haye's display of guts. In fact, it was while deliriously rushing up and down the aisles attempting to serve up humble pie to any sceptic I happened to pass that I locked eyes with one affable Frenchman merely nodding his appreciation my way. The man clapped his hands and puffed out his cheeks, as if to say, 'Oui, oui, très bien, Monsieur Haye', but with far more eloquence and sportsmanship than this overexcited reprobate could ever demonstrate. Still angling for a squabble, I pivoted to my left and right and discovered similarly respectful nods and claps of approval from all manner of French men and women. Though conversing in a different language, it now appeared France had come to realise what I'd known for years.

Naturally, Haye's following was considerably larger now than it had been when he'd walked towards the arena. Many stragglers, of both British and French origin, tagged along and stalked the new champion from the fight venue back to his hotel. A one-hundred-strong army holed up in the hotel lobby, and the Londoner would eventually appear to rapturous applause and adulation, before having his ear bent with countless tales of triumph from those who had watched the fight. Riding the wave of acclaim, Haye was being dragged this way and that, as plans were made for a celebration on his behalf. He seemed weary in mind and body, though managed to put on a brave face for anyone who vied for his attention.

Yet to utter much more than a word to him at this stage, I

watched Haye gradually manoeuvre his way closer and closer towards a hotel lift, apparently bound for his hotel room. Amusingly – to me, at least – each time the boxer edged that bit closer to the lift, someone else would interject and declare what a fantastic human being he was, before offering words of advice on what he could have done differently to avoid the fourth-round knockdown he'd suffered. Haye embraced all comments with a charming nod, smile and handshake, but was clearly in a rush to get away and spend some time alone with Natasha. Hand in hand, the pair finally reached the lift and skipped inside before the doors slammed shut. It was then that Haye, glancing out between the parted doors, spotted me in the distance and beckoned me over to join them.

'Elliot!' he shouted, high above the crowd. 'Get over here.'

In a race to beat the sliding doors, I tripped over my own feet and dived inside. The lift travelled up to floor five, and the three of us walked along to room 501, the same room we'd tidied and pretended not to panic in hours earlier. Once inside, Haye slumped down on the sofa and finished off the pasta and chicken dish he'd half-eaten earlier that evening. Natasha, meanwhile, marvelled at how clean her boyfriend's room was compared to when she'd last seen it.

'So that's that then,' said Haye, followed by a sigh and accompanying belly laugh.

'How does it feel?' I asked.

'Weird. It doesn't feel like I've achieved anything yet. It just hasn't sunk in. I can't even remember how it happened.'

'I never thought you'd one day beat Mormeck,' I said, drunk on adrenalin and joy, and thus far braver than I had been earlier in the evening. 'He was always *the man*. I just never pictured it happening like this.'

'So you're a believer in me now, are you?'

'I always was. But, yes, definitely more tonight than ever before.'

'Were you worried when I got put down?'

'Yeah. I thought you were finished. I thought it was all over.'

Haye swung back on the sofa and roared with laughter, tickled by the idea that his fragility was the cause of so much of my mental trauma that night.

'Were you hurt by that punch, Dave?' asked Natasha, now sitting next to her boyfriend on the couch. Haye rubbed the stomach of his pregnant girlfriend, then kissed her on the lips.

'My legs were fucked,' he admitted. 'I wasn't *that* hurt, but my brain just got scrambled. The shot caught me on the temple, so it knocked my brain about a bit. My left leg knew where it wanted to be, but my right leg had a mind of its own.'

The new cruiserweight champion would continue discussing the fight in this candid manner for the next half an hour or so, before phone calls began to arrive from downstairs and he was begged to attend the many parties laid on for him. Quiet moments would be few and far between in the following hours, days and weeks, and so it was unquestionably a privilege to have escaped the sudden crush and spent those reflective few moments with Haye in his hotel room. I wasn't sure why I'd been selected, but assumed he needed his scattered mind jogged by someone obsessive enough to have followed the fight with my kind of intensity and focus. He knew I grew as nervous as anyone when the first bell tolled, and was also aware of both my long-time admiration for Mormeck and my unwavering doubts going into the fight. More than that, though, Haye now seemed to value my advice more than ever before. Absurd as it seemed, the new world cruiserweight champion relied on my recollections and point of view to help align the pieces of a jumbled puzzle.

'I knew you wouldn't mince your words,' said Haye, after I'd told him his 'defence had let him down' in the frantic fourth round. 'What can they say now, though? What can *anyone* say after that?'

TRÈS BIEN, MONSIEUR

For what it's worth, I still found plenty to say and write the next day when, deadline looming, eight inspired fingertips combined to produce two thousand words of celebratory spiel for *Boxing Monthly*. I could have written ten times as much, of course, but if there was one thing I learnt from my time in Levallois it was how to remain gracious in glorious victory.

CHAPTER FOURTEEN

TWO POUNDS, TWO ROUNDS

Boxers fib perhaps more than any other sportsmen, as their profession relies heavily on the suspension of disbelief. David Haye was one of the more honest fighters I'd met on my brief travels, but was still a pathological liar in a sport of so many. Forget the bravado and biceps, Haye, like so many others, still had many insecurities and felt the need to lie his way through the process of preparing for the wholly unnatural concept of a prizefight. Not only that, Haye also had a way with words, and an understanding of semantics, which allowed him to draw on well-picked white lies in order to get the better of less loquacious opponents.

For instance, following his world cruiserweight title triumph over Jean-Marc Mormeck, the new champion insisted his days as a cruiserweight were over, mere minutes after dislodging his French opponent from his senses and titles. Haye used manipulation of words, as well as the new-found power of two belts, to rile domestic rival Enzo Maccarinelli and set the wheels spinning on a potentially lucrative cruiserweight – yes, *cruiserweight* – clash in 2008.

'I'm glad that this is my last fight at cruiserweight, and I'm glad that I was able to get the win,' Haye told Setanta Sports in the post-fight interview. 'I'm sure Enzo Maccarinelli will want to fight for these belts, but, unfortunately, I'm not going to be defending the belts at cruiserweight. We can have a fight, no doubt, but it's going to have to be at heavyweight. As you saw when I got tagged, the legs aren't there at cruiserweight.'

Sitting in a London studio that November night was WBO champion Maccarinelli, working for Setanta as a pundit and interested observer. Clearly peeved by his rival's plans for a brief tenure at cruiserweight, Maccarinelli struggled to hide his disappointment at missing out on a blockbuster payday and shot at the titles.

Although Haye struggled to boil down to the cruiserweight limit of 200lbs, Maccarinelli, an inch taller at six feet four inches, had to hustle hard to work his way *up* towards the same limit in his Newport gymnasium. Thicker-set and heavily muscled, Haye had beaten the drum about weight-making issues for the previous eighteen months, ever since missing the weight limit first time ahead of a European title defence against Lasse Johansen in 2006, and was now adamant he could no longer perform as a cruiserweight.

Haye was also convinced that Maccarinelli only wanted to face him as a cruiserweight in the hope of capitalising on a weight-drained and incapacitated version of the champion. The new cruiserweight king insisted Maccarinelli would look the other way if he hadn't shown such a susceptibility to the strains of weight-making in Paris. Haye claimed he was only at 'seventy per cent' for the Mormeck title clash, and that this percentage would only further diminish with additional ill-advised matches in the 200lb weight class.

An alleged one million pounds later, Haye forgot all about pounds of the other variety and agreed to face Maccarinelli in March 2008 at London's O2 Arena. It would be a triple-title unification clash, with Haye's WBC and WBA belts on the line, as well as Maccarinelli's WBO version. The fight was instantly hailed by its promoter Frank Warren as the biggest all-British world title fight since Nigel Benn and Chris Eubank met in 1993.

In taking the fight, Haye received the fattest pay-cheque of his career to date, and rumours ran rife that the weight-drained fighter had cashed in his body and willingly sacrificed his health for additional noughts. The prevailing wisdom was that Maccarinelli and Warren had prevented Haye from stepping up to heavyweight and dragged the champion's dry shell back down to the division in which he had once claimed to see no future. Having proved his dominance at the pinnacle of the weight class in November, one couldn't help but wonder what the motives for Haye accepting the bout were.

'The fight's on,' he revealed over the phone to me on a January morning in 2008. 'We've finally got him.'

Now, I had been aware of the fact Haye had been negotiating for a fight with Maccarinelli over the festive period, and that there was a decent chance of it coming to fruition, but was nonetheless surprised and slightly scared by the enthusiasm Haye managed to summon ahead of the bout. Like everybody else, I'd assumed the cruiserweight champion had diluted horrific weight-making issues with a bumper pay-cheque, and that he'd simply grin and bear any consequences.

'We've *got him*,' reiterated Haye for the second time, only now with far more emphasis.

'What do you mean?' I asked.

'We've got the both of them. Enzo *and* Warren. We've got them exactly where we want. They think I'm finished at the weight, and that's the only reason they've accepted the fight.'

'So you're not struggling at the weight?'

'Well, it's *never* easy. It's certainly not as bad as I've made out, though. I've been banging on about my problems for so long now, and they've fallen for it. The thing is, we've had this plan for the last couple of years. I've always planned to talk up my weight-making problems, in the hope that they'd bite and go for the fight. They've panicked, and now we've got them.'

'Okay,' I said, catching my breath for a second. 'So you'll be absolutely fine at the weight then?'

'Yes. We've planned for this to happen. I've not really had a day off since the Mormeck fight and have deliberately watched my weight in the hope that this fight would happen. I actually told Adam to go ahead and make the fight as soon as we got back from Paris. So, while I said my cruiserweight days were over on television, a few days later we were discussing ways of getting this Maccarinelli fight done. It's all been part of the plan. I'm now going to go straight into training for Enzo, and the weight won't be a problem at all. This will probably be the easiest and most pain-free weight-cut of my whole career.'

'Oh, shit,' I said, as though finally sussing an optical illusion. 'You're priceless.'

'Listen,' added Haye, 'Enzo is going to get destroyed, mark my words. This is going to be exactly like when Lennox Lewis fought Michael Grant and obliterated him in two rounds. Grant was this tall, heavy-handed, chinny contender, and the television companies had hyped him beyond belief by the time the fight came around. A lot of people were brainwashed into thinking he'd actually win. Then the fight happens and Lennox smashes him to bits and makes a mockery of the hype machine.

'Enzo is today's version of Michael Grant. He's been created by ITV and their pundits, and the hype ain't justified. He's going to get exposed on the biggest night of his life, and they're paying me nearly a million pounds for the privilege. I honestly don't know why they've taken the fight. Frank Warren must truly believe Enzo has what it takes to beat me. If that's the case, I haven't got a clue how he's managed to be this successful for so long. This is a ridiculous fight for them to take.'

I admit it, I always believed 'Big Mac' Maccarinelli was better than Haye made him out to be. Haye would, of course, have coloured me brainwashed like the rest of them, but I couldn't help but admire the Welshman's tenacity and work ethic. I liked his fast left hook, relentless pace, and his ability to bang the body like very few men of his size could. Enzo was fast, snappy and sharp with his punches, and would often string bundles of shots together with dizzying variety. He was a master of beating up sub-par opposition and doing it in style. Nobody defeated unworthy title challengers better or more conclusively than Maccarinelli. In fact, by the time Haye started telling porkies, Maccarinelli had even started to string together credible wins over the likes of Wayne Braithwaite and Marcelo Dominguez, and appeared ready to make the jump.

Unwilling to entertain the idea of Maccarinelli possibly improving or finding his groove, Haye instead pointed to farcical match-ups against the likes of Bobby Gunn and Mohammad Azzaoui as reasons why the Welsh champion would never amount to anything more than a cynical television product. David would explain how bad habits had set in with Maccarinelli and that his confidence was entirely hollow, brought on from countless one-sided beatings of overmatched punchbags. He would continually tell me how Maccarinelli was a 'master of smoke and mirrors' and that the WBO title-holder didn't possess half the belief he should have done as so-called world champion.

'I know boxing styles,' said Haye. 'I know which fighters present me with problems and which ones I can beat easily. I've always done well against fighters with Maccarinelli's style. He's tall, upright, chinny and likes to punch. He won't box on the back foot and he won't pressure me. He'll be stuck in mid-range trying to box and punch with me. That's going to lead to a painful and early night for him. All I've got to do is turn up sober and on time.'

Haye made it sound so easy. The WBO champion, meanwhile, was less bullish about his chances, but spoke with the confidence of a man who'd reeled off twenty-five straight victories since a sole pro defeat to Lee Swaby in May 2000.

'Come fight night, I'm going to be bringing everything I've got,' stressed Maccarinelli. 'I want to be *the man* at cruiserweight and to do that I have to beat David Haye.

'I'm capable of stepping on the gas from the first round, and that's what I'll be looking to do. People have been saying that Haye is stronger, faster and fitter than me, that he punches harder than me and is the better boxer, but I don't believe that, and on March 8th we will find out. We are both big punchers, but I believe I am the harder hitter. Once I drop Haye, he won't be getting up.'

Given what I'd seen and heard over the years, I often wondered how I'd advise a fighter to go about defeating David Haye. I believed I knew enough of his style, quirks and mannerisms to effectively draw up a game plan and invite a reasonably talented fighter to follow it and gain success. After all, how hard could it be? As gifted as the cruiserweight king was, we all knew he invested heavily in his right hand, kept his left invitingly low, sometimes stuck around on the ropes too long, and had trouble dealing with clusters of short and straight punches up close. Throw one shot his way and Haye would make you look silly, as he'd parry, pivot and punish you for your sins. Work the position and get inside his lengthy reach, however, and Haye was an easier target to hit, especially when committing to more than one punch at a time. Go at him after he's thrown his shots, I'd suggest, and work on the belief he lacked a second wave of attack. The blueprint had been outlined by gutsy pugs like Giacobbe Fragomeni and Lasse Johansen, who both enjoyed sporadic success against Haye in European title fights and, of course, Carl Thompson and Jean-Marc Mormeck in his most high-profile contests to date.

However, Thompson aside, Haye had managed to overcome

periods of uncertainty in each of those bouts to wind up stopping the perpetrator of the problems. He figured them out and displayed new dimensions to his game. He was a developing fighter, and one who'd benefited from the kind of arduous examinations most felt Maccarinelli had lacked in his own career. Pushed harder earlier, Haye assumed he was now the more rounded pro, the one with answers, versatility and the potential to adapt and conquer various styles.

I received the chance to back up my boasts and defeat Haye in February, as I was once again invited to spend two weeks in Northern Cyprus with the fighter and Adam Booth. Now, before anyone gets too excited, it wouldn't be *me* testing Haye's power and progress. Instead, days after arriving at Haye's latest pad in Cyprus, I met up with German cruiserweight Rüdiger May, a towering gentleman, all six feet six inches of stringy arms and liquorice legs, and, unbeknown to him, my avatar with which to sample Haye's punch power.

May was multilingual, intelligent and gracious, and never forgot to say please and thank you at the dinner table. He appeared too gentle and kind to have ever been a boxer, let alone a well-regarded one who'd twice boxed for the European cruiserweight title and also competed for the WBO version of the world title. His dimensions, awkward stance and noodle-thin limbs didn't seem to indicate a lengthy or successful career as a prizefighter, yet it was this wingspan and experience that prompted Haye and Booth to contact the 33-year-old and tempt him out to Cyprus to kickstart sparring ahead of their March date with Maccarinelli. Like the Welshman, May was gangly, upright and eager to work his left hand. He lacked the variety, punch power and work-rate of Maccarinelli, of course, yet May acted as a serviceable substitute.

'I want you to work Rudy's corner this afternoon,' Booth informed me over breakfast on a wet Monday morning. 'Just make sure he has water on hand, and keep a tub of Vaseline nearby. Also, if you see that he isn't offering much, let him know about it. Don't be afraid to tell him what he's doing wrong.'

'What do you want him to do?' I asked.

'Be as much like Maccarinelli as he can,' said Booth. 'I need him to make David work. I don't want Rudy freezing up or becoming hesitant. I need him to throw punches, otherwise he's useless.'

Easy enough, I thought to myself. I simply needed to instruct a boxer to throw punches, surely one of the prerequisites of signing up for the occupation in the first place. From there, Booth then handed me permission to improvise, work my magic, take risks and formulate a game plan to cause Haye problems. I'd finally be able to use my extensive knowledge of Haye's style to plot his downfall, albeit vicariously in sixteen-ounce sparring gloves and headguard. This was my shot, my opportunity to prove that the world cruiserweight champion was indeed human.

An hour later, Haye and May discovered that the champion's Ozankoy-based gym-slash-warehouse was flooded and out of bounds. Northern Cyprus was in the midst of storm season and, though temperatures remained high, grey clouds hovered above and rain showers were a common occurrence all week. Subsequently, the floor of the gymnasium and ring canvas were sodden with rainwater.

Booth returned from an early pitch inspection and proceeded to inform the two cruiserweights that they'd instead have to make best use of the weights gym in the basement of Haye's villa. With no option but to adapt to their surroundings, Haye, Booth and May headed downstairs and set up camp amongst the dumb-bells, benches and floor mats.

Thinking on his feet, Booth created a space on the floor and then marked out a temporary ring with numerous exercise mats. He locked the mats in place with the help of the two fighters and promptly tested them for grip and suction.

'You'll just have to be wary of them slipping out of place,' Booth explained, as he wrapped the boxers' hands. 'If the mat goes, hold back and we'll get it back in place for you.'

The plan was for Booth and me to apply pressure to opposite sides of the 'ring', in the hope of maintaining a complete puzzle and removing the possibility of a mat sliding from under one of the fighters' feet.

Reluctantly, the two cruiserweights made do with their new environment, touched gloves and eased their way into something resembling a spar. To begin with, neither was willing to commit to punches, and sudden and explosive movements were scarce, simply through fear of dislodging a mat and falling down the ensuing crack. May bounced high and low like a jouster on a horse, poking and prodding with his pesky left jab, while Haye slipped and slid away from every hesitant probe that came his way. Haye threw little in the first round, content merely to make May miss and threaten to blast him with counters.

By the time the first round ended, May returned to our makeshift corner, gasping for breath and void of ideas.

'Water,' he said, before blowing his nose on his sleeve. Taking the cue, I tilted a bottle of water his way and poured several sips into his open mouth.

'How am I doing?' asked May.

Now *this* question took me by surprise. While I'd happily assumed my role as water boy and occasional greaser, I hadn't envisaged May actively *seeking* my advice, regardless of what Booth had said over breakfast. I barely knew May, had exchanged only pleasantries up to this point, and wasn't anticipating him requesting my views. Suddenly I felt the weight of responsibility and stuttered hopelessly for an answer.

'Yeah, that was fine,' I said. 'Just stay on top of him and remain active. Keep him going backwards.'

May nodded, as though what I was saying actually made sense, and then banged his gloves together, ready for round two. Through the next three minutes, May, apparently a sponge to throwaway advice, followed my plan to a tee and walked into any number of heavy Haye counterpunches as he blindly attempted to push the action on an expert gunslinger. Sensing May had stepped up the pace, Haye simply ran alongside him, only now exerting more of his own ideas. As mats slipped, and the action stopped, May was eager for any respite he could cling to.

'What do I do now?' asked May, returning to our safe haven, nose swollen and blood dripping from a leaky nostril. He wiped away the red with a white towel and slung it over my right shoulder.

'Try not to throw single shots,' I advised. 'David's just picking you off when you throw singles. If you see an opening, throw both hands and catch him with something. You can't potshot with him. He's too quick. Also, go after him when he's finished throwing his own punches.'

'How am I looking?' asked May.

'You're doing fine,' I said, again lying. I hadn't yet summoned the courage to read the riot act to a gloved-up prizefighter. I knew the possible consequences from such a scenario. Still, it was heartening to watch May follow my instructions to a tee, even if, ultimately, they only furthered his pain and riled his foe.

Just as I'd advised, May was now jutting in and out of range and volleying clusters of punches in the general direction of Haye's head whenever he sensed an opening. A couple of times it worked, and May cornered the champion and asked him a tentative question or two, but, for the most part, Haye expertly read the attacks and mercilessly used May's pseudo-aggression against him. The sheepish German was now getting bashed about, shaken up and hurt, and fell to the floor a couple of times, due either to the power of Haye's punches or to the slippery and unpredictable nature of the floor. Whatever the reason, May was in need of help and, unfortunately for him, had only this author to turn to.

'How was that?' a shattered May asked at the end of the round.

'Not bad,' I fibbed. 'You just have to be wary of overreaching too much and getting caught falling in. David's just waiting for you. Try not to commit to every shot. Touch him and score. Stay busy.'

May nodded again and set out for the final round. He fared no better than before, but no worse either, thank God. I had visions of the German being stretched out unconscious, a result of my bogus words of advice in the corner. It would be the worst start to a trainer's career in the history of basement boxing. All in all, though, through six rounds of sparring, May had stayed alive and done me proud. I wouldn't say he won a single round per se, but he was gutsy and willing throughout and, much to my pleasant surprise, actually seemed to value and carry out the ideas I presented him with.

'Thank you,' he said at the conclusion of the sparring session. 'Do you think I did okay?'

It was sometime during that February afternoon that I finally realised just how difficult a proposition Haye was for May, Maccarinelli and most other cruiserweights in the world. As hard as I tried, and armed with as much as I thought I knew, I was still unable to deliver the kind of advice and tricks May needed to gain any kind of success against the reigning cruiserweight champion. Haye had an answer for everything, and would increase and decrease his tempo depending on what May and I happened to bring to the table. When I got May to press, Haye would step back and cajole him with counters. When I asked for more thought and patience, Haye would rapidly leap into range, bang May upside the head, and immediately instill further doubt into the mind of an already insecure German. He gazumped us at each and every turn, and would smile or nod at me as rounds came to a close, as though signalling he would always have the upper hand.

Perhaps my knowledge was wasted on someone as tentative and limited as May, yet I couldn't help but think Haye would always have a way of checkmating me, irrespective of which fighter I chose as my reluctant pawn. I'd spent six rounds attempting to bring Haye down, but, having failed miserably, now had nothing but respect for his awkwardness and ability to adapt to any possible fighting style or environment. While I believed I'd reached a certain level of expertise through learning and research, Haye was instinctively acting out what he was simply born to do. Try as I might, I'd never be able to catch up. Thankfully, I now wasn't sure Enzo Maccarinelli would, either.

Pools of unwanted water continued to accumulate on the ring canvas that February and, a mere four days into my stay, Haye and Booth decided enough was enough and uprooted sticks to Miami, Florida, where they'd be based for the remainder of their preparations ahead of the champion's 8 March date in London.

In fact, it was while out in South Beach that someone else fared far better in sparring with Haye. Weeks away from the most high-profile fight of his career, the cruiserweight champion foolishly walked into a left hook from heavy-handed Cuban Eliseo Castillo, a wake-up call that forced him to drop to his knees and reconsider his progress.

'I told him not to hook with a hooker, and he did,' recalled Booth. 'Castillo finished the session that day thinking he'd bashed up the latest hype-job from England. Everybody around the gym was calling him "champ" and mocking David.

'After his first session with Castillo, David was determined to get back in there with him and prove a point. He wanted to spar again the next day, which was something we'd normally never do. He was so hungry to make amends, though. In the end we managed to get Castillo back three days later and David sparred him again.'

This time Haye refused to swap hooks or play Castillo's game. Switching the script on the cocksure Cuban, a humbled Haye got on his bike and boxed beautifully for six rounds, landing counterpunches at will and manoeuvring himself out of harm's way.

'I don't think Castillo touched him once in eighteen minutes of sparring,' said Booth. 'David just went out there and boxed him. At the very end of the spar, Castillo stood frozen in the centre of the ring and watched David walk back to the corner, as if to say, "What the fuck did he just do to me?"'

From Northern Cyprus to South Beach, Miami, it was the hardest Haye had ever trained for a fight, a fact emphasised by the champion's overt swagger during fight week. He knew all the answers and impatiently awaited the grand reveal.

'I'm going to weigh in well under the limit,' Haye told me, as we convened at London's Victoria station on the morning of the pre-fight weigh-in. 'I've made the weight so easily for this fight. I've even got pounds to spare. I could just come in on the limit, but I want to really make a point.'

The weigh-in took place inside the O2 Arena and was scheduled for 7 p.m. on the Friday, a time both Haye and Booth were, of course, uneasy with. The pair wanted an earlier weigh-in, the sort which offered Haye time to rehydrate and rise to a more natural state ahead of the fight. Both were well aware Maccarinelli wouldn't have to work hard to hit the cruiserweight limit and could effectively make the 200lb marker at any time. It wasn't an issue for the WBO champion. More than that, though, Booth and Haye simply wanted to remain in a position of power.

Haye performed a trial-run on stage at 4 p.m., and a smile

exchanged between champion and trainer told its own story. Of course, early birds among the media looked on and were left bemused by Haye's ostentatious display of punctuality. Some assumed that arriving three hours early for the weigh-in surely meant he was struggling at the weight, and therefore required a rehearsal before shifting a treadmill into the nearest sauna.

In fact, ten minutes later Haye was flat on his back receiving a massage in a nearby holding room. No sweat jackets, bin liners or saunas in sight. Simply killing time, Haye was all smiles and a picture of utter relaxation. He watched Roy Jones Jr fights on his laptop and cracked jokes about what the reaction would be from the nation's media when he finally stepped on the scales.

'I can't wait to see the look on Enzo's and Warren's faces,' he said.

Haye's moment to shine finally arrived at 7 p.m., when he made his way back on stage and weighed in for real this time. Stepping on to the scales first, he removed his baggy black hoodie and wore only a bandana and boxer shorts. A collective gasp was released by the watching media as Haye stripped down. Not only did his physique come straight from a brochure, but he also carried the radiant glow and look of a fighter who had made the weight with plenty of room to spare. He appeared happy and mischievous on the scales. He didn't resemble the emaciated and weak fighter many had banked on seeing that day.

'David Haye weighs 198lbs,' announced master of ceremonies Mike Goodhall, as journalists made frantic notes on their pads and reconsidered ill-founded predictions. The fighter who was considered dead at the weight had indeed just weighed in 2lbs under the cruiser-weight limit. He even had the audacity to forfeit those extra 2lbs for fun and to issue some kind of statement of intent. Maccarinelli, meanwhile, looking comparatively human and fleshy, not to mention spooked, recorded a weight of 197lbs.

After they had posed and postured, Haye and Maccarinelli engaged in the customary pre-fight stare-down. Arms by their sides, both gazed hard, Haye breaking into a slight smirk, while Maccarinelli remained straight-faced. Surely a sign of inevitable defeat, the Londoner broke from the stare first.

'What does a stare-down actually mean anyway?' pondered Haye in his hotel room afterwards. 'So what if you can stand with someone and look into their eyes without blinking. It's not going to stop you getting brutally knocked out the next day.'

That day arrived on Saturday, 8 March 2008. 'The Battle of Britain' had finally materialised after some six years in the making. The size of the event was not lost on Haye, either. He was clearly even more inspired and aroused by the prospect of a fight than usual. It was The Hayemaker's first appearance on major American television network Showtime and his first opportunity to give the Stateside audience a taste of what he could do. Whereas some fighters fold or freeze under such increased pressure and scrutiny, Haye simply thrived on it.

Perhaps that was the difference at 2.30 a.m., the start time of the fight and one that fell in line with the demands of Showtime's American audience. Haye arrived sober and on time, and made his way to the ring at 2.34 a.m., accompanied once again by the strains of McFadden & Whitehead's 'Ain't No Stoppin' Us Now'. He appeared in no rush to get things started. The insouciant champion smiled, tapped hands with supporters and walked at his own leisurely pace. When he reached the ring he took the time to look around and soak up the atmosphere generated by a 20,000-strong crowd, each one of the tickets having been snapped up within hours of going on general sale.

Following quickly on his heels was Maccarinelli, who wasted no time sprinting out to the Tom Petty tune "I Won't Back Down".

Dressed in a black robe, Enzo flicked the hood over his face and charged the ring. He blanked out the crowd and focused solely on his place of work up ahead. Petty had barely reached the first chorus as Maccarinelli slipped through the ropes and bounced around opposite Haye. The entrances couldn't have been any more contrasting or arresting.

If their attitudes and ring entrances highlighted slight nuances in pre-bout make-up, one figured Haye's and Maccarinelli's fighting styles would at least complement each other. Both were big punchers with vulnerabilities, and both liked to throw hard and early. That much was a given.

Or so we thought. Pre-fight boasts and forecasts often go out the window when the threat of getting knocked out looms, and so it proved for three minutes that March evening. Though both fighters dreamed and spoke of an abrupt finish, they began with a caution and steadiness that belied their bravado. Maccarinelli caught Haye off balance with a left hook in the first thirty seconds, and Haye then returned the compliment with his own left hook midway through the round. Aside from those two nondescript flashpoints, however, the first round consisted of plenty of fakes, shimmies and foreplay, yet little in the way of clean penetration.

This pseudo-warfare evaporated in the second round, though, as both stepped up the pace slightly and Haye, blessed with the marginally quicker hands, started to make his superior range and timing tell. Edging back slightly out of danger, Haye teased Maccarinelli into throwing a shot and then timed his tentative lunges with some of the most vicious counterpunches I'd ever witnessed in a British ring. Performing this trick multiple times, Haye caught Maccarinelli with three flush right hands in the centre of the ring, the sound of each audible to those high up in the bleachers. If the WBO champion had any doubts beforehand, he was now positively petrified by the prospect of exchanging blows with Haye in range. Each and every time he attempted to step forward and probe, Haye would utilise better speed and timing to duck out, increase the gap and then launch a thudding retort. He was able to read and punish every mistake Maccarinelli was about to make.

Regardless of who you backed beforehand, we all knew the finish would be sudden and perhaps void of any prompts or clues. Haye had guaranteed some kind of conclusion in the second round and, as blood began to trickle from a mysterious slice to the side of his left eye, he hit the gas and made good on his promise. One arching right cross in a neutral corner did the damage, as Haye pounced on Maccarinelli's exposed jaw and cracked it on the move. In his futile attempts to stay upright, the panicked Welshman clung to the top rope and inadvertently positioned himself for a follow-up flurry. Then, wasting no time, Haye hurtled towards his opponent and unleashed a barrage of finishing blows. Maccarinelli had nowhere to hide and was emphatically dumped on the ring canvas.

The hurt fighter foolishly rose early, and then threatened to bump into referee Terry O'Connor while touring the perimeter of the ring on unsteady pins. Eyes scrambled and legs tangled up in knots, Maccarinelli was clearly in no position to continue and O'Connor took the wise decision to stop the contest after just two minutes and four seconds of the second round.

As only a fine stream of blood running down his face offered any indication of combat, Haye's cruiserweight encore couldn't have gone any more to plan. He'd demolished his big domestic rival and also shut down the division's second-best cruiserweight in one fell swoop. Better than that, though, he'd done it exactly the way he told me he would.

'What's your next prediction then?' I asked Haye in the changing room afterwards, as he sat draped in the glistening gold of the WBC, WBA and now WBO world cruiserweight belts.

'I'm going to clean up the heavyweight division and become

world heavyweight champion, just like Lennox Lewis,' replied Haye. 'I mean it this time, though.'

Next on the agenda for Haye was marriage, however. He wed Natasha Davis on 6 April at the Malpas hotel in Northern Cyprus and then, three weeks later, the newlyweds welcomed their first child into the world. The boy's name was Cassius. Cassius Haye.

CHAPTER FIFTEEN

THE EXORCIST

It was 2008 and boxing's once famous heavyweight division had shrunk in quality and expanded in waistline. Now a polluted sea of overweight has-beens and never-weres, images of present-day heavyweights were even included in many campaigners' pamphlets as legitimate reasons for the abolition of boxing. The sport of kings had never had it so bad.

Right in the nick of time, and fresh from his victory over domestic rival Enzo Maccarinelli in March, the rampaging David Haye had now stuck to his word and declared all three of his cruiserweight belts vacant. He would take six months off from the sport, monitor the heavyweight scrapheap, and then carefully pluck a suitable fall-guy for a winter slaughter.

In the meantime, Haye, in tandem with trainer Adam Booth, set up his own promotional company, Hayemaker Boxing, and declared his intention to begin promoting his own events, having previously worked for others. Their dual quest for full promotional independence began with a September show in Sheffield and culminated in a tentative November date for Haye's first heavyweight excursion. The so-called saviour was now ideally positioned to plot his own destiny as a heavyweight and select everything from opponent, date and venue to the way in which he slalomed his way to the top of the hopelessly divided division.

As summer ended, Haye was liberated by a new-found freedom and began to get the urge to fight again. He'd enjoyed months of good food, allowed his belt buckle to loosen ever so slightly, and was now beginning to crave human quarry.

So, on one Wednesday evening in August, Haye and I sat in his Clapham apartment and flicked open his laptop, solely with the intention of ridiculing the bloated heavyweight division via the infinitely handy boxing records website boxrec.com. Before that, though, Haye sought encouragement from the achievements of others. The fledgling heavyweight scanned the stats and reminded himself that Roy Jones Jr was only 193lbs the night he defeated John Ruiz, at 226lbs, to lift the WBA world heavyweight title, and how a 208lb Evander Holyfield moved up from cruiserweight to destroy world heavyweight champion James 'Buster' Douglas in October 1990, conceding a staggering 38lbs in the process. It wasn't just weight that captivated Haye, either. He'd also scour the tape for details on fighters' height and reach, as though somehow reassuring himself that one day his heavyweight goal would be obtainable.

'I'm taller and have a longer reach than Holyfield,' he said, eyes locked on the computer screen in front of him. 'My reach is only an inch shorter than Larry Holmes', too, and only two inches shorter than George Foreman's. It's the same as Muhammad Ali's.'

Utilising his own alleged eighty-inch reach, Haye would spend the best part of half an hour cruising through heavyweight records on boxrec.com, shouting in excitement whenever he came across an interesting tape reading or result. It would sound bizarre to imply that a six-foot-three-inch heavyweight suffered from little-man syndrome, but there was certainly the sense that Haye resented being viewed as undersized and unspectacular in this modern era of big-boned and big-boobed juggernauts. He may have come off well in comparison with the heavyweight greats of bygone eras, but Haye knew the modern equivalents were carved from an altogether weightier slab of fighting stock. The mercurial Mr Jones aside, the average height in the heavyweight division circa 2008 hovered around the six-feet-five-inch mark, and most heavyweights felt comfortable at a weight upwards of 230lbs. Pack any less than that and some critics feared for your health.

With fifteen stone and boxrec.com behind us, and a November fight date in the offing, I eventually served up a hit-list of potential heavyweight opponents, in the hope that Haye would volley back his immediate thoughts.

'Hasim Rahman?' I mentioned first, hovering the cursor over the supposed fifth-ranked heavyweight in the world.

'He would be perfect,' said Haye. 'He might not be available for November, though.'

'James Toney?'

'I'd love to fight him. He's a hero of mine. Still very slick, despite being about six stone overweight.'

'Evander Holyfield?'

'Hmm. What do you think?'

'I don't think it'd be too pretty.'

'I'm not *that* bad, am I?'

'John Ruiz?'

'Zzzzzzzz. Ruiz does have a "name", though,' he conceded upon waking up. 'That's *something*, at least.'

'Kali Meehan?'

'The guy Danny Williams sparked in a round?'

'Erm, yeah, moving on . . . How about Andrew Golota?'

'Not bad. Good name. Reckon I'd be able to "do" him quick.'

While undertaking a global tour of fallen heavyweights, Haye appeared distracted and deep in thought, a stance the fighter was rarely ever caught in. He'd answer with a grunt or sigh, caring little about the names tossed his way and unable to fake enthusiasm at the possibility of sharing a ring with the forlorn thirty-somethings on offer. He was searching for something or someone else.

After surfing from America to Eastern Europe, Haye clicked on his own career statistics and began to scroll down the page. He took me on a brief tour of his impressive 21–1 CV and appeared, for the most part, proud of his achievements. Originally interested in the latter half of his career record, Haye eventually made his way closer to the bottom and hovered a reluctant cursor over the name Carl Thompson, date 10 September 2004 and result TKO 5. The only blemish on his otherwise spotless résumé, it seemed Haye had found what he was searching for.

'Forget the heavyweights for a moment,' he said, pulling back from the laptop and resting on his sofa, arms stretched out wide. 'The world champions are going to be tied up for a while anyway.'

'There are still plenty of names,' I pleaded.

'Hear me out,' continued Haye. 'You'll think I'm crazy, but the fight I want right now, more than any other, is Carl Thompson. He'd be my ideal next opponent. I'd do *anything* to make that fight for November.'

Hold it right there. With the lure of many big-name, well-ranked and desperately limited heavyweights lying at Haye's mercy, his ideal fight would be against a retired 44-year-old cruiserweight who hadn't seen a boxing ring for over two and a half years? Moreover, Haye had since vaulted to a position of WBC, WBA and WBO world cruiserweight champion and, though as yet unable to overturn his sole pro loss, had clearly surpassed the overall career achievements of his Bolton nemesis.

'I *need* to avenge that defeat,' Haye continued, emphasising and extending every syllable. 'No matter what else I achieve in my career, that loss to Thompson will always annoy me. It pains me to look at, and I know it will always show up on my record. There will always be unanswered questions.

'Guys like Lennox Lewis and Muhammad Ali cleaned up their records by avenging defeats. They closed the book. I want the opportunity to do the same. Unless I beat Thompson, there will always be people wondering whether it was just a blip or if he truly has my number. I'm *the man* at cruiser because I beat *the man*. Carl Thompson beat *me*, though. Does that make him the real linear champion? Does that make him *the man*?'

Haye let out a heavy sigh, as though appreciating his dream fight had little chance of ever coming to fruition.

'That revenge factor will always get people talking,' he added. 'Thompson hasn't lost since he fought me, either. His win over me was no fluke. It wasn't a one-shot thing. He knew exactly what he was doing in there. I've learnt from that defeat, no doubt, but he was definitely the better man on the night. Even in a rematch, I wouldn't be stupid enough to expect an easy fight. I know that I'd have to be at my absolute best to beat him.'

With that, Haye closed down boxrec.com and shut his laptop, metaphorically slamming the door on any chances of the Thompson bout happening.

Twenty-four hours later, I reopened the door and a forty-four-year-old Carl Thompson answered his phone.

'I wish the rematch had happened a year or so ago when they originally came to me about it,' said the former champion. 'Now David's pretty much missed the boat. I've been out too long and the body's creaking a bit. Don't get me wrong, I *could* still do it. I will always believe I have David Haye's number. I just have other things to think about now. Other responsibilities.

'I always wanted to prove to people that I could beat Haye a second time. If we were to fight now I don't think David would get any credit even if he did beat me. I think he *should* get the credit, 'cos I'm a fantastic fighter, but I don't think people would give him it.'

I could tell Thompson's refusal to entertain the idea of meeting his rival again pained him as much as the response would later hurt Haye. He wanted to do it and, perhaps financially, *needed* to do it, but Carl had now finally come to the realisation that he was simply unable to. The warrior spoke like an old man that afternoon, one who'd reluctantly learnt to accept his new role in the world.

'I get the urge [to box], but I quickly try and put it behind me,' he said. 'When I hear people say nobody can take David Haye's power it gets me going a little bit, but, other than that, I'm usually okay. I just don't want my win over him being swept under the carpet, that's all.'

Four years and three world titles later, Thompson was still unsure just how much Haye had improved. I sensed Carl believed he'd always possess The Hayemaker's kryptonite, regardless of what our mutual acquaintance might go on to achieve.

'I can't say how much he's improved, because David still hasn't boxed anyone like me,' said Thompson. 'Nobody has brought the fight to David like I did. We all know he can punch hard and can knock men out who are there to be knocked out. I'll always be his worst nightmare, though.'

I was desperate for Thompson to succeed, in whatever he eventually chose to do. As much as I could sense Haye's torment when discussing a potential rematch, I never wanted to see Thompson return, especially now that Father Time had got the better of Peter Pan. The former champion was too far gone, too inactive and no longer relevant to anybody but Haye and his selfish desire to tidy up his record.

I knew I'd have no reason to contact Thompson again beyond

that day, as the doleful fighter attempted to drag himself away from boxing and focus on less punishing ways of making a living. Like a reformed junkie checking out of rehab, Thompson needed all the help he could get, and had to eradicate all those around him who might inadvertently stir up old desires.

As a parting gift, I allowed Thompson one final moment to relive his career-defining victory over Haye. Nearly four years had passed since that emotional night in Wembley, and Thompson seemed truly grateful for the chance to raid his fading memory banks and feel relevant one final time.

'I think David really underestimated me,' remembered Carl. 'David listened to a lot of people who said I was just a chinny old man, but they didn't really know my background or where I come from. I was never going to just cave in if he hit me hard a few times. I was too old and too wise for that. I'd never done it before in my career, so why should David Haye be any different? If you want to beat me, you've got to finish me off. If I've got even the tiniest chance of coming back, I'll take it.'

With that in mind, Carl Thompson had now clearly retired for good. If he'd sensed any possible route back, the brave gladiator would no doubt have grasped it with both hands.

A fan of Thompson from the age of ten, Haye knew the way the fighter operated and, from that moment on, gave up ever attempting to lure his conqueror into a potential rematch. The book was closed and Haye, clearly regretful, had to erase an old enemy from his memory, in the very same way Thompson would gradually start to release boxing and all its highs from his. It was a mutual process of letting go, and both men had to forget in order to move forward, Thompson into reluctant retirement and Haye into the gaping heavyweight division.

PART FIVE

David Haye waves goodbye to the cruiserweight division and beefs up in northern Cyprus for an assault on the desolate heavyweight landscape.

CHAPTER SIXTEEN
THE ART OF WAR (LYING)

I take no great pleasure or pride in saying this, but I set up American heavyweight Monte Barrett for an almighty fall in 2008. Not once, but approximately six times.

Let me explain. Having seen proposed dates with former world heavyweight champion Hasim Rahman and unbeaten nobody J.D. Chapman fall by the wayside, division newcomer David Haye was left without an opponent merely six weeks out from a scheduled 15 November date at London's O2 Arena. Along with manager Adam Booth, the former world cruiserweight champion searched high and low for someone to fill the void, before eventually listening to the advice of a 22-year-old writer from Aldershot.

'Who did you like?' asked Booth over the phone, with pressure quickly mounting.

'I've always wanted Monte Barrett,' went my suggestion.

'I've got a number for his manager, Lou DiBella, and that fight can probably get made,' said Booth. 'What are your thoughts on him?'

'Barrett's ideal, because he's got a decent name, he's fought on major network television in the States, and he's coming off a first-round knockout win,' I said. 'I also think that, at thirty-seven years of age, his legs have gone and he's on the downward spiral. The timing could be perfect.'

'Okay,' said Booth, brain working overtime, and with little time to spare. 'Can you get some tapes of Barrett to me pronto? I'm going to talk to DiBella right now.'

So off Booth went to speak to Brooklyn promoter DiBella, while I collected footage of the Greenville heavyweight known as 'Two Gunz'. I'd managed to locate his fights with Hasim Rahman, Dominick Guinn and Owen Beck, and then my phone buzzed, informing me a message had arrived in my inbox. The text message was sent by Booth and read: 'Barrett will do it for $250,000. I'm calling it "One Hayemaker vs. Two Gunz".'

So there it was. In desperate times, Booth and Haye had allowed me to effectively plot my first ever boxing match. Feeling a sudden pressure on my slight shoulders, I frantically rewound the Barrett videos I'd collected, in a panicked attempt to ease my mind. Had I gone crazy and assumed Barrett was worse than he actually was? Had I set David up for the biggest disaster of his career? All these kinds of thoughts swim around one's mind when they've confidently applied the seal of approval to a prizefight.

As if now second-guessing my decision, I decided to track Barrett down and get in contact with the fighter, hoping the sound of his dispirited and demoralised tones would somehow put my cluttered mind to rest. I wanted to hear the New Yorker sound old, tired and nervous, like a man who'd only accepted the bout for a quick buck on his way to retirement.

I was wrong. Not only did Barrett still carry the looks of a man in his twenties, he also spoke with the lip of one, too, and boyishly detailed the kind of lofty dreams and ambitions that most fighters had reluctantly hidden away in a time capsule by the time they reached thirty-seven.

'David Haye's made a big mistake moving up to heavyweight to fight a guy like me,' spat Barrett. 'He's skating on thin ice and is going to get hurt pretty bad. I'm actually going to do him a favour and knock him out early. That way he'll then be able to move back down to cruiserweight and get his titles back.

'David's a pretty boy, a model, a trash-talker and an actor. He's not a boxer, though. He's not a fighter. I've been fighting for free all my life. It's not that he chose it like that, either. We are what we are. I'm a natural fighter and he's not. He has a whole gimmick – endorsements, advertisements, his own cologne and the look. I give it to him. He's real pretty. Remember David Telesco? They look like twin brothers.'

'I suppose you're going to "Roy Jones" him then?' I asked, referring to Roy's landslide win over Telesco in 2000.

'Wow, you're sharp,' replied Barrett. 'That's *exactly* how it's going to go down. It's like you read my mind.'

We rallied back and forth like this for the best part of an hour, me probing Barrett for weaknesses and the fighter throwing back enthusiastic curveballs in response. Barrett was experienced, angry and armed with tales to tell. Just how I liked them.

'Even though I'm thirty-seven, I take real good care of myself and am in a good place right now,' continued Barrett. 'One day an old man came up to me and said, "Son, life is more than one day." I wrote that saying down and have been carrying it with me ever since. Sometimes you get so caught up in the stresses of one day that you lose sight of everything else. So, I said, okay, let's think about my future and let me start presenting myself the way I want to be seen. Let me fall back in love with this game. Let me take it to the next level. Don't worry about what could and should happen, let's deal with the here and now. That's when I started getting my shit together.'

Just as Barrett was getting his shit together, I was in the process of losing mine. Upon putting the phone down with Barrett, following an hour-long heart-to-heart, I instantly rang Haye, as if to re-address the power balance.

'Give Barrett another call tomorrow and say you've got some more questions you didn't get round to asking,' said Haye, keen to take advantage of my latest budding writer–fighter relationship. 'If he picks up, you then start complimenting him, praising him, and come across as if you're on his side. You could talk about how everybody is doubting my chin and my move up to heavyweight, and talk about how I'm just a jumped-up cruiserweight and haven't really grown into the division yet. Just really lay it on thick.'

'Why would I do that, though?' I asked.

'To fuck with his head. Once you've got him where we want him, we'll be in a position to feed him *anything* we want. Guys that talk as much as Barrett does usually do so in order to cover something up or seal over the cracks.'

Still unsure of Haye's motives, I nevertheless made the follow-up call to Barrett the next day and swiftly apologised for bugging him again so soon. 'Nah, man, that's fine,' said 'Two Gunz', the type who always appreciated a platform on which to speak.

'So,' I pondered, 'do you feel David is underestimating just how difficult it will be moving from cruiserweight to heavyweight, seeing as he's been down numerous times in the past from punches thrown by small cruiserweights?'

Aiming straight for the jugular, one might say, I'd thrown the hardest pitch yet. However, Barrett, if anything, suddenly seemed supportive of Haye, as though united by their shared pursuit of the same goal.

'I don't think he's underestimated it,' said the American. 'I think he's a very smart fighter and I respect him for trying to step up. He knows it's going to be a hard test. He's not fighting someone who is 250lbs and static like a robot. He's fighting someone who is fluid, faster than him and hits harder than him.'

'Exactly,' I said. 'A lot of people in England are calling it a crazy fight for Haye to take, given his vulnerabilities as a cruiserweight and your punch power as a heavyweight. How do you feel about that?'

'Love him or hate him, you've got to respect him,' said Barrett. 'I'm grateful for the opportunity. I'll thank him now and knock him out later. To be honest, this fight is not even about me being the biggest puncher he's ever faced. I'm the best fighter David Haye has ever fought, period. He has zero chance of beating me. If David Haye beats me, I'm retiring from boxing.'

'Given the big names and big punchers you've fought in the past, surely you must not hold any fear against a jumped-up cruiser-weight like Haye?'

'Absolutely. I've been in there with the best of them, man. Some I fell short with, but others I beat. I'm a throwback fighter. I'll fight anyone and everyone. I don't duck no man. Someone like David Haye has never had heavy hands laid on him before, and I'm going to be the man to do that. I'm going to be his preacher for a minute.'

'So, going into this fight, which David Haye videos will you be watching? Presumably not his loss to Carl Thompson, his struggle with Lolenga Mock or some of the other fights where he's been knocked down and put in trouble . . .'

'Listen, I'm a big David Haye fan,' said Barrett, perhaps finally sensing I was no longer on the campaign trail. 'The man's given me an opportunity to make some money and knock him out. He's given me an opportunity to get to the next level and fight for the world heavyweight title.

'I've been on his MySpace page, his YouTube channel and I've been reading all the articles about him. This is like a nine-to-five job for me. When you go to the office you've got to take your shit seriously. Some people hate their jobs, but I happen to love mine. This is what I do. I'm in the hurt business.'

In order to help Barrett with his research, Haye suggested an idea the following day.

'We need him watching fights of me at my worst,' he said, once I'd relayed my latest conversation with Barrett. 'He needs to see me against Carl Thompson, Lolenga Mock and Jean-Marc Mormeck. I want him to see me getting knocked down, cut and hurt. Do you have those fights on DVD?'

'Yeah, I've got them,' I said.

'Good,' replied Haye. 'We need to knock up a DVD of the fights we *want* him to watch, rather than the ones he *needs* to be watching. Leave out all my best performances, and just give him the dodgy ones. He won't be able to watch these fights any other way, as they weren't shown on American television and they're not on YouTube. Now that you have his trust, this is our chance to give him what we want him to see.'

A jet-lagged Barrett arrived in London the following week as part of his promotional obligations ahead of the fight. He participated in a press conference with Haye at No. 5 Cavendish Square and would endear himself to the British media the way he'd done with me days before. I'd also meet the fighter for the first time that after-noon, a moment which presented me with the ideal chance to hand over our homemade DVD.

'That's so kind of you,' said Barrett, as I passed him a brown envelope containing a disc of Haye's fights with Thompson, Mormeck, Mock, Giacobbe Fragomeni and Ismail Abdoul. To all intents and purposes a severed head disguised as a football, the enemy wouldn't get much joy from unwrapping the package and certainly didn't stand to receive the kind of insight he was no doubt hoping for.

While the crucial handover was scarily simple, the ensuing conver-sations weren't. We first met backstage in one of the hotel's lounges, and Barrett embraced me with a hug of warmth and trust while I squirmed uncomfortably. As well as massaging Barrett's ego over the phone, I'd also helped him secure an upgrade on airline tickets for his trip to England as part of another ingenious Haye ploy. Subsequently, Barrett was full of love rather than scepticism as I joined him, his girlfriend Tasha and veteran fight manager Stan Hoffman in their green room ahead of the midday press conference. I felt dirty.

'Man, you're like a Hollywood star,' said Barrett, all bowling-ball shoulders and heavyweight presence, upon finally meeting me. 'You look like Matt Damon or somebody.'

Now, at this point, I wasn't sure whether the fighter was commenting on my appearance or was instead alluding to my uncanny ability to play a less than Oscar-worthy part in this emerging melodrama. Whatever the subplot, Barrett was as cordial and engaging as I'd imagined him to be. He sat me down alongside him and his close-knit team, offered me a fruit drink and then thanked me for bumping his girlfriend and manager up to business class.

'It was no problem,' I said. 'Anything else I can do to help, just let me know. I've been a big fan of yours for a while now, and know you should be treated with respect. Some people don't know what you've achieved in the sport, but I do.'

'You've been great with us already,' said Barrett. 'If there's anything *you* need – interviews, quotes, whatever – in the next few weeks, don't hesitate to call. I'm going to be in training camp for a while, so won't be easy to get hold of, but I'll make time for you. You can call me whenever. I'll get my trainer to give you the camp number and you can use that. My cell phone will be off most of the time.'

We shook hands and I watched Barrett's girlfriend slip the brown envelope inside her handbag as her boyfriend was called to attend the press conference. As expected, 'Two Gunz' spoke lucidly and humorously that afternoon, and was quick to get many of the British media on his side. 'David is ten years my junior and my girlfriend is ten years my junior, too, but the difference between her and David is she likes it when I spank her ass,' went one of many lines an on-form Barrett fed to his defenceless microphone.

An upstaged Haye appeared uncharacteristically quiet throughout the press conference, only occasionally reacting to Barrett's barbs and unable to compete with the New Yorker's vocal gymnastics. Haye's reserved stance may have been the result of knowing he already had Barrett where he wanted him, as opposed to any sudden shyness, of course. He'd also consciously decided to wear a thin, skin-tight shirt that afternoon, in order to feed the perception of him being an undersized heavyweight. Haye wanted Barrett to see a small and meek opponent, someone who'd now suddenly come to realise what he was about to face. He deliberately talked up Barrett's chances, complimented the American's longevity, toughness and physical shape, and doubted his own ability to win the fight. Haye spoke like a fighter shrouded in self-doubt and insecurity, and he hoped Barrett would come to the same conclusion upon returning to New York the following day.

'Did you give him the videos?' Haye asked me as the press conference wrapped up.

'Yes,' I replied. 'He's got them.'

'Job done then,' whispered the instigator, before being summoned to a one-on-one interview with a national newspaper journalist.

The plan was now clearly working and, with me acting as accidental middleman, Haye was able to manipulate the thoughts of the heavyweight contender he'd face in the ring in a matter of weeks. The Englishman sacrificed the big vocal performances he so loved, and was now content to defeat Barrett on the sly, slowly interrogating his mind from afar. Little did he know, but Barrett was now fielding indirect questions and tidbits from Haye, deviously fed through the funnel of my innocent-sounding voice. I protested my unwillingness to participate and spy on more than one occasion, but Haye was adamant such mind games were well within the rules and that, had Barrett been as street-smart as he claimed to be, he'd have been doing the exact same thing.

The interrogation began gently to start with, but, as days and weeks passed, Haye's interest in Barrett's physical and mental condition verged on obsessive. He'd phone me most days, eager to discover whether I'd spoken to Barrett recently and, if so, what kind of poison I'd been slipping him.

'Maybe you could tell him you went and watched me train at the weekend and weren't that impressed with what you saw,' said Haye, days after Barrett had flown back to New York. 'You can say we held a press workout at the gym on Saturday and all the journalists that attended had the same concerns as you. I turned up late to the session, seemed overweight and disinterested, and got knocked down by a right hand in sparring.'

'He'd never believe that,' I responded, keen to swerve any responsibility.

'Why wouldn't he? If you say it happened, what reason does he have *not* to believe it? Have you told him you know me personally?'

'No. I just went with the neutral journalist line you told me to stick to.'

'Good. We should be fine then. Just give him a call and work your way round to the subject of me sparring and getting put down. Tell him I didn't seem to be taking the fight seriously and that I looked worse than you'd ever seen me.'

It wasn't so much the fib that flustered me, but more the route I'd have to take in order to finally unleash it, all the while avoiding any suspicion on Barrett's part. I couldn't just jump in with both feet and cast aspersions on Haye's training camp, as Barrett would have either twigged I was playing games or finally questioned what my beef with his opponent was.

I'd also grown fond of Barrett by this stage, a feeling only solidified when I was given the chance to meet the man in London. He seemed extremely trusting of me, despite not really knowing who I was or what I wanted. The idea of duping him didn't sit right, and I delayed and mulled over each and every strategy Haye had lined up for his opponent.

If he'd been able to pick up the phone and execute the mission himself, I've no doubt Haye would have bypassed using me in the first place. Unfortunately, though, he required my trembling voice and perceived neutral stance as a way of breaking down Barrett's barriers and infiltrating his mind.

'Damn, he really got put down?' said a shocked Barrett, as I finally recalled what had never happened.

'Yeah,' I sighed. 'It was a right hand from Zuri Lawrence.'

'Man, Zuri is *nothing*,' replied Barrett. 'I've sparred that cat countless times over the years. He can't punch his way out of a paper bag. He's ain't got shit on his shots.'

'It doesn't take much to put Haye over,' I added. 'Lawrence isn't the first guy to do it, in the gym or in the ring.'

'I guess it's true what they say about his chin then. This guy thinks he's going to hang with me? Damn, he's crazier than I thought. If Zuri is putting his ass on the ground, the dude's got no chance with me. I can assure you that.'

Not content with his latest fantasy, Haye sought to go one step further two days later, as he phoned me with news of a potential cancellation.

'Let's tell Barrett I'm having second thoughts about the fight,' said Haye. 'He already knows about a rematch clause in the contract, so maybe we can use that as a sign of my fear. You can say you spoke to me about the fight and that I said it was a fight that seemed stupid to take unless a title was on the line. Make out that I'm looking beyond this fight and that I've got one of the champions lined up for early next year. You need to make it seem like I'm about to cancel the fight and push ahead with a different one next year. Get him *really* on edge.'

This bout with Haye was a major source of income for the New Yorker and I wasn't overly ecstatic about the thought of playing with his emotions like that. With a family to support, Barrett needed the money from the fight and required the kind of assurances that simply didn't exist in the sport from which he made his living. What made this latest twist a little easier, however, was the fact that Barrett was now actively chasing *me* for information, help and money. He claimed he was owed $10,000 in expenses, required to cover his training camp, and seemed to partly hold me accountable should it fail to turn up, despite the fact I had no professional affiliation with the event's promoter. Ultimately, I was probably the only Englishman happy to give the brooding boxer the time of day.

'I'm getting nothing new from Adam or David,' I said over the phone one evening. 'Those guys aren't even contactable any more. It seems like they're having second thoughts about something.'

'What do you mean?' asked Barrett.

'They just don't seem as keen on the fight as they first were. David hasn't been training much lately and Adam has gone missing altogether. I tried talking to them about the expenses situation and they just blanked me, like it wouldn't be necessary. I know they've been talking to the Klitschko brothers about doing something next year . . .'

'Motherfuckers,' barked Barrett. 'I knew they'd screw me over like this. Let me tell you, that bitch better turn up to get his ass kicked. That's all I'm saying.'

Barrett then drip-fed my message to his trainer Jimmy Glenn, the man charged with overseeing the fighter's camp. Through the phone I heard the pair cussing in anger and disbelief. I wanted to hang up, run and confess my sins. The two of them were isolated in a self-funded training camp, and both were now embroiled in the uncertainty of whether the fight they were training for was ever going to happen.

I did my utmost to avoid both Haye and Barrett during the final days before the fight, as I no longer wanted to play the third man in their sordid game. Strangely, though, it seemed the more I lied to him, the more Barrett sought my advice, help and contact, and would often ring or email me with a fresh demand or complaint. He wanted further flight upgrades and better hotel rooms for when he travelled to England during fight week, and was also still relying on me to somehow track down his expenses. He was, in essence, now using me the same way I'd used him.

By the time the fight neared, I had grown exhausted with both Barrett's demands and Haye's Machiavellian posturing, and simply wanted to see them settle the dispute inside the ring. My initial appreciation of Barrett had now turned into a mere tolerance, while Haye disgusted and amazed me in equal measure. I refused to condone his mind-control tactics on a moral level, but could not deny the sheer ingenuity and excitement of it all, either. He'd smashed down the fourth wall and, by using me as the undercover go-between, had set up a telescope and bag of popcorn and was peering directly at the innermost thoughts of his next foe.

The day after the pair's initial London press conference, Haye led me into Waterstone's bookshop on Oxford Street and bought me Sun Tzu's *Art of War*. Although I'd heard of the book before, I'd never thought to read anything from it. Insisting he'd discovered everything he knew from the book, Haye advised me to catch up.

The heavyweight pair's second press conference, held two days before the fight, followed a similar pattern to the first. Haye sat back, unusually reserved and quiet, while the emotional Barrett spilled his heart into the notebooks and dictaphones of the grateful British media. Once again, Haye was content to let his opposite number drown himself in his own bullshit, ego and uncertainty, confident the psychological incision and subsequent damage had already been done.

If Haye required an indication that his plan had worked, Barrett's uncharacteristic outburst on the Thursday offered a unique insight into the New Yorker's turbulent state of mind. Reading from a laundry list of complaints, Barrett stood at the podium and moaned about *everything*, from his treatment in the build-up and lack of expenses to his 'shitty' hotel room and minuscule bed. Describing his temporary place of residence as 'one of those places you take your mistress to, so your wife don't find out', Barrett felt Haye had deliberately kept him in squalor to take his eye off the prize.

'He talks about coming from the streets and being this tough guy, and yet he's complaining about a hotel room,' said Haye. 'I'll give him a nice place to sleep on Saturday night.'

'They'll have to take you home in a body bag,' screeched Barrett in response. 'You wanted a rematch clause, but you ain't going to be in no fit state to have no rematch once I've finished with you. You ain't got nothing. Even Zuri dropped your ass in sparring. I've sparred Zuri before and he ain't shit. I'm retiring your ass permanently.'

Once again, Haye was unwilling to match either the speed of Barrett's tongue or the viciousness of the sentiments. Infuriated by petty games, Barrett was in kill-'em-all mode and took no prisoners. It soon became clear that we were either witnessing a fighter using the ills of the world to motivate himself or, perhaps more likely, Barrett was slowly unravelling before our very eyes. Gone was the street-smart persona he'd brought to the first press conference in London six weeks ago. Barrett was now an edgy, erratic and volatile character, and one that seemed to have an opinion on everything but the fight itself.

'I don't think he fancies the fight at all,' said Haye in his hotel room following Friday's weigh-in, where he scaled 215lbs (15st 5lbs) to Barrett's 226lbs (16st 2lbs). 'I really think we got to him. His mind is fucked right now, and he doesn't know whether he's coming or going. All that stuff we did in the build-up is paying off, mark my words.'

Far from beaming with pride, I couldn't help but feel some sympathy for Barrett, especially when I caught up with the down-trodden American fighter for a second time at Friday's weigh-in. Approaching me through a crowd of spectators, Barrett was just as welcoming as he had been when we first met, despite recent traumas and his brewing dislike for anyone associated with the upcoming event.

'Man, I tried looking for you yesterday at the press conference,' Barrett said. 'You've been one of the only guys from England that has shown me any love and support. I appreciate that massively. If I'd have seen you at the press conference, I would have pointed that out.'

I wanted to hug Barrett, apologise for my treachery, and then wish him a happy retirement. My mind was as frazzled as his by this point, torn between admiring and supporting the brash New Yorker and, at the same time, hoping he'd be stretched horizon-tally across the ring canvas the following day by the fists of my favourite boxer.

As Barrett finished with me and passed through the crowded room, I saw him apologise and warmly embrace Adam Booth, the promoter accused of so much the previous afternoon. In the space of merely twenty-four hours, Barrett's demeanour had changed from that of a suicidal on a roof ledge to that of a hippy at Woodstock. Moreover, by the time the fight came around, Barrett wasn't sure whether to be surly, happy, intense, passive, angry or simply relieved to have been given the opportunity and pay-day.

He no longer had control of his own head or emotions. Meanwhile, Haye, the master of mind control, sat contentedly in an adjacent changing room with Barrett's brain in his lap.

A boxer nervously hurdling the top rope, clipping his foot and then tumbling head-first onto the ring canvas is usually a fair indication of an emotionally and physically imbalanced human being. Agreed? Well, on Saturday, 15 November at a quarter past ten in the evening, Monte Barrett was *that* guy en route to facing David Haye at London's O2 Arena. Storming down the runway like the groom at a shotgun wedding, Barrett cleared a path with his arms, signalled his intent, and then proceeded to try and vault the top rope. Somewhere along the way, 'Two Gunz' misjudged his angles and ended up snagging the rope, tripping himself up and disrupting the planned chain of events. The head-over-heels impersonation of Charlie Chaplin triggered rapturous laughter and cheers from the 10,000 spectators, and the macho American could only bounce around in an awkward attempt to shake off the humiliation.

Back in the tunnel, opponent Haye was made aware of Barrett's crash landing via the laughter emanating from the stands and, though he never contemplated following his opponent's lead, was now sold on taking it easy. In stark contrast to Barrett, and now something of a trademark entrance, Haye swaggered and swayed his way to the ring with all the saccharine of a matinee idol. Without a care in the world, and with no intention of hurdling the top rope, Haye soaked up the atmosphere in a scene replicating his March massacre of Maccarinelli, once again backed by the chorus of McFadden & Whitehead's 'Ain't No Stoppin' Us Now'.

Former world heavyweight champion Frank Bruno stood and danced beside me at ringside that night, and the combination of his bellowing voice and lunch-box fists only further hammered home the sights and sounds of the natural heavyweight, something

I feared Haye would never be labelled as. Thankfully, Big Frank was on his fellow Londoner's side that evening, and yelped instructions his way until his voice grew hoarse. It's amazing how comforting the words of a former world heavyweight champion can be in such a tense situation.

'It's going to be all right, mate,' Bruno would inform me as the action got underway. 'David's got this. Don't worry about it, mate. He's going to take him out soon.'

I placed all my faith in Bruno's heavyweight hands, and we both sat and nervously watched as Barrett's size became inconsequential as the bout progressed. Haye, slimmer and sleeker at 215lbs, used ring savvy, speed and athleticism to keep 'Two Gunz' guessing and steal positions from which to launch blistering attacks.

Barrett tried closing the distance and bullying Haye with clubbing blows and agricultural clinch-work, while the smaller man pot-shotted the veteran whenever he overcommitted. Barrett was heavy-handed and dangerous, but also skittish and fragile. When given a target to aim at, Haye was as devastating as any puncher in the world, and, unfortunately for the American, he offered plenty of meat to feast upon.

Barrett went down off a swift left hook in the third round, and then, twenty seconds later, Haye scored the second knockdown of the fight, brought about via a cuffing right hand to the side of Monte's head. The New Yorker stumbled forward onto his knees and took a deep breath.

A third knockdown then followed in the fourth round, as Haye made Barrett miss, poked him with a left hook and spun out. Off balance, Barrett again dropped to the floor, though insisted he slipped this time around.

If the third knockdown was debatable, the fourth most certainly wasn't. With twenty seconds to go in the round, Barrett lurched forward and flurried his hands with no direction, only to walk lazily into a gorgeous Haye right uppercut. The shot sliced through Monte's non-existent guard and pierced the heavyweight's chin. Seemingly unconscious for a split second, Barrett dropped to the floor and snapped out of it. Now he *was* hurt. These were no longer glancing blows or slips. Dragging himself up at the count of nine, Barrett managed to just about survive the round on unsteady stilts as Haye went in for the kill.

Out of time in the previous round, Haye had only one thing on his mind as he entered the fifth session. Hell-bent on finishing proceedings as quickly as possible, he came out swinging – some landing, some missing – and nearly walked into trouble. Shooting wide with a right hand and left hook, Haye squared up and was caught, almost pushed to the floor, by a sturdy Barrett forearm. As the home favourite fell back onto the ring canvas, Barrett mercilessly followed up with a vicious punch on his grounded foe, and referee Richie Davies was given no alternative but to dock a point for the illegal blow.

A little shaken by it all, Haye took a momentary time-out before recommencing his destruction of the flagging foreigner. It took him only twenty seconds of the restart to finish matters. A hard left hook, followed by an even harder right hand, sent Barrett's head spinning, before Haye closed the show with a final hook. Barrett fell heavily and with no intention of rising again. He'd finally been silenced.

With Haye announced the victor, I felt I owed it to the beaten Barrett to first check in with him before joining the shindig in the dressing room around the corner. While the sounds of celebration trickled through the walls, Barrett played reluctant host to a far more sombre and downbeat gathering.

I awaited permission to enter, and the beaten fighter waved me inside as trainer Jimmy Glenn, manager Greg Leon and girlfriend

Tasha stood around despondently against the walls. Surprisingly the cheeriest of the lot, Barrett was sitting on a stool in the centre of the room, naked save for a pair of jeans, his head tilted towards the floor, face slightly marked up, but still reasonably chipper given what had just happened.

'I'm cool, man, don't worry about it,' said Barrett, as I commiserated with him. 'You win some, you lose some. I'm a warrior. I'll be back.'

'You've got no reason to be disappointed with the way you fought, Monte,' I said.

'I don't know, I just didn't feel great in there,' admitted Barrett. 'I'm not making any excuses, though. The better man won on the night, I guess.

'It was a dirty fight and he did some dirty stuff. I did some dirty stuff, too. I got penalised. We were both holding and the ref was telling me off for holding. Haye didn't get no warning. What are you going to do? You've got to give and take in this game. It's a fight. He knocked me down with a head butt, and I kind of felt the referee was fighting against me the whole fight. He should have counted Haye in the fifth round and then he should have come across and taken a point from me. I thought it was a proper knockdown. He hit me on the back of the head and also hit me when I was down. It is what it is.'

Count to ten and breathe, Monte. So much for no excuses, I thought to myself. Still, I was happy to allow Barrett the chance to reel them off, as I understood the need for some fighters to designate a reason for each and every setback. The realisation that they weren't as all-conquering as they said they were was often enough to drive weaker-minded individuals towards a new profession. Barrett knew the truth that night, but still needed some form of concealer to temporarily hide the blemish and enable him to continue with his day.

I'd later get round to spending some one-on-one time with Haye, and found a fighter not wanting to forget, but simply to remember.

'How many times did he knock me down?' asked David, as he wiped the sweat from his brow with a white towel in his changing room.

'What do you mean?' I replied. 'You went down once from an illegal shot, and then he hit you while you were down.'

'I thought I went down more than that. It felt like I got knocked down properly at least twice. What round did I stop him in?'

'The fifth. Are you pulling my leg?'

'No, I honestly don't remember. It only seemed like the second or third round. How many times did I knock him down?'

'Five times.'

'Five? That's more than I thought. Shit, he must have hit me with something big. I can't remember a damn thing.'

At that moment I realised why I'd sided with Haye over Barrett, and now felt no guilt whatsoever in the conniving role I'd played in the American's multiple falls. While the New Yorker disguised true emotions with complaints and excuses, Haye was candid and confused, a fighter speaking from the heart rather than the head. There was no cover-up from the younger man, despite the fact his post-fight comments ranged from the bewildering to the disturbing.

Slightly concussed from the illegal blow he'd received in the fifth round, Haye never attempted to shield his feelings or paper over the cracks in his memory. He was, as always, an open book, even when at his most vulnerable and forgetful. I realised there and then that Haye's delusion would be temporary and Barrett's everlasting.

CHAPTER SEVENTEEN
BITTEN

Boxing is the most confrontational sport of them all and yet I've always hated the idea of confrontation. And so it was on a Saturday afternoon in April 2008 that the confrontational David Haye spotted someone up in the distance and made a purposeful dart towards them. The mysterious figure towered above everyone, but was in the process of escaping up a flight of stairs en route to a press conference. He was snappily dressed in a suit, surrounded by minders and associates, and smiled jovially at passers-by as he negotiated the steps. Like me, this man also happened to hate confrontation.

'Wladimir,' shouted Haye, scruffily kitted out in a red hooded top, as he sprinted up the stairs. 'Knock them two bums on the head and we're going to get it on.'

'Mr Haye,' replied WBO, IBF and IBO world heavyweight champion Wladimir Klitschko, like some long-lost Bond villain.

'Yeah, yeah, Mr Haye,' sighed the hunter, shrugging off the Ukrainian's pleasantries.

'In person. How are you this morning?

'I'm perfect. Are you going to fight these two bums, or are you going to fight me?' asked Haye, referring to Klitschko's impending mandatory title defences against American southpaw Tony Thompson and former Russian amateur star Alexander Povetkin.

'First of all, what do you weigh?'

'Two-twenty.'

'Is that good enough for you?'

'That's perfect. I'd beat you at 200lbs.'

'Remember, talk is cheap. You have to deliver this service in the ring.'

'That's exactly what I'm going to do. That's why I want you now.'

'Get in the ring and do your job.'

'I don't want you to get beaten by those two bums. I've done my job, I'm the undisputed champion. Where are all *your* titles? I'm the undisputed number one. Do you want to fight a number one fighter?'

'In the heavyweight division, you are nobody.'

'No, I'm the main man. The last time an undisputed champion went up to heavyweight, what did he do? He won the title. Evander Holyfield. I'm bigger than Evander Holyfield.'

'Really?'

'Yeah, I am. You know I am.'

'You have to prove yourself in the heavyweight division.'

'I don't have to prove anything. You've got to fight the best fighters out there. I'm the best fighter out there. What has Tony Thompson ever done? What has Alexander Povetkin ever done?'

'They are the number one contenders,' pleaded Klitschko, as he attempted to climb the stairs, only for Haye to again halt his progress. 'Thompson has been waiting a year now for this fight.'

'Don't worry about that,' said Haye, quick to position himself between Klitschko and his destination. 'I was in Vegas and everybody wants me and you. Don't worry about the line of people. Fight the people that want to fight. These guys are bums. Fight the main fucking man, and that's me. The Hayemaker's coming for you, trust me.'

It sounds like the lost transcript to a forgotten *Rocky* instalment, yet the above happened and was caught on tape at Seni, an inter-national combat sports exhibition held in London's Excel Arena. Polar opposites in style and personality, the disobedient Haye cornered cagey Klitschko on his way to a press conference for the charity Fight For Peace, a boxing initiative with the aim of getting children off the streets of London. One-time London child Haye, however, was simply spoiling for a fight.

Unlike me, Haye thrived on confrontation and was keen to not only cold-call Klitschko, but also ensure the whole world was offered a ringside seat to the subsequent dressing-down. The stairs soon attracted interested observers and cameras, and in the blink of an eye various two-and-a-half-minute video clips found their way onto the internet and television. Former cruiserweight champion Haye, an unproven yapper in the heavyweight division, had ranted his way into Klitschko's head and into the hearts of boxing fans.

Ordinarily Haye would have been chastised for resisting Klitschko's attempts to make peace, but this was 2008, and the boxing world had seen far too much of Klitschko and peaceful in the same sentence. They wanted a violent and charismatic skull-cracker, a champion that chased fights rather than promoted breaking them up. In that melodramatic two-and-a-half-minute perform-ance, Haye confronted the best heavyweight in the world, stripped away his defence and pretence, and announced his own arrival on the scene, despite boasting few notable heavyweight scalps to his name.

Haye was viewed as a chancer, a hustler and the Artful Dodger of the division. Klitschko, on the other hand, was a stoic, frosty and mild-mannered character, the kind who would have been deemed a model ambassador for any other sport, but appeared woefully out of place in boxing. He lacked the dynamism, person-ality and spark of other great heavyweight champions and, crucially, these shortcomings extended beyond his character and were also frequently exhibited during his title fights. He was a methodical, intelligent and calm champion, the sort respected, but not necessarily watched or admired in a sport as visceral and dramatic as boxing. Haye was unproven in his new domain, but he'd argue the guts shown in confronting Klitschko was more significant and noteworthy than anything the Ukrainian had managed in two reigns as world heavyweight champion. In a way, he'd be right.

For the next twelve months, Haye and Klitschko would be inextricably linked to one another, as numerous fight dates were mooted and then scuppered. Having verbally made his splash in the division, Haye then settled down to proving himself physically in 2008, rounding off the year by stopping Monte Barrett in five rounds in London. With one manic dart up a flight of stairs and the slaying of an American contender, Haye had announced himself as the next best heavyweight in the world, a sign of both David's star appeal and the sorry state of the sport's blue-riband division. Haye's heavyweight induction was simple, yet ingeniously crafted. For roughly six months of 2008, he'd follow Klitschko's every move, lambast him in every interview, and then quietly watch the clinical but cautious champion defeat the aforementioned 'bums'.

He first watched Wladimir reluctantly stop Thompson inside eleven rounds in July. Then, come December, Haye was sitting ringside in Mannheim as Klitschko pounded on a bloated and faded version of former world heavyweight champion Hasim Rahman for six and a half rounds.

Weighing a shade above 253lbs, Rahman was shockingly 9lbs heavier than Klitschko at the scales, and 15lbs heavier than when he stunned the world and knocked out Lennox Lewis in April 2001. The Baltimore heavyweight was slow, lethargic, void of ambition and, dare I say it, a spent force on the heavyweight scene. He showed none of the explosive right-hand power he once possessed, nor any snap behind a jab that had previously been regarded as one of the very best in the heavyweight division. The man once known as 'The Rock' was reduced to a sinking pebble, before being put out of his misery in the seventh.

Rahman had much in common that night with Samuel Peter, the lumpy and limited Nigerian mudslide who lost his WBC heavyweight title to another Klitschko in October. Retired since 2004, older brother Vitali had watched Wladimir rise to the top of the division and, sensing the weight class was still every bit as dire as it had been when he left, decided it was worth making a return. Vitali was thirty-seven years of age when he pummelled Peter, but remained effective in all the ways Wladimir wasn't. He was sturdier, in both a physical and a mental sense, and was also more willing to swap punches and force a pace that at least resembled workmanlike. Wladimir was the prettier, of face and style, but Vitali brought the fight back to the Klitschkos and was less afraid of confrontation. Genes aside, many believed the difference in style and mentality was due to the fact Wladimir had suffered multiple shock stoppage defeats, whereas Vitali was relatively unscathed, and had yet to be viciously knocked out the way his younger sibling had. Whatever the contrast, Vitali's stiff and unsightly style was seemingly immune to the concept of ring rust and, following eight rounds of battering Peter, it was evident Haye now had two Klitschkos to goad and contend with.

Considered an offshoot of the Klitschko franchise, Haye was linked to fights with both brothers through the first portion of 2009, and order of preference seemed to alternate on a daily basis. Ultimately, with the equally confrontational Vitali and Haye often at loggerheads, it would be Wladimir who received the nod to defend his WBO, IBF and IBO world titles against the Englishman on 20 June 2009. The fight, scheduled to take place at Schalke 04's Veltins-Arena in Gelsenkirchen, Germany, was officially announced on 2 April 2009, nearly a year after Haye had first ambushed the younger Klitschko on a flight of stairs. Nevertheless, through a fog of verbiage, Haye had finally arrived on boxing's biggest stage.

I was invited to join Haye at his training camp in Northern Cyprus, first by Adam Booth, and then by the fighter himself. Curiously, Booth's initial enthusiasm for me joining them dimmed and disappeared as the weeks ticked by. In fact, as mid-May approached, only Haye showed any willingness to put me up. Booth had gone completely silent.

So, at the fighter's request, I arrived in Cyprus on Saturday, 16 May, five weeks out from the night he would face Klitschko in Gelsenkirchen, though remained intrigued by Booth's sudden display of *omertà*. I grabbed a car from the airport to Haye's home in Ozankoy and, upon arrival, was greeted by the former champion, busy pontificating on everything *but* boxing. As we shot the breeze on films we'd recently watched, Haye discovered I'd never seen *Alien 3* and immediately projected the film on his plasma television. We were accompanied by Jamie Sawyer, Haye's long-time nutritionist and cornerman, who had been living in Cyprus with the fighter since the start of January.

Midway through the film, Booth knocked and entered. He embraced and greeted me as he'd always done and informed me that I'd be staying at his home across the way. Separated only by a patch of grass between villas, Haye and Booth were now detached entities in Cyprus, but not by much.

'I didn't even know you were coming out here,' said the trainer, as we returned to his villa at around midnight.

'Yeah, I didn't hear anything from you,' I replied. 'David kept asking when I wanted to come out, but I couldn't get any response from you. I wanted to check first.'

'I didn't want you to come out here and be a part of what I'm seeing.'

'I don't understand what you mean.'

'It's not looking good. You shouldn't have to be out here seeing this.'

'Seeing what?'

Booth rolled his eyes, sighed once more, and then headed over to a video camera on the kitchen table. He removed the camera from its bag, set it up in front of us both on the sofa and then hit play, before shooting a glance at me which could only be interpreted as, 'Are you ready for this?' I'd only been in Northern Cyprus a matter of hours, hardly ample preparation time, though sensed this was a problem no amount of foresight would ease.

The tape rolled and I felt mucky, as though Booth had been secretly videoing neighbours testing out whips and chains. As the film opened on a boxing ring and two sparring partners in headguards, I realised that my original suspicions weren't exactly far from the truth.

'This is David sparring Kali Meehan,' explained Booth, pointing at the small screen. 'They did four rounds yesterday, and this is where he's at right now. Kali was a bit too slow to capitalise, but David's very static at the moment and can't generate any kind of explosive attack. His punching technique is also not where it needs to be. Have a look for yourself.'

Booth's assessment was right, of course, and Haye most definitely didn't resemble the fighter I'd come to expect and almost take for granted. He was leaden-footed, heavy, sluggish and fighting on equal terms with Meehan, a solid gatekeeper of the division, but someone an on-fire Haye would have annihilated with speed and smarts. Applying some perspective to the situation, I reminded myself that we were still five weeks out from the Klitschko fight and that Haye would no doubt improve.

'And here's him in with David Price yesterday,' said Booth, as he fast-forwarded the tape. 'Price has been doing very well against him actually, and is now getting more confident about throwing his own right hand. He's not getting much back from David, so is able to take chances. He's hurt him a couple of times with left hooks, too.'

Booth moved on the tape to reveal evidence of Haye being tagged and shaken by a Price shot, only to then rest his hand on the top rope and recuperate.

'I'm extremely worried,' admitted Booth. 'He's too heavy right now, and he's unfit. He's been doing a lot of carb-loading this year and is now struggling to get the weight off and get down to the kind of weight he'll need to be for this fight.'

'What does he weigh right now?' I asked.

'He's over sixteen stone. Probably sixteen-two or sixteen-three.'

'Yeah, that's quite heavy.'

'David always struggles with his punching technique at the start of training, because he takes time off from punching and does very little in between fights. But this is the worst it's ever been. He was hitting the bag and pads like a kid who'd entered the boxing gym for the first time in his life. He knew it, too. He knew that his punching wasn't where it needed to be.'

'Has it improved since then?'

'Yeah, it's improved, but only because he's now punching on a semi-regular basis. Unfortunately, his weight is also causing problems with injuries. His back is playing up and, as a result, we're having to miss sessions. There's no continuity. His weight won't allow him to do the things he needs to do in the fight, and I can tell it's frustrating him. You can see it just watching him train. He can't sustain any kind of tempo and he's screaming and shouting in frustration when he throws shots.'

We watched as Haye pounded away at Booth's pads and howled to the hounds of hell each and every time he unleashed a punch. Then, either when a punch fell short or a move broke down, Haye would bellow in anger, as though someone had hammered a nail into his foot. Booth knew more about Haye's training tics and mannerisms than I ever would, but the sights and sounds disturbed me. They were the screams of a desperate man, someone who'd realised he'd accidentally left the gas on, burnt his house down and was now frantically trying to retrieve lost valuables from the rubble.

'We've still got a few weeks to claw it back, but David's nowhere near where he needs to be right now,' explained Booth. 'He's catching up on basic punching drills when we need to be focusing on game plans and working out exactly what he needs to do to beat Wladimir. David's sparring for fitness and technique at the moment, and I need him working on moves. That's why you've seen him struggle and get clipped by stupid shots. He's having to start all over again, and doesn't have the fitness to see him through at the moment.'

Having now fully dragged me inside his head of demons, Booth and I sat and deliberated until way beyond four o'clock that Sunday morning. By the time I traipsed off to bed, infinitely less positive than I'd been on the plane over, my mind was filled with the kinds of thoughts that had kept Booth awake for days on end.

As my head hit the pillow, I recalled a conversation I'd once had with Klitschko's coach James Ali Bashir, a grizzled staple of the famous Kronk gymnasium in Detroit, and a man who'd rubbed shoulders with the likes of Thomas 'Hitman' Hearns and Iran 'The Blade' Barkley. Bashir later worked alongside Emanuel Steward within the Klitschko camp and had one day told me secrets which sent chills down my spine.

'Wladimir is a very strong fighter, physically and mentally,' Bashir said. 'He's like a machine. The discipline Wladimir has is unreal. Do you know how many training sessions he's missed in the five years I've been working with him? Zero. If he tells me we're training at 6.45 a.m. in the morning, he'll be waiting for me at 6.30 a.m. If I tell him to run fifty miles in five minutes, he'll give it his best shot. I've never known anyone like him. It's scary how well prepared this guy is. He's the most dedicated fighter I've ever known and I've known a few great ones.

'There was a time when we were studying fights in camp and Wladimir sat watching one round of a fight over and over again. He watched the same round at least fifty times consecutively. We were all sitting, whispering behind his back and wondering what the hell he was up to. We all thought the dude was crazy. Then, after about the fifty-third time of watching it, he got up, left to get a drink and then did the exact same thing for round two.'

I woke up in a suit of moisture the next morning, partly through fear and partly due to faulty air-conditioning. In addition to the sweltering heat, I also had to contend with at least one hundred mosquito bites on my arms, neck and shoulders.

It was Sunday and a rest day and I was thankful for the fact I'd be spared a visit to the boxing gym. The time off gave me an opportunity to seek out an antihistamine for my bites and paracetamol for my headache. Thankfully, Haye's own packed schedule that Sunday afternoon also prevented much chance of dialogue or false pretence. I was instead able to spend time with the other boxers and trainers who had made their way to Northern Cyprus that summer. Split between a local hotel and a rented house in the same cul-de-sac as Haye and Booth were sparring partners Kali Meehan, David Price and Chris Burton, super-middleweight prospect George Groves, as well as trainers and ex-boxers Dave Coldwell and Danny Watts.

Everybody was united by a common duty to help Haye prepare for the biggest fight of his life, as well as a desire to see him win it. They'd all witnessed him in the gym in recent days and weeks, and a few of them had even shared the ring with him. While nobody seemed to commit to completely writing Haye off and criticising his present form, the consensus was in line with what Booth feared. The challenger wasn't where he needed to be and had fallen behind schedule. Most of these men had been around big fights and fighters before, and they had a decent idea of progress and the so-called ideal. Crucially, none of them were speaking in glowing terms about the camp, or the fight that would emerge at the end of it. Yet, amid the doom and gloom, I started to wonder why Haye seemed oblivious, at least on the face of it, to the problems others had easily identified in training. They all passed the same concerns to one another – that Haye was too heavy, too sluggish and too far behind – but the challenger was distanced from the conversation and out running errands. He never heard the whispers.

I sat and ate a late lunch with Haye and Booth that afternoon in the boxer's apartment. The overall mood was relaxed and positive, and the relationship between fighter and trainer remained solid. Despite the anxiety and apprehension, Booth knew little good would come from antagonising Haye and risking a breakdown in communication at this stage. If ever he needed his charge to listen, it was now. So, with the drama pushed to the back of his mind, Booth and Haye swapped jokes and tales as they would any other day of the year. The fight was temporarily forgotten. After lunch, Booth and I headed back to his house, and Haye said I was welcome to return to his later that night to watch *Napoleon Dynamite*, a film he was in the process of downloading on his laptop.

Later arrived and *Napoleon Dynamite* started. I didn't make it across to Haye's apartment and instead chose to spend more time panicking with Booth in his living room next door. We watched a DVD of the 1981 welterweight championship fight between Sugar Ray Leonard and Thomas Hearns, perhaps in an attempt to distract ourselves from the problems at hand and embrace boxing at its purest. It wasn't fair on Haye, the one who'd invited me out there, to dump his plan and instead discuss his flaws behind his back, but my concern for his well-being overshadowed any desire I had to belly-laugh that evening.

At just gone midnight there was a knock on the door and Haye, ears presumably burning, entered, as chilled and blithe as he'd been earlier that day at lunch. He clocked the Leonard love-in on the big screen, sighed, rolled his eyes and then sat down opposite Booth and me on the sofa. We all watched in silence, some more interested than others, as Leonard finally brought the curtain down on Hearns in the fourteenth round with a cacophony of devastating punches. Eyes wide in admiration, Booth reiterated the need for Haye to continuously watch the fight, pointing out the tricks he could learn from Leonard in fighting a taller and rangier opponent. Haye agreed, but claimed he'd already been forced to watch it 'about one hundred times', as though now tired of the fight and Booth's obsession with it.

'Have you watched anything of Wladimir lately?' asked the trainer, as he fled from the sofa and headed over to the kitchen table.

'I watched a bit of him against Calvin Brock the other day,' said Haye.

'And?'

'It was a great fucking knockout, wasn't it?' joked David, brushing off the threat. 'Brock moved well enough, but he was petrified to throw anything.'

'Yep . . .'

'You need to give Wladimir something to fear, otherwise he'll just keep sticking that stupid jab in your face.'

Booth tapped away at his laptop, seemingly content with the fact Haye was now at least engaging in conversation about his June opponent, and had recently watched footage of him.

'So what's your expert opinion on how I go about beating him?' asked Haye, before he turned to face me.

We were now sitting directly opposite one another, separated by perhaps three metres of floor space, and Haye was grinning widely. The fighter was clearly close enough to launch a two-fisted attack on my face if the wind changed, but I somehow sensed this was my opportunity to make a stand, albeit while ironically off my feet. I remembered Carl Thompson and the unused blue ball, and recalled how nobody was willing to speak up, either through fear of being punched or losing their job. Silence had only ever created complacency. Either I reacted like Wladimir Klitschko and offered stoic silence, or I exploded in a ball of misguided passion and emotion like brother Vitali or, indeed, Haye himself would. So, *this* was confrontation, I thought to myself.

'It depends whether you turn up like I hope you do, or the way you are right now,' I said, heart racing and palms sweating.

'Oh, boy, prepare yourself for a shitstorm,' mumbled Booth from the kitchen table, and I distinctly remember being unsure whether those words of advice were directed at me or the fighter. Either way, he sensed what was coming and ducked for cover.

'How am I looking right now then?' replied Haye, his grin a thing of the past, as he squared up to me in his seat and leaned forward.

'You look like the fat and shot version of Hasim Rahman,' I said – no, *really, I did*. It got worse, too.

'Right now you look exactly like Rahman did when he got beaten up by Klitschko in December,' I continued, bravely, passionately and unwisely. 'If you fight him the way Rahman did, there's only one winner. If you turn up looking the way I hope you will, then you've got a chance.'

I barely managed to stutter out the last sentence, such was the shakiness of my voice by this stage. I felt as though I was going to break into tears each and every time I spoke, and had to frequently remind myself Haye was a heavyweight prizefighter, and I wasn't, and that I'd just apparently labelled him 'fat' and 'shot' to his face. There would be nobody to separate us if he decided to show me just how hard a 'fat' and 'shot' heavyweight could punch. I felt foolishly brave that night, but relieved I'd finally begun emptying my head.

'So, should I just pull out of the fight now?' replied a straight-faced Haye in response. 'Is it all a lost cause? What are you trying to say?'

'I'm just saying I want you to be the best you can be for this fight. I don't think you're on course to be that fighter right now.'

'How do you know? We've still got weeks left of training. No fighter peaks until the night of the fight. What have you seen?'

'I showed him the video of your sparring and training from the other day,' said Booth, butting in, as Haye's temperature soared.

'Right, one session,' said Haye. 'Is that it? So you haven't seen any of the good sessions then? You've watched one bad session and are jumping to conclusions.'

'Have there been any good sessions?' I asked.

'Yeah, of course there have. You're never going to have great sessions every time you train. It doesn't work like that. Everybody has bad days. Yeah, I had a shit session the other day, but so what? You haven't seen enough to make any judgement.'

'Why ask for my opinion then? If I haven't seen enough to warrant an opinion, what use is it? Did you just want me to say how great you are?'

'No, but I didn't expect to be called "fat" and "shot". If that's the case, maybe I should just pack it in altogether.'

'He wasn't saying that,' added Booth. 'That was just an extreme way of getting the point across. We both think you need to be lighter in order to do the things you need to do in the fight, that's all.'

'I'll get lighter,' insisted Haye. 'We're still weeks out yet.'

'You are too heavy at the moment, though,' said Booth.

'I'm sixteen stone two. How many weeks have we got left of training?'

'Four,' replied Booth.

'If I lose 2lbs a week, I'll get down to fifteen stone eight. How's that for you?'

'It's better,' I said. 'Look, I'm only saying this stuff because I care. What good would it be to leave this conversation until the week of the fight, when it's too late? I'm just saying what I feel, based on what I've seen.'

'Yeah, well it's nice to know I've got some support.'

Silence fell on the room for what seemed like an hour, as Booth retreated to the safety of his laptop and Haye and I stared blankly into space. All that needed to be said had now, thankfully, been said.

'Well, I'm off to bed then,' muttered Haye, as he rose from the couch and wandered off towards the door, without so much as uttering another word, striking a pose or issuing a glance. Once the door had clicked shut behind him, my head fell hopelessly into my hands. Booth, meanwhile, offered an uncomfortable chuckle from behind his computer.

'It's going to be interesting to see what kind of reaction you get from him now,' he said. 'Is that the first time you've had an argument with him?'

I nodded and, in hindsight, felt an unusual mixture of extreme disappointment and pride. I was sympathetic towards Haye and the fact he'd essentially visited in peace that night, only to then be bombarded with accusations and putdowns, most of which came directly from me. Regardless of how Haye had been training that summer, I didn't possess the world cruiserweight titles or reputation to knock or criticise him. I knew that, and respected the fact that Haye's opinion would always count for far more than mine ever would.

However, I also took great pride from the fact I'd gone somewhere and spoken truths many others would have shirked. I was relieved to know I was no longer part of the problem. I'd said my piece, however imprudent or extreme, and had separated myself from those content to pretend or lie. Even if I'd said the wrong things or expressed myself badly, Haye had heard my concerns and, whether he believed them or not, would undoubtedly change as a result. At the very least he'd have returned home that night and pondered, if only for a brief minute, the words and insults I'd churlishly spat his way. That alone represented some kind of breakthrough.

Perhaps unsurprisingly, Haye said nothing to me the next day, and remained cooped up in his house for much of it. When it came time to train in the evening, Booth highlighted the significance of the session by describing it as 'the most important one of David's career so far'. By way of subtle hints, I was also then informed that I'd have to stay at home and miss seeing Haye work out.

Three hours later and Booth returned, his face far less haunted than it had been the previous day.

'He pulled one out of the bag this evening,' said the trainer, shocked by the work he'd seen from his star pupil. 'I'm not getting ahead of myself yet, though, because David is always able to pull a quality session out the bag when the mood takes him. It's sustaining it and getting him to do it on a consistent basis that is the problem. Today was very good, though.'

I was pleased for Haye and Booth that evening, while simultaneously disappointed that I'd apparently been barred from witnessing any improvements. Perhaps my scathing words did inspire some kind of response in Haye, a final surge, as if to say, 'I'll show them.' Booth certainly felt that was what he had seen in the gym.

'He probably sees us as ganging up on him over here, and that's why he's reacted the way he has,' said Booth. 'He feels like his back is up against the wall now and, for the first time in a while, he's got people around him that are doubting and questioning him.'

My expulsion from the gym continued for the next week, as did my hiatus from any meaningful dialogue with Haye. We met in passing from time to time – living so close ensured that – and, while the fighter was never rude or distant, he was often unchar-acteristically short and clearly less keen to open up to me. I had expected this kind of reaction, of course, as Haye was never one to let his emotions show or talk through his problems, whatever they might be. Time would be the only healer in this dispute.

Alas, time passed slowly and, come Wednesday, I was told I'd spend the remaining days of my stay in Northern Cyprus a five-minute drive away at the Vuni Palace hotel. Booth's two daughters were due to fly in and spend a week with him at his villa, and my room was needed. This created even more space between me, Haye and the drama at large and, by this time, I was thankful for it.

Before leaving for my new place of residence, I went for a final run around the makeshift jogging route I'd followed on each day of my stay. Setting off from Booth's house, I'd venture up the hill, out of the cul-de-sac and then up and around the dirt track that hugged the town centre. Running in one continuous loop, reaching the main road and then following it back round to the house, I would complete this trail twice, clocking approximately three miles in total.

On this particular afternoon, with the first lap complete, I passed the entry gate to the cul-de-sac and continued off down the road towards the beach front. As I inhaled deeply, hit my stride and stretched my legs, I noticed two large and athletic hunting dogs menacingly poised at the top of the hill. Unsure of how to greet the inquisitive mutts, I approached cautiously, slowed my pace to a near standstill, and then meekly attempted to shimmy on by without them noticing.

The dogs glared directly at me, and I sensed the plan was destined to fail. My heartbeat gathered pace, as did my legs, triggering a dash alongside and then away from the dogs, as their overweight owner struggled to climb the hill behind them. Before I could refocus on the track ahead, the two dogs pounced and sprinted in my direction, both operating at the kind of ferocious pace I had yet to generate on my own travels.

It was about now that I screamed the sort of scream one only emits when death is knocking, and the dogs began to gnaw at anything they could touch. One ripped through my shorts and the other jumped at my torso and neck, narrowly missing both. I flailed my limbs and squealed in despair, unsure whether to run off or simply stand my ground. In the end, I did neither, and instead remained a prone target for two starved canines looking to yank open whatever hint of pink flesh they could find.

After a frantic thirty seconds of torment, the dogs' owner raced over to join us and managed to calm the dogs down and prise them from me. The rotund local seemed as emotionally overwrought and scared as I was, which only increased my suspicion that the dogs were feral and infested with rabies. As blood dripped from an open wound on my thigh, the owner offered to drive me to a nearby hospital and get patched and dosed up. I refused the offer, instead preferring to head on home and find a familiar face. En route to the villas, I weighed up whether a rabies-infested dog's bite was as damaging as Haye's earlier in the week. It was too close to call.

'You need to run at the dogs and scare them off,' advised David, as I entered his home for the first time since our spat. Adam's door was locked, while Haye's was ajar, and, bloodied and shaken up, I required the kind of sympathy I'd been unable to offer the fighter days before.

'That's easier said than done,' I replied, holding a makeshift bandage over my wound. 'They were scary-looking things.'

'Yeah, and they sensed your fear,' added Haye. 'That's what they prey on. As soon as you show that bit of fear or weakness, they'll go after you. If you stand up to them and hunt *them* down, that's when they back away. I *love* running at dogs like that.'

Before leaving Northern Cyprus on the Tuesday, I decided to hang around and watch Haye's high-octane sparring session with French heavyweight champion Gregory Tony, a former kick-boxer and long-limbed scrapper with no regard for the textbook. I ignored the hints of fighter and trainer, sat away from the ring and stayed there for the next hour as Haye and Tony sparred eight rounds. Whether welcome or not, my mind was made up. With only twenty-four hours left on the island, I was going to try my damnedest to at least see *something*.

Expecting the worst, I was instead rather impressed and proud of the work Haye produced against the wiry Frenchman. It couldn't have been easy chugging on through preparation knowing that he was a step behind schedule, and that the turncoat who'd reminded him of that fact was now sitting ringside scrutinising his every move. Unperturbed, Haye showed plenty of the kind of slickness and fluidity he'd need against Klitschko in June, though was still clearly carrying excess weight, of body and mind, around the ring with him. He cracked the aggressive and free-swinging Tony with numerous picture-perfect right hands throughout eight rounds and, despite fears over stamina, fought at a hectic pace for the duration.

Haye's performance in that particular session was a world away from what I'd seen on video at the start of my stay, and I only

hoped that the fighter had now turned a corner and was beginning to find his flow and focus. Using his own dog analogy, perhaps
Haye was now confronting the problem head on and running
towards it, as opposed to escaping into a bunker full of excuses.
After all, with the clock ticking, he had no choice. We all braced
ourselves for the inevitable bite.

CHAPTER EIGHTEEN
MUSICAL MASSAGE

With one minute to go in the eighth and final round of sparring, Adam Booth couldn't help but smile. After weeks of fractured communication, his man was now finally obeying and carrying out orders on the head of unfortunate Canadian sparring partner Raymond Olubowale. Despite falling behind on their planned schedule, Booth saw enough in David Haye that day to eradicate some of the fears that had for so long blighted their Cyprus training camp. He even started to believe again.

Then, just as scattered pieces threatened to fall back into place, fate conspired to drag dark clouds over the heads of both fighter and trainer. Drunk on minor success, Haye performed a routine move and dramatically collapsed in a heap, his ankle having given way under the pressure of carrying a recurring back injury. The gym fell silent, Olubowale retreated to a corner, Booth rushed over to assist his fallen fighter and Haye, writhing in agony, was no longer able to move or shake the overwhelming sense of negativity that had often suffocated his problematic training camp.

As pain and panic increased, Haye was rushed to the nearest changing room, his leg promptly buried in an ice bath. Booth, meanwhile, so often the magic eight-ball of Haye-related problems, shook his head repeatedly, but came up short of offering any solutions.

'It was sweltering inside the changing room that day, and I had to get out,' recalled the trainer. 'Most of the heat was stress-related, of course, and I could sense everybody's eyes burning a question mark into my forehead. They were all looking at me as if to say, "Okay, so what happens now?"

'For the first time in my life I had no idea what to do or say. The idea of being that clueless and helpless actually frightened me, so I decided to take a walk over to the Smith squat machine in the corner of the gym and stayed there for as long as I could. I placed my forearm across my forehead and closed my eyes. There was this feeling of absolute hopelessness. I knew we had no way out.'

By Wednesday, 3 June, Haye had ruled himself unfit to face Wladimir Klitschko, and the fight was off. Booth's forearm remained planted to his forehead and his eyes stayed shut. A flabbergasted heavyweight champion, meanwhile, was afforded no such thinking time or period for reflection. On the afternoon that news broke of Haye's withdrawal, opponent Klitschko was in the process of holding a press junket at his training camp in Kitzbühel, Austria, and was therefore far more visible and exposed than usual. Sitting directly in front of the British media, having just wrapped up a training session, Klitschko even spoke lucidly and positively about the fight and detailed what he planned to do to the obnoxious Brit and how victory would help bolster his legacy in the sport.

Midway through questioning, however, Klitschko's manager Bernd Boente interrupted, whispered in the fighter's ear, and then backed away, allowing the heavyweight a second to think and breathe. A look of sheer deflation was stamped across Klitschko's face in size elevens.

'We have just received an email from Adam Booth,' Boente

informed the media. 'Haye's trainer has said that Haye is injured and cannot fight on June 20th.'

'I'm speechless,' said Klitschko, when offered the chance to verbalise his thoughts. 'We will have to get someone else in. I will take whoever it is. If something like that happened to me, Haye would talk dirty, which I'm not going to do. I won't kick a man when he is down.'

Having allowed the information to marinate a little longer than his fighter, manager Boente was better positioned to issue a rational response to the development and also plot Klitschko's immediate route forward.

'They [Haye and Booth] haven't given any detail on the injury, but simply say Haye can't train,' added Boente. 'We will get someone else, but I can't say yet who it will be. Ninety-five per cent of the fans who bought tickets for this Haye fight did so because of Klitschko.'

The immediate assumption was that Boente would approach WBA-ranked heavyweights Nikolay Valuev and Ruslan Chagaev with the late-notice opportunity, a move that seemed ideal given the pair had just seen a bout of their own collapse one week earlier.

Meanwhile, speculation mounted as to what Haye's exact injury was, and whether the injury was even legitimate at all. With neither Haye nor Booth on hand to clarify, the British media ran rife with far-fetched rumours and conspiracy theories, most of which centred on the impact of the inevitable liquidation of the pair's bankrupt paymasters, Setanta Sports, the fight's broadcaster in the United Kingdom.

'Many people felt that Setanta going bust was the reason for the pull-out, but that couldn't have been further from the truth,' said Booth. 'I wish we had had that much foresight. Instead, fate handed us our only option and, ultimately, it turned out to be the right direction to head in. David's injury was the sole reason for the withdrawal, but, as we later discovered, he stood to make nothing from going through with the fight anyway. If he had sucked it up and somehow tried to fight, David would have been beaten up by Klitschko and then not made a penny, as Setanta went into administration shortly after the fight. Still, we couldn't possibly have seen it coming. I'd never heard of a situation where a fighter had a promotional agreement in place with a television network and then that network goes bankrupt. It was an unprecedented turn of events.'

As planned, Klitschko boxed in front of a reported 70,000 fans that June night in Gelsenkirchen, and produced a clinical destruction of the previously unbeaten Chagaev. A capable fighter in his own right, Chagaev, a former WBA champion, was quickly reduced to the role of surviving journeyman, covering up on the ropes and refusing to take a purposeful step forward all night. Klitschko shut the southpaw down, stripped away his ambition, and eventually halted him following nine rounds of painfully tedious, yet wonderfully effective work. Had it been Haye in the ring with Klitschko that night, I had no doubt he'd have offered more in terms of threat, ambition and entertainment, but couldn't be sure of an altogether different outcome. Klitschko impressed in all the ways I knew he would, offering zero excitement, but ultimate efficiency.

The joy of stalking brothers, of course, is that when you fall out with one, you've still got an alternative option of similar size, style and fighting stock. Having just defeated Chagaev, the likelihood was that Wladimir wouldn't fight again until December – a fact Haye quickly learnt to accept – while older brother Vitali stopped Cuban waster Juan Carlos Gomez in March, in defence of his WBC title, and was next looking to fight in early September. Sensing Vitali's schedule now aligned better with his own, Haye switched his attentions that summer and began targeting the older and sturdier of the two fighting siblings. It then didn't take long for rumours to circulate that Haye and Vitali would meet on 12 September in Frankfurt's 52,000-seater Commerzbank Arena.

My own beef with Haye also continued that summer, as neither of us spoke or saw one another for over two months. In fact, I heard nothing at all from the fighter until Tuesday, 14 July, the day he informed me he had a spare ticket to a gig at the Jazz Café in Camden Town and that I might appreciate the plus-one gesture. Dusty Motown veteran Leon Ware was playing there on the Thursday, and Haye had sufficiently brainwashed me over the years to the point where I was now a bona fide fan of the 69-year-old soul survivor. The singer's album *Musical Massage* had been a recurring feature of many car rides with Haye during the early years, and I knew most of his songs off by heart, purely due to the number of times I'd heard the boxer sing along to them behind the wheel. If anything, the album was the soundtrack to our relationship and, with that in mind, the invitation to see Ware in action was probably the most apt and meaningful way of bringing us back together.

Delighted to have first heard from Haye, and secondly to have been invited to the show, I ventured into central London that Thursday and met up with David at The Third Space in Piccadilly Circus. Adam Booth was also in the gym that day, and we caught up and chatted as though no great crisis had ever unfolded that summer. In a sign of just how out of the loop I felt, Booth also revealed to me their plans for the future.

'We've got two offers on the table,' said the trainer, leaning forward in his seat. 'We can either do Vitali Klitschko in September for the WBC title, or Nikolay Valuev in November for the WBA title.'

'*Valuev?*' I asked, stunned by the way in which a seven-foot champion had crept into the equation unnoticed.

'Yep. We're speaking to his promoter Kalle Sauerland about it. They're interested.'

'I never saw *that* coming. I wouldn't think they'd want Valuev anywhere near David.'

'That's what we thought. Seems we were wrong.'

'Well, given the choice, that's a no-brainer, right?'

I exchanged glances with Haye and Booth, and they both appeared to be thinking the same.

'The deal on the table seems almost too good to be true,' said Haye. 'How could we fail to sell a fight titled "David and Goliath"?'

As unbelievable as the proposition sounded to my ears, there was little doubt a fight between Haye and Valuev would not only sell, but would perhaps mark the only logical U-turn away from a bout with a Klitschko. As well as being seven feet tall, Valuev was 320lbs in weight and the owner of the WBA world heavyweight championship. Somewhat less scary than he sounded and looked, Valuev was a capable, if basic, operator, and someone who'd already been comfortably outboxed by Ruslan Chagaev in April 2007. That twelve-round decision loss stood as the sole blemish on Valuev's 51-fight record, but was enough to provide bountiful confidence to anybody looking to perform a similar shoeshine job on the immovable giant.

Valuev towered over the Klitschko brothers, and perhaps packed a better chin, but he remained inferior to the fighting siblings in every other respect. He lacked the amateur career, fighting instincts and athleticism of the Ukrainians and, at thirty-six years of age, was still finding his feet in a sport he'd been pushed into, rather than gravitated towards naturally. While unparalleled height, weight and reach advantages brought a certain otherworldly awkwardness to Valuev's game, the same dimensions also restricted such vital boxing ingredients as speed, athleticism, explosiveness and pace.

Stylistic issues aside, though, a bout between Haye and Valuev was so appealing simply because it was a promoter's wet dream. The allure of the pairing would transcend mere boxing circles, and engage the public on a different level to most other boxing matches. Far more than just a fighting contest, 'David and Goliath' would be an experiment, an event, a happening – something that could capture the imagination of a public alienated by the arcane nature of boxing. It broke down the complexities of the sport and returned scrapping to its purest form: big man against little man.

The Valuev fight was officially announced on Wednesday, 22 July, and took *everybody* by surprise. Like me, nobody knew Valuev was even being considered, let alone the chosen one. No man claimed to be more surprised than Vitali Klitschko, however, another champion who seemed dead set on meeting Haye in Frankfurt on 12 September.

'We had a letter from his [Haye's] lawyer yesterday and all the points were pretty much agreed to,' Klitschko's American adviser Shelly Finkel told ESPN.com. 'But then we couldn't get them on the phone. If he thinks Valuev is an easier fight or a better deal, then that's his prerogative, but be a man and don't just disappear and avoid everyone.'

The slippery Haye did plenty of ducking and diving that summer, but, by the time July came to a close, had papered over a dispute with me and appeased the frustrations of fans with an enticing world heavyweight title fight.

'David only needed a slingshot and a stone to flatten Goliath, and I'm convinced my right hand generates more power than a stone,' said the challenger when announcing his shock WBA heavyweight title clash.

Lost in a fairytale, Haye had left the reality of a potential Klitschko meeting and instead invested his dreams in a popcorn-and-coke blockbuster. David Haye was talking again. To me, and to the world.

PART SIX

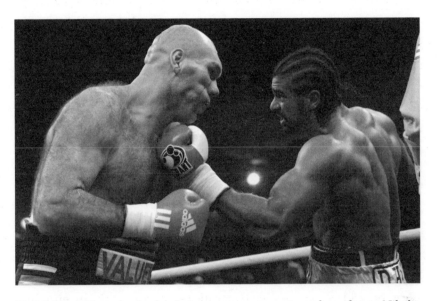

David Haye plays the lead role in a monster movie and confronts Nikolay
Valuev, a champion seven stone heavier and a foot taller than the comparatively diminutive challenger.

CHAPTER NINETEEN
LAMBS AND WOLVES

'A helpless lamb among wolves,' was how the New York writer Paul Gallico once described Italian Primo Carnera, one-time heavyweight champion and full-time spectacle, a fighter who reached boxing's pinnacle when he landed a right uppercut on the chin of Jack Sharkey in 1933. 'The Ambling Alp' was how other, less articulate, men labelled Carnera, though the moniker would never be self-applied. The six-feet-seven-inch and 265lb Carnera was a fighter through necessity, not choice.

Carcasses were somewhat larger by 2009, of course, and Carnera was no longer remembered as the world's heftiest heavy-weight champion. That accolade now went to Nikolay Valuev, a seven-foot behemoth, who topped out at 324lbs the night he defeated John Ruiz to lift the WBA world heavyweight championship in 2005. Valuev made Carnera appear comparatively minute and nimble, such was the sheer presence of the heavyweight from St Petersburg, Russia. In fact, had Carnera roamed at the time Valuev reigned, 'The Ambling Alp' would have merely blended into the stark scenery of the heavyweight division, raising barely an eyebrow in the process. Fight fans had grown accustomed to witnessing fighters of Carnera's dimensions by 2009 and so it was a mark of Valuev's genuine size and wow-factor that he reluctantly carried the 'fighting freak' mantle into the twenty-first century.

It was hard not to feel sorry for Valuev, boxing's most recent Elephant Man, and the shortest tall man I'd ever set eyes on. Commonly viewed through a perspex shield and a microscope, Valuev was an experiment, a one-man circus show known as 'The Beast from the East'. Like with Carnera, the nickname was never self-applied and represented more of a promotional gimmick than a term of endearment.

The promoter's preference was to lightly sketch Valuev as a product of Stephen King's imagination, ramming home his dimensions, fearsome facial features and carefully manufactured knockout ratio, while scrubbing out details of his humble personal life. Once you dug beneath the surface, however, you unearthed a warm, caring and incredibly sensitive individual who proposed to his five-feet-two-inch wife, Galina, with a poem, and had two young children, daughter Irina and son Grisha. A Russian Orthodox Christian, 'The Beast' led a quiet life in the St Petersburg mountains and, while he had an appreciation for hunting, would spend most days relaxing at home to the sounds of Wolfgang Amadeus Mozart or Frédéric Chopin. The cultured champion also often charmed journalists with stories of Arthur Conan Doyle, Agatha Christie and Leo Tolstoy, and insisted he'd rather unravel a murder mystery than engage in the kind of trash-talk his next challenger specialised in. Nikolay had inherited Carnera's same passiveness, a trait born of being constantly viewed and labelled as something he wasn't; rather than embrace the potential for intimidation his size presented, he recoiled from it, both inside and outside the ropes.

Valuev's record stood at 50–1 by the time David Haye glanced up at him, and he'd knocked out thirty-four of his beaten foes. However, since stepping up in class, he had resorted to countless decision wins over twelve rounds, many of which were tight and controversial. He received the benefit of the doubt in distance fights with John Ruiz, Larry Donald, Sergei Liakhovic and Jean-François Bergeron, and tasted defeat for the first and only time when finally dropping a majority-decision verdict to crafty Kazakh southpaw Ruslan Chagaev in April 2007.

It was Valuev's fifth title defence, however, that truly revealed both the mind behind the mask and the potential for a Haye victory. 'The Beast' successfully defended his crown against former world cruiserweight and heavyweight champion Evander Holyfield in December 2008, again over twelve dull rounds, but was curiously unable to mount anything resembling a significant attack during the bout. Many cried robbery, as Holyfield appeared to outbox the lumbering oaf, only to then yank the short straw at the bout's conclusion. The reason for Valuev's passiveness that night? He adored Holyfield and simply didn't want to hurt the old man.

Naturally, if you'd never seen him fight, you'd assume Nikolay Valuev was the most terrifying and destructive human being on the planet. I was finally able to offer an opinion of my own on Friday, 6 November 2009, the day I set eyes on his bulbous head at the Mercado shopping mall in Nuremberg, Germany. Present for that afternoon's weigh-in, I stood with my back to the window of a local supermarket when, pivoting slightly to my left, I caught a first glimpse of the eighth wonder in all its glory, curves in all the wrong places.

Partially hidden beneath a miniature baseball cap, Valuev's skull was enormous – twice the size of anyone else's in the vicinity. His face contained ridges and bumps that made moisturising nigh on impossible, not to mention pointless. Rather than pink and fleshy,

Valuev's skin had the appearance of a harsh metallic substance, one that allowed no give or bend. He was a faded grey colour, and neither his expression nor his complexion ever changed, regardless of whether he was smiling or scowling. Valuev appeared cold to touch and uncomfortable in his own costume.

I'd half-expected to meet the strut and piercing stare of a grotesque destroyer, a powerful man who thrived on the idea of towering over peasants, yet, conversely, found Valuev shy, fed up and meek. He sheepishly waited in the corner of the mall that afternoon, like a victim in a lunch hall, until it was time to make his way to the scales and confront his bullies. Rather than stand tall and proud, Valuev preferred to hunch and do his best to blend in. He rarely smiled, never laughed and would sigh and shrug as shoppers failed to control the plummeting of their jaws. I felt immediate sympathy towards the brute – a man who, despite having grown up with this scenario on a daily basis, was clearly overwhelmed and embarrassed by all the attention. There was a tiredness to the way in which he mingled with associates and shied away from the outsiders who chose to scrutinise. After all, he'd been labelled 'The Beast' through fifty-one professional boxing contests over sixteen years. Even the BFG got put to bed after one book. Poignantly, Valuev's unique selling point also represented his biggest hang-up and insecurity.

Keen to get the whole charade over with, Valuev was given his signal and proceeded to part the shopping centre crowd with a tentative stare, as he made his way towards the podium and scales. Rather than crowd around the champion, onlookers hung back and watched in awe, their cameras and autograph books having fallen to the floor. He's *that* kind of champion. Valuev didn't walk among people, he stepped over them. He was the world's worst hide-and-seek player, the last kid to get picked and first to be found.

Willing to do all the chest-pumping and horn-blowing in place of the reserved Valuev, the challenger took to the scales first and weighed in at a muscular, chiselled and athletic 217lbs (15st 7lbs). A well-proportioned heavyweight by anyone's standards, David Haye was about to be made to look comparatively diminutive, as Valuev finally caught up and removed his cap.

The crowd held their breath and the giant stripped off to reveal a physique that resembled a deflating bouncy castle. Cue much gasping and giggling, triggered perhaps by an uncomfortable fear for Haye's well-being, as Valuev clocked a whopping 316lbs (22st 8lbs). Fantasy had made way for reality and Haye, the fans and the watching media now realised the extent of the challenge facing the heavyweight division's designated saviour.

If the hundred or so British fans in attendance that day were starting to get cold feet, Haye was showing no signs of sudden trepidation. In fact, rather than take a giant step back and sheepishly slide off out of the venue, David stepped up to Goliath and engaged him in a stare-down for the ages. Looking up with bad intentions, Haye's gaze never left Valuev, as the pair went pupil-to-pupil in prolonged phoney warfare. Valuev's face even appeared to turn to stone at one stage, his heartbeat swiftly monitored by a nearby doctor. Meanwhile Haye, better with his mouth than his eyes, began to bait the disengaged champion.

'You're getting knocked the fuck out tomorrow,' warned Haye, cockily nodding his head and licking his dry lips. 'I'm going to make you look stupid.'

Haye was letting it be known, to the watching crowd and Saturday's opponent, that he was not intimidated by the size of foe or occasion. Whether it was because Haye was on tiptoes or Valuev was apparently daydreaming, the difference in size between the pair appeared to somehow curiously diminish by the second, as the challenger cranked up the verbal assault on the ambivalent champion. Nobody dared say it but, amid the one-sided macho posturing, there suddenly appeared a clear path from Haye's famed right hand to Valuev's chin. I could see it. We all could. The closer the pair got, and the darker Haye's eyes became, the more I started to believe that the challenger knew of a plausible way to achieve the impossible.

The underdog believed in fairytales all along, of course. One day before the weigh-in Haye had even invited me to his room at Nuremberg's Le Méridien Grand Hotel in order to show me exactly what he planned to do to Valuev some forty-eight hours later. I entered his vast suite that Thursday evening and discovered the fighter sitting by his laptop in pitch darkness, curtains drawn and radiators cranked right the way up. Before any pleasantries could be exchanged, the perspiring heavyweight implored me to sit beside him and take a look at a video he'd readied for viewing.

'What is it?' I asked.

'It's Sunday's sparring session,' said Haye. 'All fifteen rounds.'

For the next half an hour, the boxer acted as tour guide and walked me through multiple rounds of peerless pugilism, marvelling at his own movement and artistry along the way. The victims masquerading as sparring partners were American Julius Long, Canadian Raymond Olubowale and cockney Danny Watts, and none of the three landed much of note, despite alternating rounds and thus remaining relatively fresh. Watts appeared the most technically competent and spirited of the trio, while Long was frequently staggered by heavy Haye rights whenever the pair traded blows.

Haye performed a choreographed boxing routine on the bemused sparring partners, and stopped just short of shouting 'Abracadabra!' after each elaborate movement and rapid-fire punch combination. Perhaps surprisingly, it wasn't Haye's power or explosiveness that particularly caught my eye that evening, but rather his nimble foot-work and spellbinding defence. He almost appeared to be cheating in the ring. It didn't seem fair. I'd always known Haye to possess the ability to display this kind of elusiveness – and he'd often shown flashes of it during past fights – but I'd never before seen him employ such sustained slickness from round to round. He was revealing another side of his game – the key ingredient he'd need to tread the path of least resistance and conquer Valuev.

'It's weird, because this is how I spar all the time,' said Haye, 'yet I've never shown this style in an actual fight. I've never really gone into a fight and just concentrated on outboxing my opponent.'

'How did you feel, boxing like that?' I asked.

'Great,' said Haye. 'All I had to do was relax, box at my own pace and pick my shots. It's probably the easiest way you could choose to fight. I felt like I could have done another fifteen rounds like that and they still wouldn't have hit me. It's all about taking that and doing it on the night. I just need to approach this fight with a sparring mentality and it will be fine.'

It was agreed between David and trainer Adam Booth that they'd replay that final sparring session video in the changing room, moments before both were due to head to the ring. The architect of the game plan, Booth had impressively transformed a knockout-hungry power-puncher into an elusive and elastic technician.

'Pernell Whitaker mixed with Jack Dempsey,' was the mantra Booth often repeated to both David and me in the final hours before battle. 'He needs to be as defensively slick as Whitaker, but needs to also be able to explode with ferocity the way Dempsey did. He needs to go from one extreme to the other in a short space of time. If he does that, he can stop Valuev.'

I'm sure the irony wasn't lost on Booth, but on the eve of their biggest fight to date, the trainer needed his fighter to be one part instinctive and reckless bull and one part thoughtful and cautious matador. Of course, five years earlier Booth had explained to me how it was his belief that great fighters leaned towards either exceptional intelligence or exceptional ignorance, but never dallied in the uncertain quagmire between those two extremes. Now, Whitaker was Harvard intelligence and Dempsey was Manassa ignorance, and their positions were cut and dried in the view of most with an entry-level grasp of boxing styles. Therefore, in order to vault the greatest physical and psychological hurdle of his career to date, Haye would have to challenge elements of Booth's theory, wade through a potentially turbulent sea of mixed signals and styles, before combining what he knew and what he didn't know to steal a belt from a seven-foot champion. Not Dempsey, not Whitaker, not Hearns and not Leonard, David no longer resembled templates, nor even the fighter he once was. He was revamped and rounded, and there was a growing sense that Booth, once an intrigued and inquisitive bystander, knew his fighter better than ever that week in Nuremberg.

'Sleep is the cousin of death,' rapper Nas once preached in his seminal 1994 hit "NY State of Mind" and, in a sport where death is viewed as a feared end result, it can be vital to carefully monitor one's sleep patterns. Since arriving in Germany on the Monday, Haye and Booth quickly subscribed to Nas' sentiment, endured many late nights, remained wide awake while everyone else slept, and often chose to take leisurely strolls through the city centre in the early hours of the morning.

I got my own taste of this late-night orienteering on the eve of the fight as Haye, Booth, Watts, conditioner Ruben Tabares, operations manager Jon Hill and the fighter's close friends Karlton Bryan and Kamran Naqvi ventured into the town centre at a whisker beyond midnight. What began as an aimless meander soon transformed into a purposeful march through Nuremberg's red-light district, as Haye amused himself with the sights and sounds of the town's seediest hang-outs.

We walked on past rows of neon-lit windows, each one boasting a scantily clad whore on the other side – ethnicity, size and smile catering for all tastes and distastes. True to form, Haye rated the girls in passing and dished out 'solid eights' and 'weak fours' like an aroused *Come Dancing* judge. With no cinemas in walking distance, the fighter utilised this slide-show as his means of late-night entertainment and escapism. Nothing distracted Haye like the lure of cheap and accessible flesh and, even when he knew the potential for pay-off was non-existent, he still teased the senses and egged on friends to follow through where he couldn't.

'I'll give anybody €100 to go in there, finish within ten minutes and then be back out here dressed and ready to leave,' said Haye, as his eyes scanned the group. 'Anybody got a stopwatch?'

Nobody had a stopwatch, nor any intention of taking on Haye's bet.

'Come on,' he pleaded, clearly annoyed by the gang's refusal to entertain him. 'I don't think it can be done, so I'm offering one of you the chance to prove me wrong. In and out within ten minutes, that's all I'm asking.'

Haye removed one hundred euros from his back pocket and tantalisingly waved the note beneath our noses. Still no takers. As each of us passed the buck and baton, the group were bailed out by the sudden presence of two adolescent German boys, far too young to be hanging around such murky haunts.

'Is that David Haye?' whispered a voice from behind us, as the boxer continued to wave cash in his friends' faces. The first to hear the question, I turned around and clocked the two teenage boys creeping closer. I shook my head. Of course this isn't David Haye, my body language informed them. He's fighting for the heavy-weight championship of the world tomorrow. He wouldn't be seen dead out here at this time of night. The boys wouldn't relent, though, and continued to whisper and chuckle, until Haye finally turned around and spotted them.

'David Haye!' the boys shouted out.

'What's up, guys?' said the man in question, as he slipped his note back inside his pocket and walked over to the pair.

Less than a year ago it was difficult finding anybody on the streets of London who knew of Haye or craved to see his name on a piece of paper, and now he was being stalked along Nuremberg's RLD by teenagers who should have been tucked up in bed. Haye wasn't spooked to have been spotted procrastinating before his big exam, and was instead overjoyed to have two Germans on his side. The fighter's friends were also comforted by the presence of the two young boys, as it allowed them a timely escape from Haye's challenge.

In the end, the shunned heavyweight troublemaker headed back to his hotel, only to return to the red-light district some two hours later, flanked once again by friends for vicarious entertainment. Haye would fare better second time around, too, as he finally persuaded a wingman to follow through with the bet and take both the money from his pocket and his mind off the fight. For the sake of €100, Haye considered it time and money well spent.

Later the next evening, as I festered in my Nuremberg hotel room, edgy, hungry, bored and counting down the hours until witnessing either Haye's crowning moment or his devastating demise, an abrupt phone call interrupted the mental torment at approximately 5.34 p.m.

'Hello?' I said, grabbing the phone on its very first ring.

'Elliot?' replied the familiar voice of Jon Hill, the sticky tape behind the scenes and often the only sane mind in the asylum.

'Yes.'

'David wants you to go to his room now. He's in 316.'

'Okay.'

'Thanks.'

As I attempted to recall every David I knew residing in Nuremberg, I swiftly came to the conclusion that there was, in fact, only one David I was aware of. He was in room number 316 and, to only further the confusion, had cheekily checked in under the pseudonym 'Roy Jones'. As disappointed as I was to discover it wasn't the real Roy Jones residing on the floor above, the idea of Haye requiring my presence so close to the biggest moment of his career still managed to stir plenty of childish excitement within the walls of my churning stomach.

Therefore, visualising a banquet of comfort food behind door 316, I made my way out of my room, along the corridor, up the stairs and towards the future king's current throne. Once inside, I quickly discovered Haye's room was incredibly messy, and Roy Jones was, of course, nowhere to be seen. Amid the clutter, Haye was alone in the dark and in the process of sinking into a leather chair. He picked at the remains of his last supper and watched a boxing match on the hotel television.

'Here, take a seat,' he said. 'You're making me feel uncomfortable just standing there.'

'Sorry,' I replied, searching out the nearest chair.

'How are you feeling?'

'Pretty confident,' I said, half-lying as usual. 'You?'

'Yeah, good. I just started watching Mosley-Margarito.'

Just as advertised, playing on a nearby television was the January 2009 slugfest between welterweights Sugar Shane Mosley and Antonio Margarito. 'Seems as though I arrived just in time then,' I said, excited by the chance to rewatch one of that year's most entertaining ring wars.

Full of speed, explosiveness and subtlety, Mosley was always part of the template for Haye. Whenever a fight DVD was requested from this particular author's library, Sugar Shane joined Roy Jones, James Toney and Floyd Mayweather as regular lynchpins of the compilations I took great pleasure in rustling up. We were watching one of my own productions that November night and, as well as Mosley's destruction of Margarito, Haye would also digest Mayweather's one-sided dissection of Diego Corrales.

Some of the fights go unwatched, but Haye finds comfort in the ones he does view. In fact, he'd point-blank refuse to watch anything other than the boxing *crème de la crème* before fights of his own. He wouldn't watch anything of his opponent, and refused to watch any fights comprising give-and-take action and blood and guts. He enjoyed witnessing great fighters neatly demonstrate their skills in a one-sided and clinical fashion. After all, that's the position every fighter sees himself in.

'Being praised for having a great chin is not really a *good thing*, is it?' said Haye, as he watched Mosley glide through the gears and shave the facial hair off Margarito. 'It just means you get hit a lot and your defence sucks.'

Right on cue, Margarito crashed to the deck in a crumpled heap, the end result of a vicious Mosley barrage. Considered to have the best chin in world boxing, the Mexican was knocked out for the first time in his career by the canny American.

'Anyone can be knocked out if you hit them hard and often enough,' added Haye. 'No human being is designed to take punches to the head. Even one as freaky-looking as Valuev.'

That much was true, of course, yet Valuev, one could argue, was slightly different from the rest of us. The heavyweight champion suffered from acromegaly, a syndrome brought on when the pituitary gland produces excess growth hormone after epiphyseal plate closure at puberty. The disorder commonly causes a thickening of the skin and skull, pronounced cheekbones, a prominent and bulging forehead, as well as larger lips, nose and hands. So, if anybody was crafted to receive punishment, it was Valuev, an exaggerated take on the human form. While it took Mosley eight and a half rounds of severe punishment to bring the curtain down on Margarito, Haye realised it might take twice as many to put Valuev in the same state of unrest. A sobering thought for any fighter, perhaps, especially when only given twelve rounds within which to shoe-shine the dome of a deformed foe.

'Are you worried about the judges?' asked Haye, as the next meal arrived in his room, a concoction of various unidentifiable vegetables, some green, some orange and some purple, each carefully plucked and painted by nutritionist Ruben Tabares.

'No,' I replied. 'I don't think it will be close enough to be a problem. If you're going to win, it will be wide and beyond dispute. I think if the fight is close, then it will mean you're taking too many shots and being worn down. You're going to have to win cleanly and widely.'

'Yeah,' said Haye, nodding. 'That's what I think, too.'

'You've got to remember, *everybody's* going to see this fight,' I added. 'It's a lot harder to screw somebody over when the eyes of the world are on the fight.'

It was now clear to me that Haye *was* concerned about the judges' verdict that night, despite implying the opposite. Having now familiarised myself with his idiosyncrasies before battle, I realised his concerns would be revealed via questions posed to me, rather than candid musings about his own state of mind. He'd ask me if *I* was concerned, worried or nervous, in the hope that *my* answer would be in line with his thinking and therefore be enough to appease his own doubts. Like most fighters, Haye shuddered at the thought of ever appearing frightened, no matter how apprehensive he was truly feeling. I never got the sense Haye was scared that night, but he was certainly as anxious about the various unknown elements surrounding the fight as I was.

Eager to move away from any emerging trepidation, I settled beside Haye and watched two things for the next half an hour – him eat food and Diego Corrales feast on a succession of Floyd Mayweather left hooks and right crosses. There were around half a dozen knockdowns in total, and Mayweather has still never performed better. Haye looked on in awe, almost in a way that suggested, 'I'm good, but even I'll never be *that* good.' He admired Mayweather's display of speed, ring generalship and intelligent use of the left jab to Corrales' mid-section. Halfway through the fight, Haye even dropped his fork, stood up, snapped his body into a fighting stance and practised dipping down and stabbing a left jab into the belly of an invisible opponent. 'What do you think?' asked David, as he consulted the screen and then threw the punch at thin air.

'It will create you lots of time and space if you can use it properly,' I replied, preaching straight from an imaginary *Boxing Skills 101* textbook. Apparently content with the answer, Haye shook his arms out and sat back down. He picked up his fork and got back to eating something colourful. I didn't press him for confirmation or a sign that my opinion was correct, and by now realised one wouldn't be forthcoming.

Having known David for a while, and having been in this position before, I knew it was best to speak only when asked or required. If David spoke, I knew he wanted to talk. If he didn't, he didn't. Incredibly, for a man who fought so hard to distract himself from everything around him, Haye listened to me more that night than ever before.

'I've never really had to properly *box* anyone before, have I?' he said, through a mouthful of food. 'I've never had to box and move for twelve rounds.'

'No,' I said. 'You do it in sparring, though. You showed me that on tape the other day.'

Haye nodded and turned back to the television in time to watch Corrales pull himself up from the canvas once more.

'What was the reach difference between Mayweather and Corrales?' he asked.

'I don't know.'

'Do you reckon it was about the same as the difference between me and Valuev?'

I shrugged, while Haye scanned his laptop for the answer. He then discovered, much to his horror, that according to boxrec.com, Mayweather actually boasted a two-inch reach advantage over the taller Corrales. Neither of us had expected *that*.

'That can't be right, surely,' sighed Haye. 'There's no way Mayweather has longer arms than Corrales.'

'Boxrec isn't *always* right,' I said. 'They've even got you listed as six feet three, and there's no way you're that tall, even in heels.'

'I swear I'm six foot three. I've been measured.'

Whatever the actual statistics, we both knew he'd concede around a foot in height, six inches in reach and seven stone in weight to Valuev in a matter of hours. So, in order to banish that stark image, Haye distracted himself by watching humorous video clips on YouTube and hitting play on an uplifting tracklist comprising offerings from Michael Jackson, Marvin Gaye, Terence Trent D'Arby and UB40.

The closest Haye ever got to focusing on the fight was when he settled down and intently scanned the online boxing websites and forums, keen to gauge the consensus opinion before he headed to the arena. I admired his ability to read through dire predictions of his own fate, knowing full well he'd have to live up to the hopes of the believers and confound the sceptics before the night was out. I wanted to shut the laptop down and hide, yet Haye was never more invigorated than when confronting a problem head on. The bigger, the better.

Inspired by rather than afraid of the event, Haye cleared his throat with a cough and readied his vocal chords for an uninvited impression of that evening's master of ceremonies Michael Buffer. In the smarmiest American accent he could muster, Haye roared, 'Aaaaaannnnnnnd in the red corner, from St Petersburg, Russia, the reigning and defending WBA heavyweight champion of the world . . . Nikolaiiiiiiiiiiiy Valuuuuuuuuuuuev!'

Now emphasising the grandiosity of the event even more, Haye circled the room and belted out his own Buffer-inspired ring announcement, spinning out 'The Hayemakerrrrrrrr' for as long as his lungs would allow.

'I can't wait to hear how Buffer announces me tonight,' he said. 'I've always wanted to be introduced by Buffer. That's another one of my dreams.'

As silence fell and I pondered the night ahead, a yawning Haye began to pick up trash that had collected on his hotel room floor and sing joyfully to the Michael Jackson song 'Butterflies'. He placed empty water bottles in bins and arranged clothes into neater piles. The time had come to tidy his room, thus signalling both my time to leave and Haye's moment to prosper.

CHAPTER TWENTY

THE HANDSHAKE

They say the jab is the foundation, the first brick and prerequisite for everything that follows. Cheat on or neglect the jab and the entire structure falls in on itself. It's an unwritten rule, an old wives' tale and the mantra many a boxing coach has whispered in the ear of an aspiring pug.

Even *I* knew the importance of the jab. Remember the Floyd Mayweather-inspired jab to the stomach I'd expertly demonstrated and taught David Haye in the precious hours before his WBA world heavyweight title challenge? Well, so much for that. Within seconds of shooting his first jab towards the considerable mid-section of WBA world heavyweight champion Nikolay Valuev, our pint-sized challenger from Great Britain was sent scurrying back across the ring on the retreat. The giant's gut absorbed the punch like Sunday lunch, and Haye was forced to wave the white flag and rethink, rather than apply a second brick. You see, while Mayweather's lefts to the long and lean torso of Diego Corrales were flashy signs of dominance and precursors to heavier artillery, Haye was shooting for that same punch simply because it was the *only* opening available.

And so it began. Once the first bell tolled at a shade past 10 p.m. on Saturday, 7 November, the Arena Nürnberger Versicherung fell eerily silent, its German and British spectators aware the night would be long and Valuev would, in all likelihood, remain upright for its duration. If a premature climax did happen to occur, the common assumption was that it would be Haye, not the champion, spread out across the ring canvas like an unnecessary beverage sponsor.

Valuev offered little to hit in the first round as his chin was too high, his range was too long and his arms were positioned directly in front of his oversized head. Haye tentatively pot-shotted Valuev's bullet-proof belly with a further three jabs, before unwrapping his first one-two combination with ninety seconds gone in the round. Both punches missed by inches, but the intent was there, at least.

In truth, the opening round would have been a tedious dud had it not been so damn engaging. Little if anything landed from either man in the space of three minutes, yet you couldn't possibly take your eyes off the non-action. The pattern had already been set. The cumbersome champion, devoid of any semblance of explosiveness or creativity, would attempt to swat the challenger with all he knew, while Haye looked to evade Valuev's rudimentary swings and pickpocket shots on the sly. This wasn't boxing, or even a fight in its truest sense. It was an intriguing athletic encounter of styles and tactics, and one that would presumably be won by whoever could apply brains to obvious brawn.

In order to successfully bag rounds on foreign soil against a German-based champion, Haye needed to produce exclamation marks through both his punching and ring generalship. He intended to make Valuev miss by metres, not centimetres, and then exhibit defensive superiority with a juvenile wink, stuck-out tongue, nod, smile or camp wave of the hand. As the champion continued to misfire, Haye needed to retaliate only when confident of landing, and to make the punch count. The whole charade was a form of light-fingered theft and required Haye turning cocksure matador and hollering *Olé!* each time he led the almighty bull steaming towards the red rag.

In round two, Haye discovered his first clear opening and rattled a mammoth left hook and right hook off the considerable crown of Valuev. Undeterred by the punches, Nikolay merely covered up behind his gloves, shook his head and continued trudging forward. What seemed like a first minor success now appeared to resemble more of a crisis, as not only did Haye make little impression on his opponent, but he also broke the third metacarpal in his right hand in the process. By way of consolation, the challenger now at least knew he could reach the face of the giant with his pet punch.

For long periods Valuev grabbed at anything he could so much as touch, like a blind man reaching for a stray guide-dog, and even started to graze Haye in the seventh, as the challenger's reflexes finally slowed and his pace dropped. Heading into the eighth and ninth rounds, however, it seemed Valuev's token effort had taken something out of him, and Haye was subsequently able to secure a much-needed second wind. The champion was back to awkwardly conversing in sign language, while a fluent Haye slipped his way in and out of range, bouncing occasional right hands off Valuev's flashing beacon. The Russian landed nothing, and could only shrug his shoulders whenever Haye punished him for his vast limitations.

By now it seemed fine to dream and, God forbid, actually grow confident of Haye winning the fight. Blind to the scorecards, of course, I did nevertheless start to envisage a situation where David had pocketed many of the preceding rounds and thus enjoyed a reasonably snug lead heading into the final stages. Although I was aware of the potential for home cooking on German soil, I remained strangely calm and certain Haye was not only leading at this juncture, but that he'd also receive a deserved nod when the final bell tolled. I'd yet to witness Valuev score *any* major success in the bout, whereas Haye had conjured numerous flashpoints along the way.

'Clean, clean, clean,' implored Adam Booth in between rounds, as Haye slumped down on his stool and controlled his breathing ahead of the final session. It was now clear Booth was seeing the fight the way I was from ringside, and believed Haye to be riding a healthy lead going into the final three minutes. Most at ringside followed the same line of thinking, though a scant few also felt Valuev's unconvincing impression of aggression had warranted him holding a narrow lead with a round to go. Unaware of these dissenting voices at the time, I simply wanted Haye to stay out of harm's way and dance towards a clear and clean decision verdict.

As it turned out, Valuev's round twelve would prove to be an exact replica of his round one. Unable to shift his feet, pump his fists or exert any kind of pressure on his mobile foe, the champion appeared beaten before the confirmation arrived. Tired and clueless, Valuev was stuck in a rut of mediocrity, and boasted neither the imagination nor the energy to go about altering his ways. Haye, meanwhile, was jiving more than ever in the final minutes, and was mixing in wild punches whenever Valuev squared up in front of him. He continued finding success with left hooks and right crosses, thrown high and in combination, and found a flagging Valuev easier to hit and hurt in the twelfth than at any other stage in the bout.

This became abundantly clear with ninety seconds to go in the final round, when Haye loaded up on a left hook and right hand, before introducing a final hook that clipped Valuev beneath his ear and sent the giant champion scrambling towards the ropes. The crowd leapt to their feet in disbelief, as Nikolay the unstoppable was stunned, wobbled and hurt for the first time in his 52-bout professional career. The immovable object suddenly carried the flustered look of a pensioner who'd tripped over the kerb, only to then steady himself with the aid of his Zimmer frame. Valuev grabbed the top rope, shook his confused head like a child who'd unwillingly discovered Santa's secret, and then belted up as Haye attempted to make history and finish off a man never before knocked down, let alone knocked out.

A ravenous Haye bowled over two further right hands in a clinch, then another left hook and right swing upon exit, desperate to apply the exclamation mark. He then abruptly called off his attack, stood his ground, smiled, smelt the air and presumably sensed victory was just around the corner. With ten seconds to go, the challenger elected to skip around the perimeter of the ring, one arm aloft in premature celebration and the other by his side in sheer disdain for the sullen champion's lack of attack. Roy Jones Jr had done something similar in 2003 when winning the same belt from John Ruiz, though I'm sure Haye didn't need to be told that.

As the final bell rang out, the Briton shot both arms skyward, while Valuev dipped his head towards the canvas, a contrasting image which offered a glimpse into how both fighters viewed their respective performances. Valuev's robotic limitations had been exposed for the second time in his professional career by a fighter who'd shunned natural fighting instincts to box the kind of fight that felt wholly unnatural. One man tripped and finally malfunctioned doing the only thing he knew, while the other adapted to his environment and prospered in the kind of situation that would overwhelm most similarly sized mortals.

Amid the chaos of collecting and collating scorecards, I ventured through the press row and gathered the consensus opinion of Britain's ringside journalists, many of whom had begrudgingly backed Valuev to come out on top. Thankfully, with twelve full rounds acting as proof, most pre-fight doubters had now turned believers, and the general view was that Haye had done enough to take the title back to Britain. Ever the boxing purist, Claude Abrams, then editor of trade magazine *Boxing News*, even had Haye winning by a score of 120–108, meaning that in his view the English challenger had swept each of the twelve rounds. While that score seemed perhaps a little too generous, even for a self-confessed cheerleader like myself, I remained in agreement with the reporters who sided with Haye. Boxing was a sport that strived to promote the art of hitting and not getting hit and, with entertainment value perhaps sacrificed, Haye had perfected the concept beautifully through twelve rounds. He'd crafted the kind of fight he needed to box, and had received barely a lick in response.

Ultimately, I was mad at myself for not feeling any kind of post-fight tension or nerves, when everybody else around me seemed paralysed with both. Eccentric Gareth A. Davies, boxing and mixed-martial-arts scribe for the *Daily Telegraph*, assumed I was far more apprehensive than I actually was, and even kindly offered to do some scouting on my behalf. I watched as Davies snuck out from the press row, darted towards a television monitor and, with one flick of his black mane and a joyously erect thumb, signalled victory in his own inimitable way. Then, in order to provide further confirmation, he raced towards me, grabbed my arm and whispered, 'He's got it. Majority decision. Don't worry.'

He was right. By the time the scores of 116–112, 116–112 and 114–114 were read out, I felt next to no emotion. I had seen it all coming – from the performance, to the scorecards, to the sense of destiny. Try as I might to doubt him, Haye had become world heavyweight champion, just as he'd always said he would. I'd long maintained he wasn't big, tough or experienced enough, yet here he was, the black-and-red world title belt wrapped around his torso. Sure, Valuev's 48-inch strap would have to be downsized for Haye in the coming weeks but, waist issues aside, the championship was heading home with us to Britain.

Little did I know at the time, but the victory appeared to mean just as much to our great nation as it did to me. However, nothing could have prepared either of us for what would await the new WBA world heavyweight champion at London's Heathrow Airport the following evening.

'What do you think it will be like the other end?' asked Haye, as we walked through Nuremberg airport en route to the nearest McDonald's.

'I don't know,' I said. 'It's going to be a lot different to how it was when you returned from the Jean-Marc Mormeck fight, though. I know that much.'

'There was nobody at the airport after that one, was there?'

I shook my head.

'Apparently the guys at Sky Sports are saying there are already hundreds waiting for us at Heathrow right now,' added Haye. 'This is going to be crazy.'

'How do you feel about that?'

'I don't know. It's weird to think they'd all turn up to see me. I'm just a normal guy from south London who has done my job, something I've always said I'd do. I haven't created a cure for cancer or anything. It just doesn't seem *that* amazing to me. I haven't even had a chance to think about the fight at all yet. It hasn't really sunk in.'

Haye was then called to the counter at McDonald's, and spent the next five minutes reeling off a fast-food list long enough to clog the arteries of a family of Russian giants. He ordered a Big Mac, chicken nuggets and large fries for himself, and similarly hefty portions for everybody else who happened to be travelling back home with him.

'This reminds me of a time when I'd eat McDonald's on a regular basis as a kid and dream of becoming world heavyweight champion,' said Haye, as he tucked into the first Big Mac he'd consumed for years. 'It still tastes as good as I remember it.'

'So I guess you're now going to become a proper heavyweight and get fat like the rest of them,' I said.

'Today, maybe,' smiled Haye. 'Everybody's allowed a fat day from time to time, especially when you've just become heavyweight champ. You can give me that, right?'

Sure. I gave him that.

There would be no need for taxi drivers armed with boards and black marker pens at the other end. Nobody required Haye to identify himself upon arriving at Heathrow. Hundreds, perhaps even thousands, of strangers gathered in the arrival lobby of terminal five and waited in anticipation for the new champion to show his face and title belt. Some had even been congregating there for hours by the time Haye's plane eventually touched down in London.

There was a tangible buzz and excitement around the new champion, as airport security guards informed him there would be a sea of expectant faces waiting for him once he emerged through the doors. This, of course, led to an increase in staff and protection around Haye, who suddenly, in a tired blink of an eye, was transformed from friend, boxer and subject to overnight sensation and celebrity. Standing fifty or so yards from the huddle, I watched as those around him altered their stride pattern, or stopped completely, in order to flank the champion as he passed through the doors and triggered flashbulbs. In fact, within seconds of gathering his luggage and preparing to face the music, Haye was hemmed in by dozens of willing volunteers, all keen to get a first hit of the fame game. Part of me admired the hunger to be associated with Haye, yet another part of me endured a slow and inevitable death that afternoon, as I realised the fighter was no longer only accessible to me, at least not like before.

Sick of waiting and watching, I ventured on up ahead, made a break for it and bundled into the arrival area like a spat-out piece of celery, stuck between teeth and causing unwelcome distress. Nobody wanted my picture or autograph, of course, and I liked it that way. I enjoyed the comparative serenity and calm of my entrance. Stood just by WH Smith, my onlooking father waved, inspiring a frenetic dart towards him before the cavalry arrived.

'Can you believe how many people are here?' said my father.

'Yeah, it's amazing,' I replied. 'Shall we make a move? You won't be able to see him anyway.'

'We could, I suppose,' sighed Dad, clearly opposing my plans. 'I wanted to shake David's hand, though.'

I watched as my father, like a kid at Disneyland, desperately searched high above the heads of those in front, all in the faint hope of at least catching a glimpse of Haye's grand entrance before we left. Amazingly enough, Dad had never met David Haye before, despite the close association and relationship I'd shared with the fighter over the course of six years. He'd watched each of his fights on television, even attended a few in person, but had never before traded words or even handshakes.

I felt bad for wanting to direct my father away from the mêlée and break for the car. While I was tired and worn out from the hype, drama and sycophantic nature of the supporting cast, my father was new to it all and clearly intrigued. My mind then recalled a time long ago when my brothers and I waited in empty car parks after boxing events, intent on snaring an autograph or picture with the punching protagonists. My father never dared question our plans and would often wait with us into the early hours of the following morning, camera in hand, just in case we got lucky. Now the roles were reversed, and I couldn't possibly deny him the chance to meet the fighter who had meant so much to me, and to the both of us, for so many years.

It was then that the trumpets sounded and the floodgates opened. Haye and his new-found troop of tailgaters appeared in the arrival lobby and Heathrow erupted, with fans, commuters, reporters and casual lurkers all now clamouring for a bite-sized chunk of the heavyweight champion of the world.

'I'm going to get a drink,' I told my father. 'Want anything?'

'No, I'll wait here,' replied Dad, still spellbound by the carnival playing out in front of him.

I sauntered on through to WH Smith, grabbed a Coke Zero and Sprite in a two-for-one offer and then placed the beverages on the counter. Two teenage girls tallied up the total and giggled excitedly at the prospect of Haye being only metres away.

'I'd love to meet him,' said one of the girls. 'He's gorgeous. Did you watch his fight last night?'

'Yeah, of course,' said the other. 'I can't believe he beat that giant. Shall I go and get him to sign this?'

The girl held up a scrap of paper and the pair contemplated whether they could get away with fleeing from the till and pursuing Britain's heavyweight champion through a mass of people, each with similar intent.

'I could try and get him over here, if you want,' I said, sensing the girls' predicament. Rather than brazenly showing off in the company of the opposite sex, I was instead far more impressed with the fact that these girls knew who my favourite fighter was. I'd waited six long years to hear two young females discuss the wonders of David Haye, and now that time had finally arrived.

'Would you be able to do that?' asked the first girl.

'I could try,' I said, just as I began to wonder whether my initial enthusiasm had foolishly overtaken my better judgement. I looked outside the shop at the fog surrounding my friend and realised it was only growing thicker.

Meanwhile, my father had ambitiously and perhaps dangerously forced his way to within touching distance of Haye. Ready to sling him a life jacket, I spotted Dad up ahead and politely cut through the swarm to try and catch up. By this time the target was close to being out the door, and my father felt the need to make his move. He perilously reached across burly minders, pulled himself into view and then bravely offered Haye his hand.

'My name's Graham,' said my father, as he shook the new champion's hand. 'I'm Elliot's dad.'

Thankfully, any fear of Haye turning prima donna on my old man, of all people, was soon eradicated, as I watched the boxer unleash the most genuine and heartfelt smile and handshake he'd extend to anybody at the airport that day. He shook my father's hand like he'd known him all his life, and, despite being pulled this way and that by everybody around him, made a point of slowing down the procession and making eye contact with the man who'd brought me into his world. Belt or no belt, that spontaneous act of sincerity meant every bit as much to me as the conquering of Goliath the previous night. The scene was reassuring and comforting and told me that, though now mixing in the land of giants, the new champion wasn't about to leave the little people behind just yet.

CHAPTER TWENTY-ONE
BIG HANDS

The four of us crouched behind steel bars, unable to do anything about the distance that separated us from our prey. Brothers Adam and Alex and I were expertly positioned outside the car park of Wembley Arena, each armed with a camera in one hand and autograph book in the other. Dad oversaw the operation, his car on standby in an adjacent and infinitely cheaper car park across the road. We'd been waiting for nearly two hours, and then it happened. We caught a glimpse.

'That's him,' I said, clearly the best equipped to make a judgement from such a distance. 'Let's shout out his name.'

So we did and, lo and behold, a wide-shouldered minder reluctantly opened the gates, thus releasing a tidal wave on the unsuspecting heavyweight up ahead. We wasted no time in darting towards him and interrupting the supposedly seamless passage from changing room to back seat of limousine.

Perhaps the fact that he was fresh off a first-round knockout victory on his professional debut had something to do with it, but Audley 'A-Force' Harrison, our Olympic gold medallist and heavyweight hero, wooed and captivated us all that night, inside and then, more crucially, outside of the ring. After watching him defeat miserable Miami bouncer Mike Middleton from row Z in May 2001, my family's early obsession would be sealed with a signature, scrawled across multiple fight programmes, as well as a photograph and warm embrace.

'You'll be bigger than Bruno,' extolled my father behind the camera lens.

'No doubt, no doubt,' agreed Harrison, as his outstretched hand threatened to engulf the entire head of my younger brother.

The Olympic hero was already larger than Frank Bruno in a physical sense, of course. Standing at six feet six inches, and with a wingspan as wide as the stretched limo booked to escort him, Harrison, even that night in an empty car park, looked, acted and spoke like the dominant world heavyweight champion he promised us all he'd one day become.

Nine years later and Harrison was 26–4 and eleven and a half rounds into the final moments of a shock European heavyweight title challenge. It was the biggest fight of Harrison's career to date, and he was losing on all three scorecards. He'd yet to box for a world title and was, in no shape or form, bigger than Bruno. Boasting few fans or believers and even fewer titles, the Olympic hero's career had nosedived into a quagmire of lacklustre performances, unfulfilled promises and unrequited love. In fact, he'd been beaten four times, knocked out once and, at thirty-eight years of age, was now a forgetful senior citizen desperately clawing back time and memory.

Harrison was losing to Reading's Michael Sprott in April 2010, having ruptured his pectoral muscle early in the contest and been unable to match his opponent's consistency throughout. Sprott had dramatically knocked Harrison clean out three years before and, up on the cards, appeared only seconds away from ending Harrison's washout of a career for good.

Then it happened. The stars inside London's Alexandra Palace aligned and, with Sprott backed up on the ropes, Harrison cocked his left arm, closed his eyes and unleashed the mother of all finishing blows. The punch nailed Sprott flush on the jaw and sent the Reading man to the deck, out cold and with no count necessary. Harrison wheeled away, through pain and jubilation, unsure exactly how he'd managed to conjure the kind of spite and finish that had evaded him for the best part of a decade.

On the brink of retirement and from seemingly out of nowhere, Harrison had become European heavyweight champion. Sure, it wasn't the world title he'd promised everybody, and it was hardly a Brunoesque achievement, yet the come-from-behind win over Sprott landed Harrison a legitimate pro belt and a potential world ranking. Both had seemed implausible only seconds beforehand.

Watching in disbelief that April night was WBA world heavyweight champion David Haye, one week removed from the first successful defence of his crown. On Saturday, 3 April, Haye had broken down and stopped rugged American John Ruiz inside nine rounds in Manchester, to retain his belt and further demonstrate his heavyweight pedigree. Stopped only once before in a commendable eighteen-year pro career, former champion Ruiz was dropped in the first round and then floored three further times in a one-sided drubbing. He retired immediately after the bout.

Haye, meanwhile, next planned to box in either October or November, and was tentatively on the lookout for potential title challengers. Having banished mandatory contender Ruiz, the new champion was now afforded the luxury of choosing a voluntary opponent and someone ranked within the WBA's top fifteen world rankings.

For the time being, though, Haye was content to watch Harrison, a one-time friend and former training partner, win the European belt against all odds. Although he'd turned pro a year and a half later in a weight division below, Haye had since surpassed Harrison as both a cruiserweight and then heavyweight. Never one to take pleasure in a friend's demise, however, Haye was instead disappointed with Harrison's progress and, as Audley threatened to change it all with one punch, the WBA champion was one of the first to glance in his rear-view mirror and fist-pump the air in delight.

The pair had spent many long nights on the phone to one another after respective victories and defeats, but that April night would be different. Standing at contrasting platforms in their lives and careers, the relationship between Haye and Harrison had altered and soured to the extent that supportive phone calls and get-togethers were a thing of the past.

As for my own budding relationship with the one-time heavyweight hope, we reconvened again by chance in December 2006, when I took the opportunity to once more shake his gargantuan mitt. This time no gloves were involved, as Harrison and I had been invited to a thirtieth birthday party thrown for Haye's girlfriend Natasha. Acting as a mutual acquaintance, Haye reconnected the two of us with outlandish tales of car-park stalking, while I refused to confess that I'd long given up hope of Harrison ever fulfilling his post-Olympic dream.

To his credit, though, it was around this time that Harrison gained revenge over bitter rival Danny Williams in impressive fashion, and his stock had never been higher since turning pro. Just as my brothers and I had been five years earlier, most within the Clapham bar were drawn to Harrison's presence, immense frame and freakish fists, as well as his renewed ambition. Flanked by wife Raychel, the boxer spent much of the night posing for photographs and boasting of a career turnaround to any ears that would listen. While some of us knew better by now, Harrison was again back to grinning, posing, preaching and acting like the heavyweight champion of the world.

*   *   *

Haye and Harrison carried on these roles of achiever and deceiver for the next four years, and I continued to watch and flip back and forth between the pair, while admittedly investing the majority of hope and interest in the slugger from Bermondsey. David won WBC, WBA and WBO world cruiserweight titles, and Audley spoke of doing the same at heavyweight. Then, as if to compound matters, Haye beat Harrison to the punch as a heavyweight, too, when he scooped the WBA version of the crown in 2009. To make matters worse, Harrison had been knocked out in a Commonwealth title challenge, lost to an Irish cab driver named Martin Rogan, and was then denied the chance to box on one of Haye's undercards. How things had changed.

By the summer of 2010, Haye and Harrison were no longer talking. Much to the shock of the boxing world, the former friends now planned on fighting one another. Scheduled for 13 November in Manchester, Haye had taken advantage of Harrison's freshly acquired number fourteen ranking with the WBA and selected his fellow Londoner as the next challenger of choice.

Here's why. With an Olympic gold medal still lingering some-where on his mantelpiece, Harrison remained a commodity in Great Britain, albeit one with a depressing run of defeats and a fall-guy persona. Profiled heavily by the BBC upon winning gold and turning pro, Audley quickly became a prominent public figure, for better or worse. He was famous like Bruno, but not popular like him. There was a pantomime-villain appeal to Harrison by 2010 and, though he didn't have the wins to explain the fame, he possessed the face and sob story to generate interest and cash. With a European title in hand, Harrison had also fallen upon a number fourteen ranking with the WBA and yapped his way into Haye's immediate plans. He goaded the champion at any available opportunity and, through a combination of good fortune, a big left hand and simply being in the right place at the right time, landed the world title shot many felt was beyond him.

He never said it outright, but the reason for Haye accepting the fight had little to do with legacy and everything to do with cashing in on the stained reputation of a famous former friend. It's true, Haye's defence against Harrison was less of a fight and more of an event. It was Britain's biggest boxing occasion for over a decade and, with two household names vying for the heavyweight prize, touched a portion of the public most other prizefights were unable to. Whether he wanted to admit it or not, Harrison, though low on danger, was clearly the most famous fighter Haye could have possibly defended his belt against that year. He was an A-list celebrity masquerading as a D-list fighter, the kind of low-risk, high-reward proposition that appealed to most professional boxers. Criticism would undoubtedly and perhaps rightly find its way to Haye's door in the coming weeks and months, but so too would spotlight, interest and wealth.

In order to play his part in the unsightly sideshow, Harrison was guaranteed an alleged straight sum of £400,000, as well as a twenty per cent cut of the net revenue received through pay-per-view sales and money made at the gate. All in all, should the fight dupe the proportion of the public it was expected to, Harrison would conceivably walk away with upwards of a million pounds for his efforts, however risible.

Although he hated the idea of the fight at first, Haye, for his part, would take home a substantial percentage of every pay-per-view buy at a cost of £14.95 and, in addition to extra earnings, was predicted to receive around £5m for the charade. With money sorted, both champion and challenger then set about selling their squabble to the masses. A press conference was scheduled for Tuesday, 7 September in Westminster, and television partners Sky Box Office excitedly erected a stage upon which the two actors could recite lines, spin stories and, above all else, flog their product.

As with all big box-office motion pictures, wardrobe and cine-matography would be key components in Westminster that September afternoon. In order to accentuate the size difference and simultaneously heighten a sense of peril, Haye decided to dress in a skin-tight T-shirt and flat shoes, while Harrison rocked a weighty designer suit. A three-inch disparity appeared almost twice as much, and the illusion clearly worked.

Haye, the smaller man, made up for his lack of inches with a spiteful tongue and numerous verbal putdowns, promising a 'public execution' and at one point explaining how he'd 'violate' Harrison in the ring. The champion then went one step further and predicted the fight would be as 'one-sided as a gang rape' to a group of national newspaper writers. Hours later and the quote and its impli-cations took the country by storm, landing Haye column inches and criticism from pundits and rape victim support groups. Haye merely shrugged, accepted the lashes and began to count his pennies.

Meanwhile, Harrison seemed to rattle Haye when he reminded the belt-holder he'd been knocked out by southpaw Jim Twite as an amateur, and stopped by Carl Thompson as a pro. He also frequently mentioned how he'd 'groomed' the younger Haye in their early days together and that David had merely grown up to become a clone of the one-time Olympic gold medallist. Both cham-pion and challenger screeched at one another like warring neigh-bours over an invisible fence for the best part of half an hour, and nobody in the room had any reason to doubt the authenticity of the spat.

The dispute and fight, titled 'Best of Enemies', was then further legitimised by two key plot points. The first was Haye's point-blank refusal to host an abject Audley on one of his promotional company's undercards in 2009, and the second centred on an infam-ous sparring session the pair shared in Miami in 2006.

'When I lost to Danny Williams, my confidence was at an all-time low,' explained Harrison to a pack of British boxing writers, who were all tuts and rolling eyes, long fed up with the Olympian's tiresome 'Yes I Can' spiel. 'David happened to be in Miami and we hadn't seen one another for about two years. He was roughly a week away from defending his European title and turned up in the gym one day. I was training for a fight of my own at a different gym and Lennox Lewis was there. David asked to join in and do some sparring and I said, "Sure, why not?" Besides, Lennox was there and I wasn't about to argue.

'I had been sparring with a novice boxer just to get back into the swing of things and work on some moves. This was my first proper spar ahead of my next fight. David gets in there, sharp as a razor, tries to knock me out, and I'm like, "Wow, okay, so that's how it is." Lennox was at ringside and David was obviously very excitable.

'It was then that I realised David was never a friend and was just trying to use me. If he could have knocked me out that day, he would have done. He was ready to go past me and take advantage of our situations. He would have never attempted that back in the day. The experience didn't shake me up, but it took me away from where I was going. I was trying to get my mojo back and I never got it back.'

Haye, of course, was later given his own opportunity to explain himself, although chances are, very few of the congregating journalists required a counterclaim to doubt Audley's version of events.

'I went down to Audley's South Florida boxing gym on my own with my gumshield, headguard and gloves, just like I'd do on any other day,' recalled Haye. 'Once I turned up, I saw Audley in the ring sparring a guy who had never had a boxing match before in his life. I then noticed Lennox was at ringside watching on. I asked the sparring partner how many fights he'd had and he shrugged and said, "I haven't – I've done a bit of karate, that's all." Well, I figured I'd be able to give Audley a far more beneficial workout than the karate kid who'd just made way for me, so I put my gloves on, jumped in the ring and had a little move-around with him. Audley makes it through one round and then tries getting out of the ring at the end of it. I didn't blast him out or smash him up, I just hit him with a few nice body and head shots, that's all. His corner then forced him to come out for rounds two and three, before it all came to an end after the third.

'Audley took something from that whole experience and must have thought I was trying to take the piss out of him in front of Lennox. The thing is, I just sparred the way I always sparred and the way I'd been sparring all week in Miami. I'm used to sparring all-comers and taking myself out of my comfort zone, whereas Audley was now used to his comfort zone and was hand-picking useless sparring partners. He didn't want to be tested.'

It was hard not to believe Haye's version of events. When throw-away words offer the only explanation, it's best to keep in mind one's track record and reputation. Unfortunately, in Audley's case, he'd already tried the patience of the onlooking boxing writers one too many times and was now viewed through cynical and judge-mental eyes. *Nobody* trusted him.

However, midway through his many declarations of destiny, Harrison inadvertently hit upon something genuinely *interesting*.

'When I look at the situation from David's point of view, I kind of think maybe he wasn't actually taking liberties,' reassessed Audley, only minutes later. 'Maybe he was thinking the Audley he once knew used to go back and forth like cats and dogs and that I'd be up for it like I'd always been in the past. When we'd spar as amateurs, I'd be the bigger guy, the natural heavyweight, and I'd be able to put David in positions I wanted him to be in. David may have looked for something of the same in Miami, but, unfortunately, I *wasn't* up for that spar. There's a chance David turned up as David and I just didn't keep my end of the bargain. When I look back at that situation now, as a mature man, I think maybe I just wasn't up to the task that day.'

In the space of five minutes Harrison had transformed from righteous purveyor of justice to insecure defeatist, and there was an innocence and honesty to his final revelation that had long been absent from previous declarations. For perhaps the first time since that cold night in a Wembley car park in 2001, I found myself warming ever so slightly to the reformed Audley Harrison.

CHAPTER TWENTY-TWO
SEASONED VETERANS

David Haye became a 'seasoned veteran' on 13 October 2010. He turned thirty years of age. Three days before that landmark, the heavyweight champion was sucker-punched by a surprise birthday party at London's plush No. 5 Cavendish Square. Seventy of Haye's closest friends and family sprang out from the dark, party poppers in hand, and stunned the fighter, who had entered the premises under false pretences. Then, half an hour later, Haye and company were treated to a nostalgic slideshow of photographs taken through the years. Orchestrated by long-time friend and photographer Cressida Jade, the album played out like the opening credits to *The Wonder Years*, as Haye appeared in numerous guises from the halcyon days of his youth, the images drawing admiration, sympathy, ridicule and delirious laughter from everybody present. Some contained gloves, while others celebrated time spent away from the ring and in the company of those not seeking to punch him in the face. One picture placed a young David at the feet of his father Deron, as Stevie Wonder's *Hotter Than July* LP sat in the background, while another showed the future fighter enjoying a trip to the beach with older sister Louisa and younger brother James. The next saw the toddler beneath a table, snuggled tightly in the grip of his mother Jane, an image poignantly followed by that of a 27-year-old Haye mimicking the infantile mood swings of his own son Cassius at their luxurious home in Northern Cyprus.

It was a photograph of David and next opponent Audley Harrison that most captivated me, however. Pictured together in an anonymous nightclub somewhere, Haye and Harrison posed together like lifelong friends, embracing, with drinks in hand. The image generated rapturous laughter and cheers from those in attendance, and once again highlighted just how close the two heavyweights had previously been.

Haye couldn't believe how time had twisted relationships and complicated goals. He never imagined he'd one day fight his former training partner and drinking buddy. Likewise, he never believed he'd one day bear the responsibilities of a mature thirty-year-old man. The fighter felt old that Sunday evening, and we frequently joked about the fact I now possessed just cause to tag him a 'seasoned veteran' in future journalistic endeavours. David had humorously used that phrase to describe many a peer, opponent and woman in the past, and now shuddered at the thought of it being applied to him. As a former undisputed world cruiserweight champion, WBA heavyweight title-holder and eight-year professional, Haye was certainly creeping towards veteran status, regardless of whether the label was a running joke or not. Yet, despite the number of candles on the cake, I was never able to imagine the man as anything but a cavalier and carefree juvenile. The idea of him becoming an elder statesman and father figure – to son Cassius and daughter Sienna – was an otherworldly notion to accept. Before my very eyes, Haye had reluctantly grown up.

This sense of responsibility seemed to extend to his flourishing boxing career, too. Adamant he'd be finished with the sport by his thirty-first birthday, Haye had one year left to fulfil his remaining goals and escape with both his reputation and his faculties intact.

*　　*　　*

Prior to the surprise party I had watched the champion's final sparring session as a 29-year-old take place inside the boxer's latest gymnasium, a dolled-up garage located beneath a railway arch in Vauxhall, London. As late-night trains rumbled overhead, occasionally drowning out the stark sounds of leather on flesh, Haye pitched a stupendous eight rounds against two southpaw American heavyweights and looked better than I'd seen him at any other juncture of his eight-year professional career. Three-bout novice Nate James and former world heavyweight title challenger Tony Thompson were the unfortunate crash dummies that Monday evening, as both plotted and failed to execute game plans in the eye of a considerable storm.

It quickly became clear that, despite his extensive experience, the 39-year-old Thompson was unable to spook Haye inside the ring, and would instead attempt every trick learnt throughout a ten-year pro career to indirectly claim some form of one-upmanship.

'Can I change this music?' Thompson asked Haye, as the pair prowled around the ring shadow-boxing before their spar.

'Why?' responded Haye. 'This is *my* music.'

'Yeah, I know,' said Thompson, 'but I don't like it. I'd prefer *my* music on.'

'No way,' scoffed Haye. 'You aren't changing anything. You'll mess up my chi.'

The truculent Thompson didn't care about Haye's chi and wasn't bothered about upsetting it, either. Affectionately nicknamed 'The Washington Hustler' by Adam Booth, six-feet-five-inch Thompson was 34–2 as a pro, and a bona fide contender in the heavyweight division. He was paid $2,000 a week to travel to London and spar with Haye and, had it not been for that weighty pay-packet, Thompson would have never entertained such a proposition.

'I'm no motherfucking sparring partner, man,' the Washington southpaw told me. 'If his trainer has a request of me, sure, I'm going to do my best to follow that request and give them what they want, but, in the meantime, I'm going to be Tony Thompson and that guy's one of the best heavyweights in the world. I'm going to fight like I always fight, and I'm going to try and give David hell for every second I'm in there. I think me being me is enough to get any heavyweight ready for a fight.'

A pleasant fellow without gloves, Thompson was bitter and grumpy in all the ways you want from a so-called sparring partner when his foot touched the canvas. He scowled at Haye across the ring, frowned at his shadow-boxing attempts and continually tried to disrupt the gym's jukebox and overall mood. Thompson carried the air of a man insulted to even be asked to spar with the heavyweight king. After all, Thompson was coming off three decent back-to-back victories and still had title aspirations of his own.

'I told David that if he can hit me with right hands and beat the hell out of me in practice, he will kill Audley Harrison,' explained Tony. 'Audley is leagues below where I'm operating, and that's just common knowledge. I've achieved, beaten good guys and mixed with the best. Audley has achieved nothing so far.'

When it came time to finally spar, Thompson didn't want to be Haye's friend and wasn't keen on sticking to the unwritten code of conduct. Rather than retreat to his own corner at the start of sparring and in between rounds, Thompson would instead hover near Haye and Booth by the opposite corner and proceed to linger like a fox around a bin liner. As Booth applied Vaseline to the face of his fighter, he also attempted to fend Thompson off the scent and send him scurrying back towards his own corner. The disobedient American was shameless in his pursuit of a reaction, and remained upright and beside Haye for as long as he could. Occasionally he would even push, prod and poke both Haye and Booth in futile attempts to rile the pair further.

'I do that stuff everywhere I go,' said Thompson, when asked about his unconventional brand of gamesmanship. 'I want the other guy in the ring to know that this is my ring also. David's the heavyweight champion of the world, but I'm one of the very top heavyweights myself. I came here to work, I didn't come here to kiss his belt, bow down and call him "Godfather". He's getting ready to defend the title and he doesn't need no ass-kissing or back-slapping. He needs to be in shape and he needs to be scared. He's a good guy, I'm a good guy, we're all family people, but when we're in that ring, it's all professional. I'm not just a professional in title, I'm a professional in action and deeds, too.'

Despite the austere exterior and wealth of experience, Thompson was led a merry dance that Monday night and in subsequent sessions. Working predominantly off the back foot, and with the emphasis on speed and agility, Haye lured Thompson in, shut down the veteran's offence and then buzzed him with countless right-hand leads and left hooks. The puncher became boxer, and seemed to find comfort in the role.

'I think David's looking pretty damn good,' assessed Thompson, eyes bloodshot and bruised, as we trudged back to the American's riverbank hotel. 'He gave me a pretty good beating today, which I don't like one bit. I'll kick his ass on Wednesday, though. That's my real get-back time right there.'

While Thompson's ring nous and ruggedness allowed him to escape the clinic relatively unscathed, countryman James was less fortunate. The novice lefty was game well beyond the call of duty, and possessed no little talent, but was routinely being sickened and stunned by numerous Haye counterpunches. To his immense credit, however, James remained upright and spirited throughout.

'Every time David throws something at me I'm trying to work on it and come back with something either in a later round or in the next sparring session,' said the bespectacled James, dabbing at a bloody nose with a piece of tissue. 'He does a lot of things very fast, though, and it's hard to adapt to the speed. He's sharp with everything he does, and he doesn't just rely on one thing. He's able to do lots of things, simply because he's that much quicker and so agile. He can move, show defence and punish you at the same time. I don't know any other heavyweights that can do that.'

Despite the best intentions of both, Wednesday played out just the same as Monday. The only difference being that, by the middle of the week, the Vauxhall gym had swollen with visitors and interested parties, and a world champion southpaw was now present at ringside. Former world super-middleweight and light-heavyweight king Joe Calzaghe, a man unbeaten in forty-six professional bouts, was invited to the gym by Haye to oversee his final sparring session with Thompson. Perhaps the ultimate southpaw of the modern era, retired Welshman Calzaghe knew the intricacies of the portside style better than most and, though he hadn't fought professionally since defeating Roy Jones Jr in November 2008, remained barely an ounce above his fighting weight of twelve stone.

The 38-year-old watched Haye spar that October night and seemed suitably impressed by what he saw. Crouching only metres from the ring, Calzaghe fidgeted and winced with each right hand Haye slipped through the guard of his two hapless sparring partners. He nodded his head in approval as the heavyweight champion suckered his taller foes in and then spun away majestically, making the Americans miss desperate punches by inches. Ever the competitor, Calzaghe also knew where his two left-handed comrades were going wrong.

'What do you think, Joe?' barked Thompson, as he wearily climbed down from the ring and joined Calzaghe at ground level.

'You did well,' praised Calzaghe in return, eager to inspire a dejected prizefighter.

'No,' sighed Thompson, as he shuffled up next to the former

champion. 'What do you *really* think? What should I try and do with this motherfucker?'

A former world title challenger in his own right, Thompson wasn't looking for hollow praise or a mere slap on the back. He was seeking answers from one of the greatest southpaws in the game. He was flicking through the pages of the southpaw manual, eager to figure out an old way of deciphering a new problem. So now, switching on to the true intentions of the American, Calzaghe's smile dissolved and he edged that bit closer.

'He just keeps you coming along that line and then nails you on the way in,' whispered Joe, one hand cupped over his mouth, as if Haye might somehow overhear. 'David needs that space to let his punches go. He can control you from that range. You need to stay off that line, work on the angle and then get close. He won't be as effective up close, I promise you.'

And there it was. For the record, Thompson, having soaked up Calzaghe's advice like blotting paper, duly went out for the next round and digested Haye's punches to both face and body in a similar fashion. As wise as Calzaghe's words seemed to all within earshot, it would take a certain type of fighter to efficiently carry them out. Try as he would, Thompson wasn't that fighter on that particular day. The most gifted left-handed pug in the gym was the man sitting on a comfy chair, positioned metres from the ring, and void of even a speck of sweat, let alone blood, on his Ed Hardy T-shirt. While happy to delve into his knowledge banks to aid a fellow lefty, Calzaghe was certain of his new-found role and content to watch and explain without a single urge to step back in the ring and demonstrate. Haye was convinced he'd be feeling the same way in less than twelve months.

Many miles across the Atlantic, 38-year-old opponent Audley Harrison claimed, 'I'm as serious as a heart attack,' and, perhaps to begin with, he was telling the truth. Aware that his shock title chance was both undeserved and highly lucrative, Harrison endured a six-week training camp at high altitude in Big Bear, California, surrounded only by snakes, bears, team-mates, wife Raychel, daughter Ariella and his own thoughts and fears.

Ominously, though, while Haye forked out nearly £10,000 to swap dress-rehearsal blows with a former a world heavyweight title challenger in London, the less adventurous Harrison settled for spars with Israel Garcia and Joell Godfrey, two American fighters accustomed to competing at a cosy club-fighter level. The former was a forty-year-old heavyweight journeyman, while the latter was a comparatively light-hitting cruiserweight.

From what we now knew of that infamous 2006 spar with Haye, it was clear Harrison required a certain confidence generated from sparring and, in choosing two substandard fall guys, the challenger would be able to garner plentiful dollops of hollow self-belief. The last thing an individual as complex as Harrison needed was to be beaten up or exposed in the gymnasium. He required confidence on a drip. Furthermore, the presence of loved ones would have also helped Harrison retain a sense of comfort and familiarity, as well as providing a constant reminder that he was the alpha male and dominant force. Naturally, the sensation of getting beaten up in sparring quickly eradicates such feelings.

Haye saw through it all, of course. At the end of one session at his Vauxhall gymnasium, the champion returned to his hotel room and watched Sky Sports footage of an open workout held by Harrison at his Big Bear ranch. He hunched forward in his seat as the video began and proceeded to watch his foe rattle off infrequent left crosses against the pads of trainer Shadeed Suluki. No right jabs were thrown throughout the five minutes, and Haye stayed silent, occasionally twitching his head from side to side, as though avoiding incoming punches. When the film ended, Haye shut down his laptop, shook his head and released an almighty and almost comical sigh.

'Oh dear, Audley,' said Haye, as he rose from his seat. 'I know *exactly* what he's going to do. All those left hands are bullshit and a disguise. He's going to be trying to jab with me and keep this thing as low on punches as possible. He won't throw his left hand once, believe me. He's so predictable. Jesus, this might be even easier than I thought.'

They say anything can happen in boxing, and it's true. However, on Saturday, 13 November I was about as confident of a result as I'd ever been in my life. Like David Haye, I knew far too much about Audley Harrison to even entertain the idea of a competitive fight or upset. A potentially mind-altering concoction of Harrison's tongue and Sky Sports' public relations team would attempt to tell the uneducated otherwise, but most saw nothing beyond a comprehensive Haye victory. I was certain of it.

I'd studied both boxers for the best part of a decade and, immune to customary pre-fight bluster, knew by now what both could and couldn't do. That was what made the bout so appealing to me in the first place. No, it wouldn't be the greatest, most competitive or stirring ring collision of all time, but it was a wholly twenty-first-century phenomenon and a fight I'd watched develop from the ground upwards. I'd criss-crossed between fighters, admired both at various junctures, and would now prepare to watch them settle my own argument in the only manner two fighters could. I'd never envisaged Haye and Harrison boxing one another, and yet here they were, merely days from doing just that.

As a close confidant of Haye, I'd often been told Harrison was our friend and someone to be supported, not ridiculed, like so many others chose to do. He was once on *our* side. A good guy. It sent a chill down my spine, therefore, to now imagine Haye meeting this so-called friend inside the ring and introducing his fists to Harrison's suspect chin. I wondered whether Haye would be able to mentally prepare himself to punch me in the face if he ever became that way inclined. How would one go about preparing to flick the switch from friend to foe in a blink of an eye?

Yet, despite this fear for Harrison's well-being, I also grew slightly concerned about Haye's mindset and the true nature of the fight. I knew how much he had previously cared for this man and how he had been genuinely disappointed by Audley's many past failings. David was never a malicious or spiteful person, and I questioned whether he would be able to generate the malevolent streak needed to ruin a former friend.

In fact, I raised that very point with Haye on the afternoon of the fight, just as he began to tidy his Manchester hotel room ahead of battle. He was topless, shadow-boxing and obviously proud of his physical condition. Twenty-four hours earlier he'd weighed in at a staggeringly light 210lbs (15st and 8oz), his lowest mark yet as a heavyweight. Built for explosive speed, Haye had informed journalists and those close to him that Audley would be dealt with inside three rounds.

'I just see him as any other opponent right now,' said Haye, as he stared coldly into my eyes. 'I don't feel *anything* towards him. He's not a friend and he's not an enemy. He's just someone that needs to be knocked the fuck out. He's no different to John Ruiz or Nikolay Valuev. Just another slab of meat for me to hit hard and often.'

Goosebumps broke out along my arms and back as I copped a reminder of just how cold and clinical Haye could be that close to a fight. Harrison had looked a bundle of nerves at both the pre-fight press conference and weigh-in, and was now about to meet Haye at his most evil. Although I was by now certain of which side of the fence I stood on, I couldn't help but slightly sympathise with Harrison's inevitable plight.

'This is just going to be fun,' Haye would repeat over and over again on the day of the fight. 'I can't wait to punch his face with my right hand.'

Haye briefly watched a video of Roy Jones Jr bamboozling south-paw light-heavyweight Richard Hall, before claiming he was no longer interested in watching boxing. The champion was impatient and in a doing mood. He viewed Harrison as someone he could look spectacular against, and I detected no sign of the nerves or anxieties I'd sensed before the fighter's other heavyweight encounters. He knew too much about his opponent to be wary and too much about himself to be doubtful. If training was anything to go by, Haye had never been better and Audley had never been older or more cautious, following recent setbacks and shattered confidence. It didn't seem fair.

Once back on English soil, Harrison had traded an air of calm for one of an aggravated madman juggling mixed messages. He started fight week surrounded by family members and training partners, content and comfortable in his country hotel, before ending the week on edge and unable to string coherent sentences together. Eyes bulging, the challenger cut interviews short, growled, grunted, chewed gum like an under-pressure football manager and hollered his 'Yes I Can!' mantra relentlessly, as though now trying to persuade *himself*. Harrison was preaching to the supposedly converted and yet couldn't even win an argument within the courtroom of his own mind. No amount of propaganda or campaigning could change the way Harrison's fists spoke when the microphone was moved away.

He weighed in for the contest at a heavy 253lbs (18st 1lb) and presumably hoped the three-stone advantage in weight would somehow help soak up Haye's unquestionably quicker blows. Scale-reading aside, it was during a brief stare-down at the weigh-in that Harrison's mask finally slipped and his fancy dress costume split at the seams.

'He was embarrassed to look at me,' said Haye, late on Friday night. 'He did a little blink, cracked a smile and then looked away. I don't normally read too much into what happens at weigh-ins, but I know enough about Audley to read *a lot* into that. He knows he's in way too deep and that he's fucked. He pretty much accepted defeat there and then. He's terrified.'

Haye tucked into a bowl of fruit fit for a king and then slouched back on the sofa in his hotel suite. 'This is going to be so much fun,' he said to himself. 'So much fun.'

The talk lasted eight weeks and the fun lasted less than eight minutes. In truth, it wasn't much fun for Haye, Harrison, myself, the 20,000 people crammed inside Manchester's MEN Arena or the reported 800,000 customers who paid £14.95 to watch the fight at home on Sky Box Office. Haye ended Harrison's ludicrous world title dream when he wanted to – in the third round – and received only one solitary jab back from Audley in return.

Harrison froze and crumbled on the biggest night of his pro career, just as we all knew he would. He attempted nothing in the first round, only the infamous solo jab in the second and then a stop, drop and roll in the third. In the controversy-filled aftermath, the British Boxing Board of Control even considered withholding Harrison's predicted £1m purse on account of his feeble effort. In truth, nobody should have expected any different.

To his credit, Harrison took one finisher to the jaw in the third round and managed to stay upright for a few seconds of subsequent mayhem. He was eventually clubbed to the floor moments later, but, with his gumshield spat out, gallantly rose and beat the count. Honestly, I hadn't even expected *that* much. The ransacked challenger didn't last much longer, of course, but he took his lumps and stayed upright and alive for as long as his unreliable chin allowed him to. Salesman rather than pro fighter, Harrison had lived up to his end of the bargain and then folded the way most had assumed he would.

The beaten challenger then took his opportunity to talk at the post-fight press conference and continued to do what he did best. He talked a lot and said little, to the point where I no longer even cared to write, record or remember what he spewed. It just washed right over me. Rather than simply annoying, Harrison's delusion was now just downright disturbing, as he talked about continuing his career and praised himself for apparently 'frustrating' Haye in the opening two rounds.

The only ones frustrated in Manchester that night were the many thousands of fans who'd paid top money to witness the first all-British world heavyweight title fight on UK soil for seventeen years. Robbed of a fight and delivered a pantomime, the fans booed Harrison's walk to the ring, berated his no-show during the fight and then showered him with chants of 'You're shit and you know you are' as the battered boxer sloped off back to the changing room. The epitaph was every bit as brutal and embarrassing as the swift beating Haye had unleashed on him.

Needless to say, I didn't join in that night. I was beyond caring. I barely even broke into applause as Haye rained down the final insults on the shell-shocked challenger. It was the most subdued I'd ever felt watching Haye punch his way to victory and, to begin with, I wasn't sure why. In many ways, this rotten fight meant more to me than most. Harrison and Haye had been two of the foremost reasons why I found myself immersed in this sport in the first place, and here they were, ten years down the line, pretending to confront one another in the squared circle.

Perhaps the closer you get to the ring, the more *real* the action seems to get and the less susceptible you are to the copious amounts of bullshit flying overhead. Distance allows for skewed perceptions and room for manipulation. When you're close enough to see fear in the eyes of a man, no sport is more terrifyingly honest. Audley Harrison always required and demanded distance, as both a fighter and a salesman. He wanted to keep people at arm's reach with his jab, in order to control their punches and mould their thoughts. For a while, he got away with it. On 13 November in Manchester, however, David Haye closed the distance on him and delivered reality to a man who had for so long avoided it.

Sitting only one metre from the ring, I'd never felt more at ease. Normally a wreck of nerves and anxiety at the first bell, I'd grown close enough to both Haye and Harrison to avoid their nonsense from point-blank range. There was no longer anything either man could have said or produced that would have swayed my opinion or surprised me. For one night only, the pair had become carica-tures to me.

'Wasn't Audley your role model once?' asked Haye at the break-fast table the following morning.

'No, that's not quite right,' I replied, eager to claw back some self-respect.

'You told me once that you waited in a car park for him after he'd had his first pro fight,' continued Haye, clearly not content with just one fight that weekend.

'That's true. I got him to sign my fight programme.'

'Yeah, and how long did you wait for it?'

'A couple of hours. I also got Marvin Hagler's autograph that day, though. I think that counterbalances Audley's one.'

As much as I was thankful for Audley's rise to prominence at the beginning of the decade, I was also glad to have now seen the light. Harrison's slump at the feet of the truth closed the book on his career and also a chapter in my own ring education. Gone was the naïve and impressionable kid sat way up in the bleachers, bin-oculars pressed to his eyes, eager to believe every tall tale thrown his way. I was now sitting in the row of kings, cynical, cold and already reminiscing about days gone by. I had made it. I was a 'seasoned veteran', experienced beyond my years. Haye called me an 'expert'.

As far as seasoned veterans go, Roy Jones Jr, our mutual hero, inspiration, obsession and first subject over which we bonded, was now positively burnt to rubble.

Days before David Haye shattered a boxing myth in Manchester, a 41-year-old Jones was skipping from city to city in England giving after-dinner speeches for five-figure sums. Both Haye and I had been alerted to our hero's presence – for entirely different reasons – and, indeed, the fighter himself had been warned that Jones was on his trail in London. In a scarcely believable turn of events, it was 2010 and idol Jones requested a sit-down with disciple Haye in order to talk while in the same time zone. I'm sure the lure of a heavyweight title shot and six-figure pay-day also had something to do with the plan, but it excited me nonetheless to envisage Haye and Jones sitting across the table from one another. The champion was less enamoured of Jones' sudden advances, however.

'It's quite sad, actually,' said Haye, as he strolled to his Vauxhall gymnasium one chilly November evening. 'I'm not sure I can sit down with him and talk business with a straight face. I love him to bits, but we should not be talking about fighting each other.'

Now is probably the time to confront my own delusion and reveal that the Roy Jones Jr walking around in 2010 was a world apart, in appearance, performance and lustre, from the version Haye and I had both grown up adoring at the start of the decade. The boxing legend hadn't been anywhere near a world title since 2005, and had recently suffered defeats to both Bernard Hopkins and Danny Green, the latter of which occurred within a mere ninety seconds of the first round. It pained me to admit, but Jones was a spent force, and someone seeking a date with Haye through desperation rather than realistic competition. A source of inspiration had now become one of irritation for Haye, who had also recently fended off similarly audacious advances from both Hopkins and James Toney. It felt surreal to witness Jones and the like pursue Haye in this manner, as all three had been and, indeed, still were, part of the template for the Bermondsey fighter.

As queasy as the mooted fight made me feel, I couldn't help but hope Haye and Jones got together in London, if only to realise my own vision. I sat patiently by my phone for days after Haye received his initial heads-up, quietly hoping Jones would follow up on the tease. Though he'd never let on, I imagined Haye, too, was eager to finally spend some intimate alone time with his hero, having followed and admired him from afar for so long. In fact, an hour after beating up American southpaws Tony Thompson and Nate James in sparring, Haye retired to his Westminster hotel room, let his guard slip and exclaimed to me how he 'wished Roy could have been there to see that'. It soon became clear that Haye wasn't looking to talk figures, negotiate or entertain the proposition of one day boxing Jones; he simply wanted to impress the pioneer of the fighting attitude he'd since adopted. He needed to show Jones what he had become and highlight just what an overwhelming influence the great American had been on both his style and his success. Moreover, I desperately wanted to watch Jones watch Haye.

Alas, as is so often the case in the anticlimactic world of professional boxing, the dream never materialised. Jones left for America without so much as saying 'hello' or 'goodbye' to either of us. Haye continued beating up sparring partners and I continued to watch him do so. Part of me was disappointed by the no-show, but another part of me was relieved not to have witnessed Jones at forty-one, weathered, tired, desperate and a smoky shell of his former self. It didn't feel right to finally meet the legend under such humiliating terms. There would be an unavoidable sadness to the whole spectacle and, desperate though I was to touch and stare long-ingly at the future Hall-of-Famer for an afternoon, I couldn't help but feel, watching Haye spar one evening, that the man in front of me had now taken hold of the baton anyway. A forty-one-year-old Jones would never be able to live up to the idealised image I had of him, whereas this thirty-year-old Haye, now at his athletic peak and in his fighting prime, was living and breathing right before my very eyes. He was performing moves Jones had indi-rectly taught him as a young boy and even using the Pensacola native's name to check into hotels. Maybe Haye would never scale the heights of Jones, Ray Leonard or Muhammad Ali, but it was 2010 and the current WBA champion was *my* version of those boxing greats. My grandfathers had Ali, my father had Leonard, Haye had Jones and I had Haye. He'd unashamedly replaced Roy Jones in my affections, and I didn't feel an ounce of guilt.

PART SEVEN

Although a clenched fist ultimately settled the score, an open hand and broken toe provided the greater stories surrounding David Haye's 2011 clash with Wladimir Klitschko.

CHAPTER TWENTY-THREE
TOE STORY I

He liked Eric Cantona, but hated football. Perhaps even more bizarrely, he had never even seen Cantona kick a ball. The alluring sight and smell of freshly cut grass failed to stir in David Haye the same joyous feeling dancing around my belly one May afternoon in Hamburg. The fighter merely saw a field on which to walk, whereas I saw pitch perfection. If you couldn't play football on a green carpet like this, you had no right attempting to play it anywhere. It was turf meticulously crafted for the discerning footballer, yet the groundsman's efforts were entirely lost on a man with far more violent and visceral leanings that day. The immaculate pitch and accompanying goals belonged to Hamburger SV, and WBA world heavyweight champion Haye stood waiting in the players' tunnel of the 54,000-capacity Imtech Arena without a single urge to showcase his Cruyff turn.

'Football just never grabbed me as a kid,' said the fighter, as he watched a trail of young children in Hamburger SV shirts walk past him towards the pitch. 'I was never any good with team sports. I used to get pissed off having to rely on other people to get the job done. Also, football was never physical enough for me. Because I was one of the bigger boys at school, I'd always get people falling over whenever I went near them. One day I went in for a tackle with my own team-mate and accidentally broke his leg. I didn't like the idea of somebody else having the ball, even if they were on the same side.'

In adulthood, the closest he ever came to showing even the slightest sign of interest in the beautiful game arrived one listless night in London when, peering up from his laptop, Haye successfully eavesdropped on a conversation Adam Booth and I were having about former Manchester United forward Cantona. The flamboyant Frenchman had long been one of Booth's footballing heroes and, more than any skill or success, it was King Eric's single-minded approach to retirement and goal-setting that most appealed to the trainer. Upon learning that Cantona had retired from football at the relatively tender age of thirty, Haye was suddenly all ears.

'Did Cantona ever play in Germany?' he asked, as we continued to stand and stare from our position in the Hamburg tunnel.

'No, he never played for a German side,' I replied. 'Kevin Keegan played here, though.'

'Who?'

'Never mind.'

'How old was Cantona when he retired?'

'The same age as you. Thirty.'

'That must have taken some guts to do that. Was he still at the top of his game?'

'He'd just won another league title at United.'

'That's crazy. So he ended his career in his prime and yet is still remembered as one of the all-time greats? That's how you do it, man.'

'Just think, he could have won even more titles . . .'

'Fuck that,' said Haye, butting in with an aggressive shake of his head. 'He'd already won titles and become the best player in the league. What else was there left to prove? If he wants to swan off to Brazil and play football on the beach for fun, what right has anybody to tell him otherwise? He made his money, he proved his point.'

Suddenly Haye was an expert – on both Cantona and the ethics of football. While David was viewed as an anomaly in his own sport for even contemplating retirement at the age of thirty-one, the mercurial Frenchman with the upturned collar had already nonchalantly strolled that same path and done so in a blaze of glory and acclaim. Haye had few examples to follow in his own sport – as most boxers sadly remained stubborn and active for too long – whereas Cantona boasted just the right amount of foresight and arrogance to shut the door when those around him advised otherwise. He'd never watched Cantona play, and admitted his only reference point was an unsightly kung-fu kick on a Crystal Palace fan, yet Haye was now clearly an admirer.

As I prepared to elaborate on Cantona's long-time omission from the French national side, a dark cloud hovered overhead and banished the resplendent sunshine we'd bathed in for much of that afternoon. Rather than pursue further Cantona-related small talk, I pivoted to my right and spotted another heavyweight figure approaching in the distance. This one was altogether more upbeat and welcoming than Haye happened to be at that moment, as he engaged in a peculiar tickling contest with Hermann, a fluffy blue dinosaur masquerading as a football mascot, and then posed for pictures. The jovial gentleman stood at around six feet six inches and was well turned out in a grey designer suit. With not a hair out of place, he almost looked too good to trust. If somebody had told you the man was a prizefighter, you'd assume they meant the sweat-soaked soul inside the hyperactive dinosaur. Yet Wladimir Klitschko's aura and sheer presence that afternoon were enough to unsettle and silence both Haye and me.

'What's wrong?' I asked Haye, as he rolled his head from side to side and bounced on his toes ever so slightly. Klitschko was, by now, approximately ten metres behind him, and both were separated purely by will power and politeness.

'My Spidey senses are tingling,' replied Haye, with the slightest hint of a smile.

Never one to follow Marvel Comics as I perhaps should have, I asked Haye for a clearer explanation of his mood, prompting the boxer to inform me that he was 'ready to knock somebody the fuck out'. That overt display of emotion was then followed by a routine nervous yawn and crack of the knuckles. Haye sensed his adversary was behind him, but never once turned around for confirmation. Nobody told him Klitschko was present, nor did anyone even dare. His sixth sense – or, to use his own parlance, Spidey sense – had picked it up in an instant. Haye's body then slipped into the same trance he'd grown accustomed to experiencing on the night of a fight. I couldn't relate to him at times like these. He was too intense, too malevolent and too evil. I'd spent enough time around the fighter to know what kinds of thoughts were running around his head and, instead of embracing the same sentiments, I broke for the nearest exit.

The 35-year-old Klitschko, in stark contrast, had no visible desire to bump heads with Haye that day. He laughed and joked and even offered me, the supposed enemy, a respectful nod as we first locked eyes in the tunnel. Though having never before traded words or handshakes, at that very moment, Klitschko and I shared more in common with each other than I did with the British fighter I'd followed for the best part of a decade. I was more familiar with the décor of Klitschko's mind than with Haye's own turbulent head space. With the heavenly green grass acting as backdrop, Klitschko was play-fighting the mascot, while Haye was left to play-fight his own animalistic need to lock horns with an approaching threat.

I was suddenly scared for Klitschko, and had visions of Haye walking on the pitch and employing the same kung-fu kick Cantona planted across the face of an imprudent Matthew Simmons in 1995. Yet, despite this apprehension, I also derived a guilty sense of satisfaction from the unnerving sight of Haye foaming at the mouth to plug himself in and throw punches. It pleased me to know that, despite setting himself a Cantona-inspired retirement date of 13 October, Haye hadn't gone soft at the point where the credits started to roll.

The thinker and the fighter stared at one another for two minutes and forty-five seconds, neither willing to break, blink first or concede ground. It meant nothing. From New York and Hamburg to Westminster, Haye and Klitschko struck the same poses and repeated similar soundbites ahead of their anticipated 2 July showdown, both keen to gain an early advantage, yet only too aware that little of it would be remembered in the aftermath.

Klitschko asked for a handshake and Haye looked the other way, promising, 'I'll come to your hospital ward and shake your hand after the fight.' Undeterred, Wladimir shot an outstretched hand in David's direction whenever future opportunities arose, and the more he made a point of doing it, the more motivated Haye became to ignore it. Klitschko claimed the refusal was a sign of disrespect, while Haye assured us all that, by neglecting customary pre-fight pleasantries, he'd gain a form of one-upmanship on a champion always keen to control his opponents.

'I do not like the way this man carries himself,' said Klitschko, who would later christen his avoided right paw the 'magic hand'. 'Shaking the champion's hand is a sign of respect. I want to teach him a lesson on July 2nd. My brother and I are both doctors, and I'd like to give David Haye therapy when we fight. I don't like the way he talks or walks, and don't get a nice energy from him. I respect him as a fighter, but not as a person.'

By nature, Klitschko was unable to match his opponent for putdowns or cutting remarks. He neglected playing that game and even apologised whenever he paraphrased Haye and stumbled upon a curse word in the process. Nevertheless, one got the sense Klitschko was about as riled as a gentle giant could get when in the vicinity of Haye, the churlish maverick who'd chipped away at him for the best part of three years.

'Emotions are important, so long as you don't take them into the ring,' said Klitschko. 'Emotions in preparation can be great for motivation, as they help you train harder and longer for a fight. But, of course, once that first bell rings, emotions are no good. You need to be clear-headed and cold. Emotions only complicate things.'

Klitschko was the gentleman, Haye the rogue, and that dynamic hinted at an obvious contrast in the way each would go about selling his product. The multilingual Klitschko charmed, preached about peace and assured us all that bad guys would always get their comeuppance. The closest he came to traditional trash-talk arrived in the form of a sheepish declaration that Haye would be his fiftieth knockout victim and that he planned on giving the brash Brit a 'pizza face' following twelve rounds of methodical slice and dice. Meanwhile, Haye spat, snarled and growled like a starved carnivore, never once in the mood to entertain Klitschko's high-brow patter.

As much as I was spellbound by Klitschko's eloquence and all-round pleasantness, this explicit contrast in character only helped increase my confidence in a Haye victory. It was a given that Klitschko would defeat the moody mauler in any other court but the square ring, and I was just fine with that. Haye spoke and acted like a fighter, and we were readying for a fight.

'I became a boxer for the challenge, but I never loved boxing,'

Klitschko explained to me, while on a whistle-stop trip to London. 'I was always a fan of it, but only became involved in the sport when my brother decided to become a fighter. I wanted to be a doctor. My brother was born to fight, whereas I became a fighter in time.

'I truly fell in love with boxing after my 2004 loss to Lamon Brewster, believe it or not. I was at the bottom of the sport and was written off by *everybody*. Even my own brother, Vitali, spoke to me after the loss and said, "Wladdy, look at your face, look at your soul – I think it might be time to retire from boxing." Suddenly I realised where my career was heading and realised that, if I didn't turn it all around, I could lose boxing from my life. That was a scary thought for me. You don't realise how important something is until you are on the brink of losing it.'

Fighters are supposed to fight, not think. Yet Klitschko thought about fighting more than any other heavyweight champion.

'I am always scared before a fight,' he added. 'I am scared of losing and I am scared of not being able to do what I do best. That is the key to making me perform, though. I use that fear to ensure I am the best fighter I can be on the night. It is only human to fear failure. If we weren't worried about certain things, we'd never get anywhere in life. Fear of being late to work helps us find the motivation to get up and get ready in time.

'Boxing is very much like chess and we are all chess players here. Some of us know the moves and think things through, while others work on instinct. I like to take my time and make the right move. David Haye just moves. If we were pieces on the board, I'd like to think I was the king and he was the knight. He is a wild man with a cowboy style. The horse is one of the most dangerous pieces in the game and, although it's not as powerful as the king, it can still do damage if you do not stop it.'

*   *   *

In order to fulfil his dream of becoming king, Haye trained like a pawn. Essentially embarking on a six-month training camp, he avoided potential boredom and staleness by splitting headquarters between Miami and London. While Stateside, he worked out at South Beach's famous Fifth Street Gym, often under the watchful eye of its founder and Hall-of-Fame trainer Angelo Dundee, the 89-year-old who'd once taught Muhammad Ali how to float like a butterfly and sting like a bee.

'David's a great and humble guy, and I'm talking above and beyond fighting,' Dundee told me. 'I saw him being interviewed on television wearing one of my Fifth Street Gym T-shirts and I couldn't believe it. That made an old man very happy. It just went to show what a class act the kid is.

'Whenever I saw David around the gym, he was just one of the guys. If you didn't know who he was, you'd never guess the kid was heavyweight champion. There are no airs or graces about him and he treats everybody equally. Muhammad was the same. If we could clone David and have one of him in every country, the boxing world would be a far better place, believe me.'

Armed with the Dundee seal of approval, a trim and conditioned Haye returned to Britain in May and prepared himself for eight weeks of sacrifice, dedication and flirtations with the pain barrier. By the time he began sparring midway through the month, he already boasted the warm glow of a man at peak fitness.

American heavyweights Deontay Wilder and Kelvin Price, both unbeaten and six feet five plus, were the first sparring partners charged with testing and tasting the rate of Haye's progress. A former Olympic Games bronze medallist, Wilder was loose, languid and often reckless, whereas Price, the more considered and tentative, preferred jabs to crosses, and fiddled rather than fought. One evening Haye overcame caution in the only way he knew how. He slipped one of Price's many uncertain leads and allowed the American to fall right into the tip of a devastating right hand counterpunch. Price collapsed to the deck in a heap, limbs crossed and eyes elsewhere. As trains rumbled overhead, Price rose gallantly to his feet, before being checked over by on-site physiotherapist Kevin Lidlow. Whatever the final assessment may have been, Price was done for the day. Game though they undoubtedly were, neither Wilder nor Price offered the kind of impersonation Haye was after.

The WBA champion later employed the services of fellow Brit David Price and Finland's heavyweight contender Robert Helenius, in the hope that upright Europeans would better replicate the kind of conundrum he would attempt to solve in July. Ultimately, though, Helenius offered little in the way of anything over the course of two spars, while Price, clearly the best of the bunch, couldn't stick around long, as he had a fight of his own to prepare for.

Blessed with technical skills in abundance and a fine left jab, Olympic bronze-medallist Price had been a go-to sparring partner for Haye since their respective amateur days. The six-feet-seven Liverpudlian was long and upright and, though not yet in Klitschko's class, was able to control range with similar stinginess and mimicked the Ukrainian better than anybody. He refused to give Haye so much as an inch, and forced the comparatively minute heavyweight to dance, duck and dive around his consistently effective lead hand. Because of his size and length, Price always seemed within punching distance of Haye, and a sense of claustrophobia forced the nifty champion to think and react quicker than usual.

This became apparent during the second of two spars the pair shared, when Haye ransacked the taller man's range in the blink of an eye and cracked Price with a sweeping right hand to the chin. It was the sort of shot that would vaporise most other heavyweights, yet Price miraculously shook off its thunder in the form of a funny jig, before recomposing himself, straightening his headguard and biting down on his gumshield. He was somehow still upright and alive. Encouragingly, though, Haye had found his range and, if only for one brief moment, cut down the barricades and penetrated the sweet spot of a heavyweight behemoth.

Sparring came to an end on Wednesday, 15 June, following ten rounds in the presence of Helenius, a lanky but limited Finn who regrettably offered more in the way of apologies than punches.

'I know what I need to do against Klitschko, and no amount of sparring is going to help me,' said Haye, who raised concern and intrigue when announcing that sparring had ended two and a half weeks out from the fight. 'I have done enough sparring to sharpen up my timing and punching, but now is the time to focus on what I actually need to do in the fight. Sometimes you can get so caught up in sparring that you lose sight of who you are fighting and what you need to do to win the fight.'

As for my own view on why sparring had ended unusually early, I only assumed the production line of Klitschko clones had run dry. Save for the two Prices, Wilder and Helenius, most of similar stature had turned down the chance to work with Haye, for either financial or health reasons.

There was also the small matter of a mystery toe injury that had left Haye requiring local anaesthetic before all training sessions. One evening, moments after training had ended, Haye removed the padding around his right foot to reveal a swollen and disfigured little toe, accompanying blisters doing their worst to make leisurely walks all the more uncomfortable. His choice of flip-flops hadn't been as incidental and image-led as I'd first thought.

'The toe's broken, but it's nothing to worry about,' said Haye, grimacing and contradicting his way through the excruciating pain that followed the removal of the strapping. 'You always get injuries like this in the build-up to a fight. You've just got to battle through it. Once the anaesthetic kicks in, I can't feel a thing in my foot.'

'How did you do it?' I asked.

'I honestly don't know,' he replied. 'It happened one afternoon when I was in the gym. I felt a sharp pain in my toe and couldn't walk properly. It's probably just the result of wear and tear.'

Haye made a point of playing down the broken toe's impact, as if to not concern me, but I couldn't help but think it was far from an ideal state of affairs. Kevin Lidlow arrived at the gym armed with numbing agents and anti-inflammatories ahead of every training session, and it was only Haye's continually impressive form that allowed me to put the toe troubles to the back of my mind. He said the injury didn't impact his performance, and it was easy to believe him. One June evening I watched him go fifteen rounds on pads, bags and body-bag and can safely say I'd never seen him hit harder, faster, louder, or with as much savage intent and unwavering focus.

For perhaps the first time in his professional boxing life, Haye was frighteningly serious about training. He'd enter his Vauxhall gym late at night, dump his bags by the ring and then tour the perimeter in his own fuzzy and introspective haze. Once he hit play on his iPod and absorbed the opening beats of Candi Staton's "Victim" or Teena Marie's "I Need Your Lovin'", all chance of conversation and distraction disappeared. Haye drifted into his own space, one soundtracked by soul and ambushed by vague outlines of the waiting Klitschko.

He also spoke and listened to Adam Booth in a way I had never before witnessed. Casual conversation and lewd jokes were unnecessary stalling tactics of the past as the pair now used each and every breath for a purpose. A mutual fear of what lay ahead had brought them closer than ever, and Klitschko was the first and last word on their lips each time they stepped beneath the railway arch.

Physically, Haye had never looked slicker or quicker in sparring and, at barely a sweat bead above fifteen stone, was backed by the kind of lithe structure necessary to carry out the strategy he and Booth had been hatching for months. When sparring came to an end, Haye then took the same ferocity into pad and bag work, eventually working his way towards throwing fifty consecutive punches in 8.6 seconds on the heaviest of heavy bags towards the back of the gym.

To conclude sessions Haye would step back inside the ring and wrestle his way out of body-locks slapped on by Tomasz, a Polish wrestler and friendly giant with a world peace smile and world war scowl. With fellow grappler Davide Nicolosi looking on from ringside, six-feet-five-inch Tomasz stringently followed instructions and attempted to move Haye around like an empty shopping trolley, replicating the strong-arm tactics we all expected from Klitschko in Hamburg. He taught Haye escapes, tricks and holds of his own, and then toughened the lean fighter's neck muscles by pushing, pulling and yanking his head in various unnatural directions.

Haye grafted and grazed like a wild beast, refusing to shave his unruly beard or trim the locks that were freely running down the back of his neck. He cut an older, rougher and uglier figure than before, but now projected, for perhaps the first time, the conventional image of a striving fighter. There was no longer anything prim, pretty or pristine about the thirty-year-old.

'I'm almost waiting for something to go wrong,' whispered Booth, as he sipped on a hot Ribena in the gym's office, following yet another stellar training session. 'It never usually goes *this* well. David always has peaks and troughs during a training camp, but we've had far more highs than lows this time around. It's almost going too well right now. I'm having to stop myself becoming overconfident about the fight.'

The forecasts of the inner circle were infinitely more positive than they had been two years before, when the heavyweight pair were originally scheduled to square off and Haye was a stone heavier and a stone less interested. I feared for his well-being ahead of his first date with Klitschko, but, by May 2011, was joyously performing butterfly in a pool of optimism.

It was only when driving home with Haye late one evening, following another torturous training session, that the WBA champion unknowingly disturbed my walk in the clouds and reminded me of why I'd previously been so concerned.

'Remember how my fight with Nikolay Valuev was so clean and precise?' said Haye, turning down the volume of Michael Jackson's 'PYT'.

I nodded.

'Well, this fight with Klitschko isn't going to be *anything* like that,' he warned. 'This is going to be uncomfortable for every minute of every round. I know it is. It's going to be a horrible, gruelling kind of fight and I know I'll have to take some serious shots at some point.

'That's why I need to toughen up. I need to go through the pain barrier in training, because I can't afford to be weak or soft on the night. I know that I need to be at my absolute best for this fight. Any less and I'll lose badly. I need to be the fittest I've ever been and the toughest I've ever been. I'm actually looking forward to killing myself in training for this fight. I want to feel tough and fit. I want to be a machine.'

Tracks changed, allowing for a few seconds of thought, reflection and silence.

'I know Wladimir won't be grafting like I am, though,' muttered the champion, almost to himself. 'He'll train hard, sure, but it will be technical and scientific. He won't be trying to kill himself in the gym like I am. No way. That's not him.'

CHAPTER TWENTY-FOUR
TOE STORY II

Although their boy was about to confront the most dangerous heavyweight opponent of his boxing career, neither Jane nor Deron Haye revealed any sign of trepidation at the breakfast table that July morning. Sipping on carrot juice and coffee, they were comfortable and confident, two emotions I'd always struggled with in the agonisingly slow hours before David Haye stepped into the ring and traded punches.

'I'm always surprised when people ask me how I deal with watching David box,' said Jane. 'Weirdly enough, his dad never gets asked the same. I think it's because dads are seen as being tougher. They are used to the rough and tumble.'

'We are able to get through it simply because we have faith in David and are confident in his ability,' added Deron. 'If we weren't, we would worry and say something. We wouldn't let him do it. We've always told David that he should aspire to be the best he can possibly be, but we have never steered him in a particular direction. If he wanted to be the best road-sweeper in the world, that would have been fine with us, so long as he put maximum effort into achieving that.'

Sitting at a nearby breakfast table were Natasha, David's wife, and Louisa, his sister, both of whom were by now clearly fending off pre-fight nerves. They talked of sleepless nights and necessary diversions, eager to escape the suffocating crush one feels on the morning of a fight.

'As parents we always said that if somebody hits you, you must hit them back twice as hard, but only if they started it,' said Jane. 'We never wanted to see David instigate a fight, but, if one happened to break out as a result of somebody else's actions, we also knew how important it was for David to make a stand and show he wouldn't be intimidated.

'His school friend Kulpash once told me, many years later, that he was thankful for knowing David at school, because he was the one that stopped Kulpash getting bullied. He knew the biggest, strongest and most athletic boy in school and, as a result, Kulpash would always be safe from harm. That was nice to hear.'

Of course, Saturday's fight with Klitschko wasn't the first scrap their son had been involved in, either in the boxing ring or on the school playground. Preparation was something both parents had in abundance.

'I remember David once beat up the school bully after school,' added Jane. 'The bully had said some hurtful things about me, and David reacted. I then received a call from the headmaster, who let me know what had happened and said the boy's family were very upset and angry. The thing is, this lad was the school bully and was known to be a bit of a menace. He was always picking on weaker children and thinking he was untouchable. David took a stand that day, and I'll always remember the headmaster saying, "Between you and me, the little blighter deserved what was coming to him. David did us all a favour."'

Deron smiled, and did his fatherly best not to laugh. A former karate teacher, Deron had always had a soft spot for combat and an appreciation of the dedication it took to thrive in martial arts. Bruce Lee flicks and Nigel Benn fights would often litter the living room floor.

'I always remember David watching boxing on my lap with his thumb in his mouth,' said Deron. 'Even as a young kid he showed an interest. He'd know all the boxers and their styles and would know what punch would work and which punch wouldn't. He even knew what southpaw meant from an early age. David spoke like a trainer.'

School threw up alternative options and diversions, of course, but none grabbed David or his dad the way boxing did.

'It annoyed me to see David playing rugby, because the teachers would always expect him to be everywhere on the pitch,' continued Deron. 'He was the most athletic and quickest boy in the team, and a lot of pressure was put on his shoulders. There even came a point where the other kids were given merits if they could take him down and get the ball. Nobody could do it, though. Funnily enough, even the teacher tried tackling him one day, and I'll always remember David shaking off the tackle and leaving the teacher drenched in a puddle on the field.'

Jane nodded in agreement, fondly recalling the moment Haye left a senior member of staff in slush. After all, speed had always been a valued commodity in both their son's school life and boxing life.

'They used to do a one-mile run at school, which was basically four times around the track,' said Jane. 'James, David's brother, was younger and in a lower year, so he only had to do two laps, while David had to do all four. As you can imagine, David sprints ahead like a maniac and is huffing and puffing and pumping his arms. After one lap he has emptied his tank, is struggling to breathe and gradually starts to slip back. The rest of the field catch up. It's then that he sees James running past him and waving. James wasn't a sprinter like David, but was more measured and took his time. He knew what race needed to be run, whereas David just saw victory and was in a rush to grab at it. David never did like running.'

Eagerly arched forward in his chair, Deron revealed: 'That played out in the way they both boxed, too. David was always in a rush to end things. I used to say, "Take your time, son, think about what you're doing." Because he was so fast and powerful, he fell in love with the idea of knocking *everybody* out quickly. He felt he had failed if he didn't score a first-round knockout.

'James was the complete opposite, though. He would glide around the ring and counterpunch, wait for his moment and then sting. He would also apologise for hurting kids and knocking them out. James didn't have that same intensity and fire that David had. He wasn't as bothered by winning or losing. David had to win at all costs.'

The stereotype paints all prizefighters as hopeless products of broken homes and dead-end situations, but Jane recoiled whenever the same generalisation was made of her boy. It quickly became clear to me that David's love of boxing was built on the competitiveness of his father and the compassion of his mother, as opposed to any scarring trials or tribulations on the streets of Bermondsey.

'I don't like seeing David described as a "street child" or somebody who had it rough,' said Jane. 'At one point he was the only child in his class whose parents were still together. Gatehouse Square was great for us and gave the kids a nice place to play and grow up. David was well-mannered and bright, and certainly wasn't knocking around in a gutter somewhere.

'I once wrote a letter to a newspaper that published a story about David's "tough upbringing", asking for an amended story and an apology. I never got an apology, but nobody has run with that line since.'

As Jane sat back in her seat and practised the whimsical smile and shrug she'd later employ to evade approaching anxiety, Deron stared down at the table and tightly clenched his right fist. I watched as he rubbed, caressed and cracked his knuckles in the exact same way I'd seen his fighting son do at numerous points during our journey together. Though calm of voice and manner, Deron was a natural scrapper, and primitive instincts were taking over.

It was then that Jane placed her soft hand upon Deron's twitching fist and whispered, 'Why don't you get yourself another coffee, love? It will set you up for the day.'

Mum and Dad had every right to be in good spirits that morning, as their middle child was well on course to fulfilling his dream and becoming the undisputed world heavyweight champion. With training all wrapped up and the hard graft complete, Haye checked into Hamburg's Park Hyatt hotel buoyed by an overwhelming sense that nothing had been left to chance. Even more encouraging, though, was the way in which the British hope had successfully crawled his way inside the mind of Wladimir Klitschko.

The games began for real on Monday afternoon as Haye, backed by an entourage of twenty, bowled into the official pre-fight press conference forty-five minutes after the scheduled start time. Conversely, Klitschko, true to form, made a point of arriving to the same function fifteen minutes early, only to then have to sit alongside an empty seat and lonely place-card for over an hour.

Of course, the instigator was beyond caring who he upset by this stage. That was the whole idea behind deliberately turning up late in the first place. Now was the time for antagonism, not punctuality. Therefore, once the door finally opened, Haye continued his verbal assault on Klitschko's eardrums, Adam Booth offered the media only one-word answers, and Irishman Paddy Fitzpatrick, Haye's third man in the corner, even decided to incite a squabble with legendary trainer Emanuel Steward, the man given the job of invigorating Klitschko on fight night. A lot of it made no sense to anybody but Haye and Booth, but the master plan appeared to be working. By the end of Monday afternoon, Wladimir's older brother

Vitali had allowed himself to become emotionally involved in the event, and now both were keen to teach the Brit with the braggadocio a lesson.

The next twist in the theatrics occurred on Wednesday, as both Haye and Klitschko visited a Mercedes-Benz showroom to conduct workouts for the public and media. With unpredictability still the name of the game, the Englishman arrived ten minutes early for the workout, taking everybody, including the onlooking Klitschkos, by surprise. Haye and company were then shown to a nearby holding room, where they were sharply instructed to wait.

After a while, events coordinator Yvonne Muller burst through the door to inform the cavalry that Klitschko and his team had lined the stairs and were anticipating the Briton's imminent arrival. Muller explained how, eager to intimidate on home soil, the opposition had purposely positioned themselves on the stairs to interrupt their opponent's grand arrival.

'Fuck it, let's go a different way then,' said Haye, as he unlocked the closest window to him.

So they did. Well, all except Kevin Lidlow, that is. The singular moral strand in the group stuck to the prescribed way of doing things, as everybody else climbed out of the window, scurried along the rooftop of the showroom and then ventured down the steps the other side. They walked through a Mercedes workshop, waved at startled engineers, and then entered the showroom via a trapdoor.

Perhaps keen to even the score and save face, both Klitschkos took their place at ringside, alongside trainer Emanuel Steward and countless other members of the entourage, as Haye warmed up inside the ring in the middle of the showroom. They were present to watch Haye work out, regardless of whether anybody wanted them there or not. Haye and Booth sensed the scrutiny and, within minutes, were plotting a second counter-attack. Booth leaned over and told me, 'He's going to wrap his hands in the ring for twenty minutes, shadow-box for ten and then hit the pads with one punch. We will celebrate like he's won the world title and then leave.'

And just like that, Haye wrapped, shadow-boxed and then punched, just once, before taking a bow and departing the ring. Klitschko merely smiled the same rueful smile he'd produced on the stairs, before begging Haye to stick around and watch his own workout. It was too late. Haye was out the door, his work done.

'These are the worst kind of sessions,' sighed a weary Haye, as Adam Booth wrapped his hands ahead of a pre-fight punching session at a downtown Hamburg boxing gym. It would be his last before the fight, signalling the end of a six-month training period. 'I just want to punch as hard and fast as I can at this stage, and yet I can't afford to do that. I'm only operating at something like thirty per cent right now, simply because you don't want to peak too soon. I'm just ready to go now.'

The focus that Thursday was on visualisation and restraint. Booth watched Haye shadow-box for four rounds, before slipping him a yellow gumshield and advising him to start rounds exactly the way he expected to on Saturday night. I felt privileged to watch Haye rehearse scenes and moves in his head that evening, complete with all the tools he required, including the same ten-ounce Grant fight gloves he'd use to try and rattle Klitschko with. I'd never seen him more concentrated or quiet and, for once, I stared up at Haye and familiarised myself with the 'lonely man in the ring' image so many people often speak of. The fighter appeared lost in his own thoughts, impatient, drowned in tactics and uncertainty, and yet was shadow-boxing with a beautiful instinct and childlike innocence. Everything came naturally and easily to him, the result of years of drilling and rehearsing the same moves over and over. Right there before my very eyes, Haye was back to being a ten-year-old kid with a lightweight frame and heavyweight dream.

Booth then promptly strapped on his leather platform boots, increasing his height by a few inches, and began to prod the champion with a boxing glove on a stick. Built to replicate the size and length of Klitschko's venomous left lead, this device kept Haye out of range and forced him to explode in close. Booth waited in one corner, pad in one hand and poking mechanism in the other, while Haye prepared himself for war in the other. The buzzer signalled the beginning of the round, and Booth instructed his man to 'start as you plan to on Saturday.' With that, Haye pressed forward on his front foot, moved his head from side to side, twitched endlessly and then looked to throw himself forward in a zig-zag movement. This essentially required him to dart off an invisible 'line' with his head, and then create the letter 'Z' with his feet. The idea was for this rapid motion to swiftly and cleanly transfer Haye from safety into punching range, thus positioning him for a potential ambush. He perfected the sequence countless times that Thursday night and, in doing so, made Saturday's task appear worryingly simple.

Once punching was concluded, Haye picked up the nearest skipping rope and again lost himself in another instinctive rhythm he had practised his entire boxing life. There was no need to think or fear, the rope acting merely as an extension of his arm. He skipped longer than I'd ever seen him skip that night, and no doubt used the exercise to blur the complex sketches Booth had so meticulously etched into his mind. The time for thinking was over. Animal instincts were about to kick in, and Haye was ready to enter his dark place.

The heavens opened outside, the clock read half past five and Haye was alone again. D'Angelo's 'Untitled' played on his hotel room's stereo system, and would be just one of many icky, pedestrian-paced jams we both listened to that uncomfortable July evening. The fighter was less than two hours away from leaving his hotel and heading to Hamburg's Imtech Arena, and I had been called to his room moments before, accompanied by Dael Poulter and Ben Anderson, on hand to film a documentary, and also Jerome Haye, the boxer's young cousin and photographer. Yet, despite the extra numbers, and the presence of nutritionist Ruben Tabares in an adjacent room, Haye still remained locked up and alone inside his own head.

'I definitely think we've got to him this week,' said Haye, as he devoured a hefty bowl of rice at the dining table. 'He will have been unsettled by everything that has gone on. I *know* he will.'

I didn't respond. Truth be told, I had no indication as to whether Haye had won the mind games or not. I simply sat opposite and nodded. Haye needed Klitschko to become emotionally entangled in the fight and for him to change the habits of a lifetime, becoming reckless and wild in the process. He needed to unsettle Klitschko in order to improve his own chances of landing the necessary bingo punch. Haye was looking for confirmation and reassurance that his plan was working, but I couldn't help him. I didn't know.

Detecting my indecision, Haye changed tack.

'You've never been a fan of Lenny Kravitz, have you?' he said, as he sang along to 'It Ain't Over 'Til It's Over'.

'No,' I sighed. 'If I wanted to hear somebody impersonate Jimi Hendrix, I'd go listen to Hendrix.'

'I've watched Kravitz in concert twice. He was a really good musician and played a few different instruments on stage.'

'I'm sure he was "good". Good doesn't cut it if you're trying to look and sound like Hendrix, though. Most of his songs sound like bad versions of old Hendrix stuff.'

'Well, not everybody can be *great*. You can't just respect the greatest to ever do something. There will always be people that use the greats as inspiration, but never reach the same level. I'm not saying Lenny is as good as Jimi, but he's still good in his own right.'

Haye's ongoing reluctance to listen to Hendrix, the originator and god, rendered his opinion almost worthless, but I appreciated where he was coming from. More than that, though, I welcomed the light-hearted nature of the conversation at a moment like that.

'It's weird, I haven't even checked any of the online boxing forums or websites once today,' said Haye, as he huddled over his laptop and began compiling a changing-room playlist, channel-surfing from song to song, eager to nail the right kind of mood.

'That's very unlike you,' I replied.

'Yeah, I know,' he said. 'I'm usually *always* looking at those sites before my fights.'

'Why do you think you haven't done the same this time around?'

'I'm not sure.'

'You haven't watched any fights today, either,' I said. 'Why do you think that is?'

'I just haven't felt like it,' said Haye. 'Maybe it's because I know what I need to do tonight and don't want to complicate things. Watching Roy Jones or somebody else isn't going to help me in any way. It's probably best not to confuse things and try to copy someone else.'

'That makes sense.'

'I always used to watch those guys back in the day because they were doing things better than I could in fights that were bigger than the ones I would be preparing for. That's not really the case any more, though. I feel like I've got to step up to that level tonight. I've got to prove to myself that I belong there and that I am as good as all those guys I used to watch.'

There was suddenly a feeling in the room that Haye was on the brink of surpassing the role models he had once looked up to, learnt from and so admired. He slumped back in his seat and yawned the kind of anxious yawn I'd grown accustomed to seeing at this point before a fight. More than anyone else, he sensed it. The magnitude suddenly dawned on him right there and then.

'What do you expect to happen in the first round?' I asked.

'I don't know,' said Haye. 'I think he will be the same old Wladimir. I don't expect him to be aggressive just because I have wound him up. He knows how dangerous I am, and he won't take risks against someone like me. That just wouldn't make sense.'

I agreed, and decided to let that final thought sink without a trace. Haye, however, had other ideas.

'Game plans mean nothing when you're in the ring anyway,' he added. 'We can sit and talk about what he is going to do and what I am going to do, but nobody really knows. Once you are in there, you kind of make it up as you go. The weeks of training and tactics help you prepare for certain situations, but it soon disappears when the first bell goes. Then you are just working with what you know. You're all alone and it's all instinctive.'

A hard, hurtful and ominous rain continued to fall that night and, by the time I'd reached ringside at Hamburg's Imtech Arena, the downpour had reached biblical proportions. The press row was empty, the seats covered in plastic. The invisible journalists who'd spent weeks lobbying for pride of place at ringside were now content, nay, elated to take up a dry seat in the bleachers and open their laptops without fear of electrocution.

Similarly, those who'd paid upwards of €1,000 for outer ringside positions were also left out in the cold, as neither the canopy above the ring, nor the roof, covered their seats on pitch level. Subsequently, both the seats and their drenched inhabitants were wrapped in plastic and moved as close to the barricade and overhead protection as possible.

Even at ringside, the kings and queens of the affair were left with glum faces and lying brochures. Haye's wife Natasha, positioned in arguably the best seat in the house, flattened her pink dress to reveal giant brown scuff marks along the bottom of it. She sighed dejectedly, before unwrapping a wholly unglamorous rain mack and throwing it over her designer attire, thus waving goodbye to any delusions of glamour.

All in all, a crowd of approximately 38,000 were packed inside that once glorious football stadium. Thankfully, though the previous day's sunshine had made way for sobbing clouds, the vociferous British support created an artificial warmth and elevated the occasion to unprecedented levels of anticipation. Then, as news filtered through that Haye was planning on delaying his ring entrance by up to ten minutes, the tension became almost unbearable.

'We had to delay,' explained Haye. 'Kevin [Lidlow] gave me a local anaesthetic in my foot, but thirty-five minutes later it had worn off and I was in agony again. I had already warmed up and was ready to go. So I had to remove my boot, receive another injection and start over again.'

Haye was bundled out of his changing room ten minutes later, kitted out in the England football team's latest away strip and a beanie hat. The flustered fighter was then asked to traverse through a swarm of inebriated British fans, as his designated ring walk took him on a shortcut to potential disaster. Flanked by bodyguards Davide Nicolosi, James Thompson and Mustapha Al-Turk, the fighter was not exactly short on muscle, yet still struggled to escape the flailing arms and aggressive exuberance of fans en route to the ring.

Klitschko, on the other hand, dressed in his traditional super-sized red robe, complete with body warmer, took a different route and breezed through his ring walk relatively unscathed and with minimum fuss. If Haye had spent all week scoring points in dress rehearsals, the spotless Klitschko unquestionably had the last laugh, just moments before the first bell tolled.

Whether it was brought on by the delayed start, the sight of an England football shirt, the perilous entrance to the ring, the circling dark clouds, the rain-sodden seats and faces or the sheer magnitude of the event, I was by now as low on confidence as I'd been at any point leading up to the contest. Whereas one week before, everything seemed so right, it now all seemed so wrong. Call me superstitious, but the signs were there.

Once the first bell rang, tactics Haye had practised and perfected for months suddenly seemed drawn in Crayola by the hand of a toddler. Granted, he moved intelligently and dipped and faked menacingly, but, crucially, the WBA champion wasn't able to join the dots the way he had done so seamlessly in the gym.

The beneficiary of a two-stone weight and three-inch height advantage, Klitschko used both to control the centre of the ring behind his jab, and would then shove Haye towards the floor whenever the marauding Brit attempted to get close. Klitschko's physical strengths opened the door to basic consistency, whereas Haye's deficiencies in those same departments required him to take risks and aimlessly catapult attacks from out wide in order to close the gap.

In fact, Haye wouldn't land his first significant blow in the fight until midway through round three, when range and timing finally shook hands and allowed the Englishman to bounce a high and hard right hand against Klitschko's cheek. The wild shot forced Wladimir to hold momentarily, before Haye slipped out and grinned, the yellow of his gumshield evident. Two further cuffing right hands late on in the round helped Haye steal the session on the scorecards, but Klitschko still remained upright, composed and six feet six inches tall.

Alas, the veteran champion used these dimensions expertly in the fourth and fifth rounds, too. He flicked jabs and thudded occasional right hands in Haye's direction, well aware that so long as he kept his range, the typically aggressive Brit would be unable to counterpunch. Klitschko's persistent use of the left jab kept Haye's mind occupied and his body unable to set and propel attacks of his own.

When the doctor's steel hammer of a right cross did occasionally connect, as was the case in the fifth and tenth rounds, Haye showed a surprising and impressive resistance to it. The common consensus beforehand, of course, was that whenever Klitschko landed hard and clean on his smaller foe, the fight would be as good as over, yet Haye frequently soaked up thudding shots and begged for more.

In the end, though, it was predictability, rather than a lack of toughness, that hampered the one-time heavyweight saviour through many of the middle rounds. Wary of the big right hand of his opponent, Klitschko would half shoot his jab and then, when sensing Haye was primed to counter, raise his left shoulder ever so slightly to deflect the incoming roundhouse shot. Frustration ensued for Haye, as time and time again he misfired, only to end up on the floor as a result of a Klitschko push. Referee Gino Rodriguez even took the whip to the home favourite in the seventh, when docking a point from the German-based champion for persistent bulldozing in close.

Encouraged by a better seventh round, Haye baited and waited again in both the eighth and ninth, but came no closer to landing the decisive shot required to sever a mounting deficit on the judges' scorecards. Klitschko was similarly reticent, however, and refused to throw, let alone land any notable power punches. He instead decided to rack up points behind a stiff left arm, thrown in the form of a tentative and controlling jab.

A knockdown was then scored against Haye in the eleventh

round, following yet another push and resulting flop to the floor. Rather than take a point from Klitschko as he had done in the seventh, though, referee Rodriguez instead decided to even the score and administer a mandatory eight count in Haye's direction, despite the fact no punch was even thrown.

With the scorecards taking a turn for the worse, Haye entered the final round in need of a knockout to hold on to his WBA title. He began the session with a renewed vigour and purpose and, after only fifty seconds, managed to step inside and uncork the kind of punch he had misplaced all night. Haye bowled over a high and agricultural right hook that struck Klitschko bang on the chin and forced the Ukrainian to cling on immediately. He secured Haye's arms in a hold, walked him backwards and then dumped the smaller man on the ring canvas. His experience and know-how prevented any attempted Haye follow-up, and Klitschko used an impromptu time-out to regain his senses and once again consult his trusted left jab. David tried desperately to replicate the early success, but instead watched the round and his title reign dwindle away at double speed. The final bell rang, and Haye had been defeated. He raised a solitary arm in hope rather than expectation, but scores of 118–108, 117–109 and 116–110 sealed the Englishman's fate. He had been beaten for the second time in his professional career, and the first time as a heavyweight.

The former champion's choice of comfort food that night was a pack of Maryland chocolate chip cookies and a bag of Cadbury Clusters. Laid up on the sofa in his hotel room, Haye alternated between cookie and cluster, before offering the half-eaten bags to surrounding family and friends. Physio Kevin Lidlow knelt down at one end of the leather sofa and carefully removed the cast that had encased the fighter's right foot. As the foot was finally granted freedom, Haye winced and did his best not to scream. Pain was etched across his face, though, and even the comforting sight of his mum and dad failed to ease the anguish.

'You can grab my hand if you like, son,' said father Deron, stood nearby with a look of concern.

'No, it's fine,' said Haye, with a grimace.

'Yeah, I know,' replied Deron, understanding his son's need to win this small battle.

We'd all since heard Haye use the injured toe as the reason for his constant misfiring of the right hand through thirty-six minutes in Klitschko's presence. He had even removed his boot to reveal the broken toe in more than one post-fight interview. Some saw this as the sad climax to an enthralling three-year heavyweight adventure, while Haye claimed he had simply and honestly answered the questions that had been asked of him. I could understand both interpretations of the scene, of course, and winced uncomfortably as I recalled the many conversations I'd previously had with the fighter relating to the very same subject.

'I can't stand fighters that make excuses after a fight,' Haye had once told me. 'You never hear the winning fighter make an excuse or talk about an injury after the fight. It is only ever the beaten boxer that comes up with the excuses.

'If you're injured going into a fight, don't take the fight. Some hard-up fighters can't afford to pull out of fights because of an injury, but I'll never be in that boat.'

Haye had preached those truths to me after a hamstring injury forced him to withdraw from a British and Commonwealth cruiser-weight title fight against Mark Hobson in July 2005. We were now six years down the line and, while Haye's bank balance had only increased since then, his get-out card, especially in the company of Klitschko, had well and truly expired. He'd already cancelled a June 2009 clash with the Ukrainian through injury and, under-standably, fans and critics alike were poised with their 'scaredy cat' tags should the Briton so much as dare call in sick for a second time. Irrespective of whether the toe injury was severe enough to justify a cancellation, Haye unfairly felt the pressure throughout training camp.

'I *have* to get through it,' said Haye, as he sat on the edge of the boxing ring one night after sparring. 'There is no option to pull out or postpone. If I could cut my right foot off and still go through with the fight, I'd do it without hesitation. My reputation would be in tatters if I pulled out of this fight again. I can't even let the thought enter my head.'

To nobody's surprise, the British press morphed from ambivalent angels into stake-wielding slayers at the post-fight press conference, eager to proclaim Haye the sore loser with a sore toe, but the one-time national hero was, by this stage, beyond caring. He finally shook Klitschko's 'magic hand' – though would have loved to amputate his left one – and praised the champion for shutting down his offence and crushing his dream. He then limped back to his hotel.

Gathered around the fallen warrior upon his return were his mum, dad, wife, sister, uncle Donovan, auntie Sabeela, cousin Jerome, trainers Adam Booth, Jamie Sawyer, Ruben Tabares, Paddy Fitzpatrick and Pete Marcasciano, Booth's wife Claire, boxer George Groves and girlfriend Sophie Modhej, as well as David's best friends Karlton Bryan and Kamran Naqvi. Nobody so much as frowned or sighed, let alone cried. There were other passing visitors, too, armed with rehearsed commiseration speeches, and Haye treated each to the same packaged smile and meek handshake. Spirits remained high despite the result, and the boxer periodically sang along to the same sombre playlist that had accompanied his final hours before the bout. If anything, even in defeat, Haye seemed happier at that moment than he'd been earlier in the evening, perhaps liberated by the fact it was all over.

'At least now I know my chin isn't as bad as they all said it was,' joked Haye, through a pained smile. 'Everybody said I would be knocked out cold by the first right hand Wladimir landed. There were some people even saying he might floor me with a jab.'

'You showed you could take a good shot,' I said.

'Yeah, I guess. That's probably the worst compliment a boxer can receive, though, isn't it? That just means I got hit too much.'

Haye rubbed the side of his fist along a welt beneath his right eye, with Klitschko's jab to thank for the discomfort.

'I'm gutted,' he sighed. 'I just couldn't close the range on him. My legs wouldn't cover the ground quick enough and my toe was hurting from the first round onwards. I couldn't explode off my back leg the way I'd normally do. It was like that dream I have where I'm unable to do the things I'm supposed to do. It's really frustrating, because I know I had chances.'

'You can at least take satisfaction from the fact you did all you could under the circumstances,' I reasoned.

'That's not good enough, though. I lost.'

He was right. He'd lost and I was, as usual, talking like the perennial loser. As if to then compound matters, 'It Ain't Over 'Til It's Over' resurfaced on Haye's playlist. Only now I was strangely less disturbed by its presence. The affirmative song title and clichéd lyrics resonated more at times like these and, though I'd never dare reveal such a weakness, my earlier debate with Haye had given me a fresh perspective on the concept of greatness and the harsh standards by which I judged also-rans. Nobody wanted to hear Hendrix more than me, but, as I'd come to realise that day, sometimes one must be content to settle for Kravitz, a serviceable and talented imitation of the real thing. No, he'd never be Hendrix, but who would ever be?

Haye himself fell short of his legendary heroes that night in Hamburg, but remained as upbeat and philosophical as he'd been earlier in the day. He lost a fight he wasn't supposed to win, in a division he wasn't meant to conquer, having already lassoed the world's cruiserweights three years earlier. World titles are owned by few boxers in Great Britain, and yet Haye had already deposited four of them on the mantelpiece of his parents' home in south London. Context and Kravitz allowed for positivity and, eight years on from when I first met the skinny cruiserweight, I was now stuffed on titles, trauma and chocolate, having wolfed down the remains of his half-eaten junk food. It was then that I glanced over at Haye, through proud rather than pitying or judgemental eyes. Perhaps wrongly interpreting the look, David nodded his head, reached across to his laptop and skipped to the next song.

'Okay,' he said, 'just for you.'

I never let it be known, but the song was starting to grow on me.

EPILOGUE

A thoughtful David Haye reconnects with his roots in Jamaica and contemplates whether boxing is still the game for him.

EPILOGUE

A sweat-soaked world champion prowled before a mirror, challenging and deceiving his reflection, all the while shooting rapid left and right punches into thin air. The underdog was twelve weeks away from a world title unification clash, and shadow-boxing allowed him the chance to prise open the pores of combat. Then, once the play-fighting was over, he'd bury his head in a clean towel, sip on a cup of water and tour the gymnasium for further challenges.

David Haye sat and watched Carl Froch work out that July afternoon, perched on the edge of a dormant treadmill, silently contemplating his friend's chances of victory. Nottingham's Froch, a two-time WBC world super-middleweight champion, was due to face America's WBA king Andre Ward on 29 October, and Haye knew his former amateur team-mate was up against it. Ten years ago Froch and Haye had both medalled at the 2001 World Amateur Championships in Belfast, and now the long-time friends had reconvened on a family holiday in Hanover Parish, Jamaica, Haye intent on relaxing and Froch keen to utilise the sticky climate to kickstart his fight preparations.

Alas, Haye remained rooted to the treadmill with neither a title nor a craving to join Froch in a communion of sweat and aggression. He was an idle spectator and an exhausted soul, vision and judgement skewed by Appleton rum, infamous right toe still maimed and inflamed. Three weeks on from his own world title unification fight in Hamburg, the defeated former champion was in no mood or fit state to move, let alone punch. He had spent over twenty years of his life drenched in sweat and expectation, and wasn't about to invent a reason to continue that routine on holiday. Boxing was still very much on his brain, but his body had long since left the premises.

'He just wants to safely control you, Carl,' said Haye, rising to his feet and mimicking Ward's style. 'He won't want to mix it with you.'

'Yeah, I know,' replied Froch. 'That's nothing a hard right hand around the back of the head won't sort out, though.'

'You've got to be on him from the first bell and let him know he can't get away with any of his bitch moves.'

'There's no way he will be tougher or fitter than me on the night, Dave. Yeah, he might be quicker and more skilful, but that's out of my control. If I go out there, put it on him and fight my fight, I'll be happy. If he still manages to beat me, I'll hold my hands up and admit he's the better man.'

As they shared thoughts and forecasts, it became clear, at least to me, that while Froch's mind was naturally on Ward, Haye's remained on Wladimir Klitschko, the giant Ukrainian he'd faltered against three weeks before. The required game plans and complications were eerily similar for both Haye and Froch, and the heavyweight offered advice through experience and regret as opposed to any penetrating insight.

Froch wasn't the only one sweating that day, either. Haye's parents Jane and Deron were also being put through their paces on elliptical trainers, while wife Natasha joined Froch's girlfriend Rachael Cordingley for a spot of circuit training. The one-time heavyweight champion, meanwhile, was content to simply watch and advise, occasionally shuffling from station to station to kindly assist those with the energy to work.

'Let me ask you something,' said Haye, as he sidled up next to Natasha and Rachael by the lat pull-down machine. 'Why do you bother training if you don't have to? I genuinely don't get it. Why even make the effort? I couldn't think of anything worse right now.'

The boxer's question was greeted with wide-eyed amazement and open mouths.

'We do it because we enjoy it, Dave,' replied Natasha. 'You probably don't see training as something to enjoy, because you've been doing it as a job for so long now. You need to reach a stage where you can enjoy doing it even when you're not preparing for a fight.'

Haye shrugged, took a deep breath and then returned to his safe haven on the edge of the nearest idle treadmill. He continued analysing everybody around him, and then honed in on Froch, proudly flexing in front of the largest mirror. Haye gazed at his friend and said nothing. He listened intently as Froch spoke of training plans, pre-fight mind games, fight tactics and potential ring entrance music. They shared a mutual enthusiasm for what lay ahead, but Haye, having seen his own unification clash end in disappointment, could now only watch from an exterior position through a cloud of nostalgia. He was back to being a fan without a belt, a contender unsure whether he still wanted to contend.

His holiday tipple of Appleton rum and apple juice helped alleviate the pain in his toe and any lingering emotional trauma, but Froch's sweat beads and six-pack acted as a constant reminder of what Haye would leave behind should he stick to his promise and retire from boxing before his thirty-first birthday on 13 October. As Haye silently monitored Froch's progress one evening at the gym, I couldn't help but feel he was in equal measures jealous and repulsed by the sight of a fellow fighter in the throes of preparation, only too aware of what his friend was about to put his body and mind through in the coming weeks. Haye still loved the idea of being a fighter in front of a mirror, but recoiled at the thought of heading to that dark place all fighters must visit ahead of a world title fight.

Blink and you'd miss it, but the transition from awe-inspiring athletic specimen to temporary workshy layabout was swift and dramatic. Haye was about as perfect an athlete as I'd seen heading into his July bout with Klitschko – his body a temple, his mind a war room, fiercely focused and animalistic in his desires – yet three weeks on and the same fighter found himself in Jamaica, a destination as far removed from those emotions as possible. He'd drained every ounce of pent-up aggression and frustration on the flight over, and both body and mind were now grinning in a relaxed state of deflation. He ate and drank everything that had been off limits to him earlier that month and lost himself in the listless labyrinth of unemployment.

'I've never been as free as I am right now,' said Haye, hair wild and unkempt, one evening at a luxury £8m villa, situated high up on Hanover's Tryall Club golf resort. 'I can literally do whatever I want and go wherever I want and it won't matter one bit. I'm so used to being kept to a schedule, and this feels really weird. I don't have to follow a routine or think about who I'm fighting next. I don't have to monitor *anything*.'

'Doesn't that scare you a bit, though?' I asked.

'Not really,' he replied. 'I don't know what it means yet. I don't know whether the time off is going to be good or bad. It might make me lazy and not want to do anything with my life, or it could lead me on to something better. I don't know, and have never been in this position before. It's a nice feeling, though. I'm not scared by it. If anything, I've waited twenty years to feel like this.'

Haye never said it outright, but it became clear by implication that competing, at least in a sporting capacity, was something he'd now left in the past. By the time he touched down in Montego Bay, hit the sun lounger and began staring at palm trees, Haye talked less of Klitschko and more about carving a niche in the film industry or as a television personality. Plans were still sketchy at this stage, but meetings had been arranged with both the BBC and Sky Television for his mid-August return. Wife Natasha and trainer Adam Booth, two pivotal influences, were very much steering the career change and, though I sensed Haye would forever regret departing the sport on a defeat, he had few reasons to continue.

'Neither of the Klitschko brothers will fight me next, and I'm not going to drop down a level and start working my way up against bums,' said the former champion. 'The only way I'll fight on is if Wladimir gives me another shot, or Vitali calls me out.'

'That's unlikely, though, isn't it?' I asked.

'Wladimir won't do it immediately,' said Haye, 'but he might start to realise in a year or two that he simply can't make the kind of money he made against me by fighting these other guys out there. I'm happy to sit back and watch him beat a couple more bums for peanuts, because I know that at some point he will start seeking me out again. Even if that takes two or three years, I'll be ready and waiting. All I've got to do is make sure I train and keep myself in decent nick alongside whatever else it is I choose to do in the meantime. I'm going to build a gym in my house and use that to stay sharp. I can't afford to get fat and out of shape to the point where I'm unable to jump back in and fight him.'

'So October 13th doesn't *really* stand as the retirement date?'

'That's the date I'll retire on, but it doesn't mean it's the end, at least as far as the Klitschkos are concerned. I will retire from fighting everybody without the Klitschko surname on that date, but Wladimir will always interest me, simply because he holds a win over me. If I could fight Carl Thompson again, I'd probably do that, too. I hate looking at my record and seeing twenty-five wins and two defeats.

Despite everything that I've achieved, the number two haunts me and pisses me off. I've lost two fights and may never be able to get the chance to avenge either of them. If my career does end on October 13th, that will probably be the only regret. What can I do, though? Sometimes you've just got to keep on moving.'

Two days later Haye rediscovered an urge for competition and stepped back into the firing line. Casual to the point of laziness in slacks, shirt and flip-flops, he plucked his weapon of choice, lofted it high above his head and began to stretch out. Then he stopped, checked up ahead, cracked each of the knuckles on his left and right hands, and rolled his shoulders like a shifty henchman in an itchy trenchcoat. Another glance into the distance shortly followed. It was a look of serious intent second time round, though. The boxer bit down and loaded up. He lifted the driver high up above his head and then, in one brisk and purposeful motion, Haye brought the club down and connected with a petrified white golf ball trembling on a tee.

Meticulous preparation and explosive action should have resulted in the ball being catapulted into the yonder, but instead, eleventh-hour doubts conspired to scuff Haye's approach and pitch the ball a mere fifty yards from where it was struck.

'For fuck's sake,' cursed the fighter, as he marched to collect his splintered tee and ego. 'It's going to take me a while to find my flow again, I think.'

Haye's latest brain-freeze was infinitely less painful than the one suffered in Hamburg earlier that summer, but appeared to bemuse and hurt him just the same. Only four people watched him fluff the opening shot that Saturday afternoon, and yet the embarrassment that ensued clearly preyed on his mind. Of the four spectators present, myself and the BBC's Ronald McIntosh, mere newcomers to the game of golf, failed to register on Haye's radar, whereas father Deron and fellow fighter Froch were both slow-clapping and hissing inside his head each time he sized up that little white ball. Like most competitive young men, Haye could think of nothing more unbearable than losing a game of anything to his father, while Froch, clearly his closest rival in the talent stakes, boasted a parallel mindset and attitude to victory. Therefore, as the three of us patiently waited our turn, Haye growled and muttered something X-rated, before fetching a second ball. Unfortunately, this one fared no better.

'You guys can start hitting over there,' said Haye, while kicking up a tuft of turf and motioning for another ball to be sacrificed. 'I'm going to be a while.'

We promptly went our separate ways and the pattern was fairly predictable to begin with. McIntosh and I both produced a flukey humdinger of an opening shot before slipping into a quagmire of abused turf and stray balls, while proud Deron huffed and puffed and nailed his fair share of respectable pings. It was the cocksure Froch, however, who caught the attention of everybody, not least Haye, who soon split time between eyeing up his own quivering ball and scouting the emerging hotshot beside him.

'It's just like boxing,' explained Froch, as he strolled confidently towards ball number one. 'The power is all in the technique. If you try hitting it hard, you'll screw up the technique and struggle to hit it at all. The key is to concentrate on the technique and then let nature take its course.'

As each of us waited for the inevitable egg-on-face moment, Froch fluently wound his club back and struck a textbook drive right down the middle of the range, the ball eventually landing way beyond the 150-yard mark.

'That's a winner,' said Carl, as he spun around to receive feverish acclaim from us mere beginners. Rather than clap, Haye simply acknowledged his opponent's opening effort with a respectful smile and nod. He then turned his attention back to the ball he was about to punish.

'That's what I like to call setting the bar,' added Froch. 'Reckon you can match it, Dave?'

'I'll get there,' said Haye, 'don't worry about that. Just watch.'

'Remember, try not to force it. I know you'll really want to go out there and smash it now, having watched me do that, but don't fall into the trap. Just relax and swing.'

'Tell me where you want me to hit it.'

'Somewhere beyond fifty yards would be a nice start.'

'We'll see.'

'Don't make it a competition, Dave. That will just make you tense. You need to relax and clear your mind.'

It was peculiar witnessing two professional fighters roam a serene golf course and exhibit the same brand of macho posturing they'd both routinely carry into the boxing ring. The peaceful and tranquil backdrop of Tryall Club's 6,800-yard, 18-hole course failed to dilute the absurdity of the narrative, too. Few words were spoken, and punches were strictly forbidden, yet we all sensed the simmering competitive edge return to Haye in the presence of a tangible threat to his athletic prowess. These two men had been Britain's pre-eminent boxing stars for the best part of a decade, and, while weight restrictions would always prevent them from demonstrating superiority over the other in their own domain, both were offered a shot at bragging rights that Saturday afternoon on the driving range.

So, mind switched to combat, Haye shook his arms out, shrugged his shoulders and lined up a retort. Undeterred by mounting scrutiny, Haye neglected his customary rehearsal swing and abruptly dived straight in for the kill. He pulled back and released in one smooth motion, and the four bystanders, Froch included, could only watch as the ball soared up, up and away, far beyond our collective eyeline.

'Where is it?' asked Haye, using his hand to shield his eyes from the sun. 'I can't see it anywhere.'

'It's over there, son,' shouted Deron, a raised finger directing us to its path. Sure enough, the ball dropped like an injured bird somewhere between the 200-yard sign and the end net. The humbled Froch, gracious as ever, merely stood and applauded his rival's supreme effort.

'Warmed up now then, have we?' said Carl with a wink.

'I'm back, baby,' roared Haye. 'It all just came flooding back to me.'

Wasting no time, the pair rushed to their respective buckets, fetched more balls and forgot all notion of peering over the neighbour's fence. Indications of the other's success simply arrived in the form of childish hollering and clapping each time a ball fell from the sky. Haye and Froch were now competing directly against one another, and, though boxing and golf shared little in common, neither man wanted to lose at anything that day in Jamaica.

For the record, despite the nip-and-tuck start to proceedings, Froch's promising early form eventually fizzled out and allowed a resurgent Haye the chance to light up the blue sky with an array of inspired drives. As Froch struggled to reclaim his knack, Haye found accuracy and potency and began to consistently hit high, straight and long like the pros. Passing caddies even stopped to watch the muscled boxer unveil his rudimentary swing, and each could be seen nodding their approval upon witnessing the end result. It may not have been technically correct or even legal, but Haye's combination of raw strength and competitiveness helped him overcome a talented rival and, in doing so, dupe locals into thinking he was a veteran at Augusta.

'How far do the pros hit these things?' asked Haye.

'I think the best of them usually hit upwards of 300 yards,' replied Froch.

'Some of these are going way beyond the 200 mark.'

'You're right there. A few are getting very close to 300.'

'How long would it take for me to reach a decent pro standard?'

'With a drive like that, it would probably be quicker than most. All you've got to do is work on your putting and you're halfway there.'

'That's the hard part, though,' added Haye. 'What is it they say? Driving's for show, putting's for dough? I could blag this shit all day, but it takes years to master putting.'

That sentiment rang true moments later, as Froch restored his own pride with an admirable return thrashing on the putting green. The reverse in fortune came as no surprise to either Froch or Haye, of course. We all knew the maverick heavyweight had long mastered the concept of driving in his own sport. He hit harder and faster than most, habitually went for broke, discarded foundations and sought success as quickly as possible, both inside and outside the ring. Haye was the king of shortcuts and shocking climax. He never did have time for the more patient art of putting.

However, by the time the summer of 2011 swung around, I grew aware of the need for Haye to eventually encounter and conquer the putting green, perhaps not that Saturday afternoon in Jamaica, but in subsequent challenges away from the boxing ring. Natural talent and physical gifts had partly helped remove the need for foundations in the boxing arena, but Haye would be afforded no such luxuries in future endeavours. Whatever the next step, he would have to listen, learn, hustle from the bottom up and ensure his putting game was up to scratch, a daunting proposition for anyone defined by their expertise in another field.

In all the years I'd known the man, there were still two emotions I had yet to see surface. One was fear and the other was contentment. Before leaving Jamaica in mid-August, I was lucky enough to finally stumble across both on a day trip to Westmoreland, the westernmost parish on the island, and birthplace of David Haye's father, Deron.

Home to sugar-cane fields and vast tracts of farmland, Westmoreland offered a stark indication of how Haye's forefathers had prospered and spiked the gene pool he would so blissfully later bathe in. Roads were perilously bumpy and steep, and skinny kids dived in and out of nearby streams with no regard for safety. Meanwhile, the heavyweight tourist was offered bracelets, coconuts, sugar, chicken and rice en route to his eventual destination, as numerous locals clocked the magic tour bus and followed its path up the hill.

Waiting for David at the parish's highest point was a small shack and a lean black man with wispy grey hair and a wide smile. His name was Lorenzo. He was eighty-six years of age. The boxer had never before met the local, but wasted little time falling into his warm embrace upon arrival.

'It's great to meet you,' he said.

'You came home, David,' replied Haye's great-uncle.

'You're in incredible shape,' said Haye, as he touched the top of the man's shoulder. 'Fit and healthy. I've seen guys in their twenties with less muscle definition than you've got.'

'We make him cycle to his farm every day,' said Dale Haye, Lorenzo's grandson. 'He is always keeping active and still works. He has no problem walking up and down that same hill we just drove up.'

After posing for photographs outside the man's house, Haye paced just twenty yards and unearthed another extension of his family name. David Haye approached David Haye with a stiff handshake and a familiar glint in his eye. Grandson to Lorenzo, this David Haye was twenty-two years of age and, as far as we were aware, had never boxed professionally or even thrown a left hook.

Still, the younger, Jamaican-born David was elated to meet and touch his famous namesake, having heard so many tales of his prizefighting prowess on the dirt tracks of Westmoreland.

'I had no idea there was another David Haye in the family,' said the boxer, as his bus moved back down the hill. 'It's strange to think there is somebody else with the same name as me living out here. Although we're related in some way, this David Haye goes about his life on the farm anonymously. Nobody wants his picture or autograph.'

After immersing himself in a scrapbook that had for so long been hidden, Haye carried on through to the blue hole, a bottomless lagoon consisting of baby-blue water and topless young locals, and then the roaring river, a gushing mineral spring with bullish current. Keen to familiarise himself with the same water his father once swam in, Haye handed me his designer sunglasses and straw hat and then lowered himself into the river without so much as a second thought. Perhaps he found comfort from the sight of sister Louisa already positioned in the river and thriving among the jagged rocks and argumentative current. Whatever the impetus, seconds after greeting stone with flesh, a stunned Haye jolted upright and grimaced in pain. He panicked, gripped the nearest rock and used every ounce of strength and power to retain his position. The current had buckled him and there was no going back. He remained admirably stoic and straight-faced, but was doing a lousy job of appearing unflustered. As he shifted over rocks and tried to progress, his eyes widened and his body nervously twitched with each additional painful step. Haye had never before shown this same level of uncontrollable terror in any of his ring battles, and dry spectators were paralysed by a mix of surprise and concern, unable to lend a helping hand or do anything about the looming predicament.

This wasn't the David Haye any of us had grown to know. While he could punch, move, lift, duck, dive and run with the best of them, this supreme athlete was now thrown into a situation where none of those honed and perfected elements were required. Swimming had never been a forte, and a little right toe, the current bane of his life, was being crushed against the sharp obstacles lurking at the bottom of the stream. He now wanted to exit as swiftly as he'd entered.

'It was one of the most uncomfortable experiences of my life,' Haye would later tell me. 'I felt so far out of my element. The current was ridiculously strong and it was very hard fighting against it. There were also some really sharp rocks that were cutting my feet up as I tried to hang on for dear life. If I'd let go and allowed the current to take me, those rocks would have done some serious damage.'

Following an initial struggle to first stay upright and then make his way to the nearest dry spot, Haye suddenly came to a halt and remained hopelessly rooted in one place for around five minutes. Through pride and machismo he said nothing and refused help, despite an array of outstretched hands in close proximity. This was a problem he'd have to overcome himself. Seeking assistance would be just as horrifying as losing his footing and tumbling downstream, a feeble victim of the current's relentless pull.

To further the humiliation, local Westmoreland kids dipped in and out and somehow mastered the flow of the river with the same effortless expertise Haye had once demonstrated with punches on dry land. He glared at them with envy and despair, before signalling for his own overzealous son Cassius to stay well back and forget all notion of joining him in the stream for a light-hearted paddle.

Eventually this five-minute respite concluded, and a stranded and humbled Haye, kidnapped from his comfort zone and robbed of the necessary tools to flourish, had no choice but to simply keep moving. So he did.

*   *   *

It was while stationary and presumably dry, however, that Haye, two weeks on from his Jamaican journey of self-discovery, phoned me with his latest revelation.

'There may be a few more chapters of your book left to be written,' he said, cryptically, on the last day of August.

'Oh, really?' I replied. 'We're pretty close to deadline ...'

'I had a dream,' he interjected, 'but not of the Martin Luther King variety. I had a dream that I returned to the ring and destroyed Vitali Klitschko.'

'Okay,' I said, reaching for the nearest pad and pen. 'Go on ...'

'It sounds strange,' he begun, 'but my perspective has completely shifted since I've been back in England. I hadn't felt the need or desire to even think about fighting, let alone talk about it since my fight in July, but now I'm consumed by it and haven't been able to think about anything else for the last few days. I want that boxing routine back in my life. I want to fight again.'

Although I'd witnessed David at one with the retired way of life in Jamaica for four weeks, this latest bombshell and U-turn still failed to catch me by surprise. I knew boxing had historically prevented its warriors from strolling out the exit door and Haye, a month shy of his thirty-first birthday, still seemingly had plenty to offer, should he intend to stick around. The self-imposed retirement date of 13 October would have to fall by the wayside, of course, but the Londoner, arguably in the prime of his fighting life and still rattled by constant reminders that his last ring outing had ended in defeat, appeared ready to lick his wounds, rip up the supposed ideal and get dirty once more. He talked of fighting Vitali Klitschko in February of 2012 and revealed a wish to revisit the painful sensations and emotions commonly associated with rigorous boxing training and competition.

By Saturday, 10 September, Haye was even sitting on a sofa alongside Adam Booth watching the older of the two Klitschko brothers distort the facial features of Tomasz Adamek in ten punishing rounds. A week ago the pair couldn't have cared less about the outcome of Vitali's WBC world heavyweight title defence in Poland, but now Haye, eager to remain involved in the Klitschko sweepstakes, was nervously swaying away from every hopeful Adamek fist.

'I saw nothing new from Klitschko,' he said to me later that night. 'Adamek was a big disappointment. I don't think he even tried moving his head once. He was just a sitting duck for every shot. You can't fight Vitali like that. I think you've got to be even more awkward than Vitali to beat him. He's used to fighting those small, tough, come-forward guys. If you try to just *fight* Vitali, he'll always get the better of things. He's bigger and tougher than everybody in the division. You can't play his game.'

'Adamek gave it a go, at least,' I offered.

'What does that mean, though? So what if he 'gave it a go'? Giving it a go only resulted in him getting beat up, hurt and smashed to bits. That's not too smart in my book.'

'Given what you saw, do *you* still fancy giving it a go?'

'No,' said Haye. 'I won't just give it a go. I'll take Vitali apart.'

The WBC world heavyweight champion vehemently disagreed, of course.

'David Haye is world famous, not for his boxing skills but for his long tongue,' Vitali told Sky Sports following his seventh straight title defence. 'He is the world's biggest trash-talker. He touched me and my brother personally and I want to knock him out. I'm serious. I want to knock David Haye out.'

Intrigued by this latest twist, I checked in with Haye at his home and found an in-built gymnasium ready to be put to use, yet no sign of the man himself. The gym remained empty that morning, its owner absent in body, but, encouragingly, present in spirit. While various weights and fancy machines hinted at vanity training, key boxing essentials were also on hand, including a black heavy bag with a large fist-shaped indentation across the middle. *Somebody* had been hitting it. There were also size eleven running trainers by the front door, those clunky flip-flops a forgotten nuisance of the past. Haye's toe had healed and returned to normality at precisely the same moment the fighter had embarked on a similar journey.

It was then that I was told David's other pair of running shoes were currently occupied and that the man of the house had been out pounding the roads for the past half an hour. Toe and mind on the mend, on the spur of the moment he'd simply decided to go for a jog. There was no point running that morning. Nobody had told him to do so. After all, it meant and proved nothing at that stage. Furthermore, the boxer in question hated running. He hated training. Two weeks ago he even hated boxing. Yet, for whatever reason, he was out running. I had no clue as to where David Haye was headed or when he'd turn up that day, but, like everybody else, was content to just wait, watch and wonder.

ACKNOWLEDGEMENTS

Firstly, thanks to David Haye, the heart of this story, for answering my initial phone call and not letting me run to voicemail. And for not punching me that one time I spoke out of turn. And for taking me to my first strip club. And for giving me some of the greatest experiences of my young life. More fool him, but I'd have been happy with just the one interview all those years ago. Now he's stuck with me.

Thanks also to Adam Booth, my go-to outlet whenever I grew tired of Haye, required a dose of sanity or simply wanted to learn more about a sport that meant so much to me. In all my time following boxing, no man has taught me more about what happens when two men step inside a ring and throw punches. For that I owe him plenty.

Another important piece of the Haye puzzle is his wife Natasha, the left brain to the boxer's big right hand. Thanks for letting boys talk boxing and never once saying he couldn't come out to play.

Ultimately, while I'd like to think this book was always likely to get published, a number of important people directed it from my bottom drawer towards glorious sunlight. I extend thanks to David Luxton, literary agent, Leeds United fan and my torch into darkness, as well as the entire team at Quercus, most notably Richard

Milner and Iain Miller for their boundless show of support and passion towards the project.

On an author-related note, special thanks must go to Donald McRae, not just for producing *Dark Trade*, the first book I ever read on boxing, but for also being a valued source of advice and guidance throughout my own journey. I hope I did you justice.

High-fives in the direction of Roy Jones Jr, too, for giving me something to tell my friends about at school, even when none of them *really* cared.

And finally thanks to Mum for being Mum, and Dad for being Dad. It would have been strange any other way. *Making Haye* may be my creation, but I was theirs.

INDEX

INDEX

INDEX